Carib

Goajiro

Cuna

Guaymi

Chibcha

Arawak

Arawak

Cañar

Omagua

Timbira

Chimu

Mundurucú

Inca

Nambicuara

Cayapa

Sherente

Inca

Mojo

Aymara

Sirionó

Atacama

Coroado

Diaguita

Guaraní

Araucania

Abipón

Charrua

Puelche

Tehuelche

Alacaluf

Ona

Yahgan

Indian Terms
of the Americas

Indian Terms
of the Americas

Lotsee Patterson
Mary Ellen Snodgrass

Original Illustrations by Dan Timmons

1994
Libraries Unlimited, Inc.
Englewood, Colorado

LIBRARIES UNLIMITED, INC.
P.O. Box 6633
Englewood, CO 80155-6633
1-800-237-6124

Stephen Haenel
Project Manager and Art Editor

Alan Livingston
Design and Layout

Connie Hardesty
Copy Editor

Pam Getchell
Pasteup

Ann Marie Damian
Proofreader

Kay Minnis
Production Assistant

Judy Gay Matthews
Production Advisor

Cover design and interior beadwork ornamentation: Joan Garner
Endsheet maps: Joan Garner and Alan Livingston
Lewis and Clark map (p. 127) and Long Walk map (p. 130): Raymond M. Barrett, Jr.
The following illustrations were provided by the Western History Department of the Denver Public Library: Little Robe (p. 45), horse (p. 102), Mandan lodge (p. 129), Powhatan (p. 184). John Ross (p. 194).

Library of Congress Cataloging-in-Publication Data

Patterson, Lotsee.
    Indian terms of the Americas / Lotsee Patterson, Mary Ellen Snodgrass ; original illustrations by Dan Timmons.
        xvi, 275 p. 19x26 cm.
        Includes bibliographical references (p. 251) and index.
        ISBN 1-56308-133-4
        1. Indians--Terminology. 2. Indians--Dictionaries. 3. Reference books--Indians--Dictionaries. I. Snodgrass, Mary Ellen.
    II. Title.
    E54.5.P47   1994   93-47170
    970.004'97'003--dc20   CIP

To Native Americans,
who have set an example
of reverence for all creation

Contents

Acknowledgments

The authors would like to thank the following individuals and organizations for their assistance with this project:

Knolan Benfield
Dr. Carol Blessing
Lynne Bolick
Bernadette Carey
Cherokee County Library, Cherokee, North Carolina
Cherokee Museum, Tahlequah, Oklahoma
Janey Deal
Cindy Detweiler
Dennis Detweiler
Charles Mason
Susan Mason
Burl McCuiston
Corki Miller
Tom Moon
National Museum of Natural History
Wanda Rozzelle
Dan Scott
Mark Sinclair
Thea Sinclair
Roberta Smith, Fort Bragg Schools, Fort Bragg, North Carolina
Margaret Snodgrass
United States Department of the Interior
United States National Archives and Records Administration

Introduction

In too many books and movies, the Native American is treated as an eccentricity to be studied, discussed, analyzed, reflected upon, counseled, and, if possible, improved. Other works of fact and fiction reflect upon the Indian as a static museum display, for instance:

- the days of the mighty forest tribes;

- the quaint diet and lifestyle of the Eskimo and Inuit;

- the emergence of the mounted plains Indian;

- the magnificence of the Mayan and Aztec cultures;

- the defeat of Sitting Bull and Crazy Horse;

- the dispersal and extinction of nations like the Thule and Beothuk, which succumbed to changes in climate and contact with European diseases.

These examinations imply that Indians, like butterflies pinned to balls of cotton, are currently devoid of life, drained forever of blood, and ready for the bell jar.

Whatever the purpose or point of view, such studies, in an effort to accommodate specific philosophies about human societies, often miss an important point—that in the past, Indians, like people of all cultures, followed normal, standard rhythms of living.

- People got up in the morning, dressed, and ate breakfast with their families.

- They went about their work; fulfilled their patriotic, religious, and home duties; and enjoyed free time by relaxing, entertaining, sharing food, playing games, exercising, and talking with friends.

- They took medicine when they were ill, attended weddings and funerals, patched their shoes when they wore holes in them, kept an eye to the weather, offered a prayer of thanks for a good meal, and taught their children how to lead happy and productive lives.

In these respects, Indians were no different from anyone else who is alive or ever lived.

As is true of all animistic worshippers, Indians evolved gods from the most important objects in their lives, be it sun, river, maize, snake, whale, bear, horse, or buffalo. Today, their religious garments, icons, totems, amulets, dances, re-enactments, and other ritual items and functions repeat themes that even the youngest tribal member can identify—love of parents, respect for others, and reverence for nature and the Almighty. Native philosophies speak the desires of all people—to know the comforts of a full stomach and safe bed, the love of sympathetic people, the acceptance of peers, and the assurance of a reward for loyalty and attention to duty. To offset the most serious tribal concerns, Indians enjoy their jests, whether in drawing, song, story, pantomime, or riddle. Their mythic tales, filled with tricksters and heroes, boogers and spirits, attest to complex belief systems. Their community networks remain stable through the members' commitment and will thrive so long as the people exist, respect each other, and hold fast to their beliefs.

This book, which grew out of a study of numerous native terms gleaned from children's and adult literature, reflects the authors' interest in accuracy. Within the alphabetized, illustrated text are these entries:

- names for objects, such as pirogues, prayer sticks, kayaks, blowguns, dumas, mukluks, quipus, and medicine bundles;

- methods of doing things, such as stone boiling, diapering babies, building igloos, burning off a field, healing sunburn, and fletching arrows;

- names of significant people, places, and events, from Bright Eyes to Datsolali, from Wounded Knee to the paintings of George Catlin, from Sacagawea's trek west with the Lewis and Clark expedition to Catawba clay workers' search for a better way to make pottery, from the diaries of Christopher Columbus to the ingenuity of Comanche and Navaho code talkers who baffled Japanese intelligence networks during World War II.

In addition, the text includes words imposed by speakers of other languages as a means of naming or describing aspects of Indian culture, such as arroyo, bandolier, Yankee, Nez Percé, travois, savvy, and bois d'arc. In time, these words have permeated the English language and become a part of traditional terminology.

This compendium is meant to present a realistic picture of Native American lore—neither Pollyanna sweet nor obsessed with strife and barbarity. The entries answer questions about everyday activities, from cleansing a newborn to coating the runners of a sled to speed it through snowdrifts, from treating indigestion to playing double ball and lacrosse, from seeking a vision quest with ritual sweat bath to honoring the Great Spirit with prayer sticks and the contents of a medicine bundle.

Each entry includes a term, in most instances with pronunciation, and variances of form or alternate spellings. In some cases, people and tribes are known by several names. We have begun with what appears to be, in our estimation, the most common designation. Wherever dates or time periods and places are available, we name them to pinpoint the entry as surely as fact, tradition, or legend allows. Illustrative sentences conclude the entries, denoting how the term might be used in actual conversation, speeches, letters, journal entries, songs, prayers, or myths. The people in these sentences are either historical or current figures or characters taken from myth, film, or fiction, for example Montezuma II, Tecumseh, Nancy Ward, Keokuk, Ishi, the last of the Yahi, dancer Maria Tallchief, singer Buffy St. Marie, my Carrier friend Bernadette Carey, who lives in Yellowknife, Canada, or True Son, the central figure in Conrad Richter's *The Light in the Forest*. Where no historical figure came to mind, to preserve accuracy, we searched reference books for genuine names. Because the preponderance of literature deals with Indians of North America and, to a lesser extent, Central America, terms relating to Indians of South America are comparatively few in number. The pronunciation style, an h-based system commonly found in children's books, is easy to understand and requires no knowledge of diacritical markings. A reference line appears at the bottom of each page to associate phonetic spellings with 12 common words.

Lotsee, Dan, and I offer this work as a source book for readers who want to know more than a dictionary, encyclopedia, or glossary entry may give. Numerous cross references are intended to guide the searcher to additional or corroborating information, for instance, the relationship between the snowshoe and babiche, various rituals and methods of healing, or Charles Eastman's role at Wounded Knee. The source list that follows the text illustrates the wide range of works consulted, from encyclopedias and compendia of myths and verse to atlases, almanacs, art histories, biographies, story and picture books, diaries, and classic American works by Dee Brown, James Fenimore Cooper, Hal Borland, N. Scott Momaday, Conrad Richter, Henry Wadsworth Longfellow, and Scott O'Dell. Our backup materials derive from a variety of places: the Department of the Interior and the Smithsonian Institution in Washington D.C.; superintendent of schools in Point Hope, Alaska; the Cherokee Museum in Tahlequah, Oklahoma; the American Automobile Association; interviews with Dennis and Cindy Detweiler, a missionary team to the Tarahumara in the Sierra Madre Mountains of Mexico, and with Mark and Thea Sinclair, scientists who studied pueblo sites in the southwestern United States, records and tapes of ceremonies and rituals; travelogues, photo albums, films and videos; museum fliers and brochures; Native American newsletters; editorials from Sequoyah's *Phoenix;* and newspaper articles and features from Charlotte, North Carolina; Atlanta, Georgia; Los Angeles, California; Denver, Colorado; Louisville, Kentucky; Carlisle, Pennsylvania; Seattle, Washington; Point Hope, Alaska; and New York City.

We hope that this book will open a new world to you or broaden your understanding of a subject that has intrigued almost every visitor who has come to the Americas from a foreign shore. Just as Columbus took notes and asked questions of the Caribbean tribes he encountered, we have compiled our facts, drawings, maps, and narratives out of curiosity, wonder, and enjoyment.

Introduction

Yesterday and today, the American Indian—whether pounding acorns into flour for bread or pulling a load of buffalo meat on a travois, holding a potlatch or stomp dance or sprinkling sand designs around an ailing grandfather, braiding the hair of a bride or recounting stories about Old Man Coyote—has maintained and will continue pursuing a sincere interest in life. We honor that spirit with our book.

Mary Ellen Snodgrass

Pronunciation Guide

The following chart demonstrates the vowel sounds used in this dictionary:

a	as in	[**sak** and **sand**]	for	sack, sand
ah	as in	[**sahb** and **sahk**]	for	sob, sock
aw	as in	[**sawlt** and **saws**]	for	salt, sauce
ay	as in	[**sayk** and **sayl**]	for	sake, sail
ee	as in	[**seel** and **seet**]	for	seal, seat
eh	as in	[**seht** and **sehlf**]	for	set, self
ih	as in	[**siht** and **sihp**]	for	sit, sip
oh	as in	[**soh** and **sohk**]	for	sew, soak
oo	as in	[**soop** and **soon**]	for	soup, soon
ow	as in	[**sownd** and **sowr**]	for	sound, sour
uh	as in	[**suhch** and **suhm**]	for	such, sum
y	as in	[**sy** and **syd**]	for	sigh, side

Key to Entries

pronunciation (pronunciation symbols are listed in the guide above and at the foot of every page)

alternative form or spelling

pauluk [pow' look] or **poaluk** [poh' uh • look]   a waterproof **Inuit** glove or mitten, which was made of skins lined or padded with soft down, moss, or felt for extra warmth. [See also **sphagnum**.] *The elder put on his anorak and boots, then stuffed moss into his pauluks before pulling them on.*

bold words in the definition refer to other terms in this book

see other related terms for more information

italic sentence illustrates use of the term

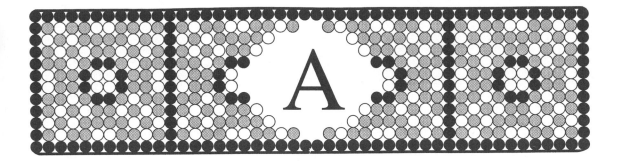

abalone [ab' uh • loh' nee] a mollusk or shellfish common to the Pacific Coast. The abalone is the source of a sweet white meat and glittering mother-of-pearl shell, which is easily carved. The **Olmec** and **Maya** used the abalone as a source of materials for beads. **Mission Indians** floated their canoes at low tide alongside rocks and used pointed sticks to pry loose the mollusks. After forcing open the shells, they sliced and pounded abalone meat into steaks, which were roasted on sticks over an open fire. [See also **beading**.] *Pacific Coast tribes found shiny abalone shell a useful material for ornaments, buttons, fishhooks, and knives.*

Abeel See **Cornplanter**.

Abenaki [ah' buh • nah' kee] or **Abnaki** a confederation of **Algonquin** hunters, fishers, and traders spread from Nova Scotia to Maine and allied with the **Micmac** and Maliseet. The Abenaki, including the Penobscot branch, served as strong allies of French traders in the early 1700s. French Jesuit missionaries converted the Abenaki to Catholicism. As loyal warriors for the French, they helped establish New France as a stronghold against the British. After decades of warfare, the depleted groups migrated toward Quebec and the northern Great Lakes. In 1980, U.S. courts gave the Abenaki $81 million in restitution for loss of their lands in 1790. *Abenaki elder Mdawilasis teaches children through storytelling; Abenaki poet and novelist Joseph Bruchac keeps native lore alive through his work, particularly his gentle poem "Birdfoot's Grampa," which describes how an old man helps toads cross a road because "they have places to go to too."*

Absaroke See **Crow**.

a = s**a**ck; ah = s**o**b; aw = s**au**ce; ay = s**a**fe; ee = s**ee**k; eh = s**e**t
ih = s**i**t; oh = s**oa**k; oo = s**ou**p; ow = s**ou**nd; uh = s**u**ch; y = s**i**de

1

acorn the smooth-shelled nut of the oak tree, which Indians gathered, capped, and shelled, then pounded. Nuts from the willow oak and white oak were sweet enough to be eaten straight from the tree. The **Pomo** and Hupa Indians poured the pulp of the red oak into a leaching pit or a hole in the sand and rinsed the nut meats with water to remove the bitter, poisonous tannin, a substance used to tan leather. They ground the purified pulp into flour and baked it into loaves and cakes or used it to thicken stews and soups. When the acorn pulp was cooked into mush, diners ate with their hands or dipped into a common pot with a wooden or bone mush spoon or paddle. [See also **chemuck**.] *One of the Mono woman's daily chores was the gathering of acorns, which she stored in a large mocuck until she could pound the nut meats into flour.*

adobe [uh • doh' bee] a reddish brown brick common to North and Central America that is made of sun-dried clay mixed with straw and gravel or sometimes with ash from sagebrush fires. Brick makers pressed the stiff mixture into molds or shaped it into oval lumps called "turtlebacks." Houses made of these bricks, called adobes, were built on stone foundations. The bricks were held together with a mud plaster, which families refreshed each year. Adobe was cheap, fireproof, strong against extremes of weather, and resistant to warping and cracking. [See also **Anasazi, horno, pueblo**.] *On a warm, sunny morning, Lola leaned her head against the adobe wall and toyed with a blue-striped lizard.*

short-handled adze

adze [adz] a gouging or scraping instrument made by joining a shell, bone, stone, or metal blade to a handle with rawhide strips or rush lashings. The farmer used the adze much as a modern gardener uses a hoe or mattock—to dig trenches, uproot weeds, chop up clods, or harvest tall plants. The adze also served as a hatchet, ax, plane, or carving tool useful to carpenters. [See also **dugout**.] *Taino Indians used a crude shell adze to remove the burned-out core of the cypress to form a pirogue or to shape serving bowls or platters, cradleboards, and other wooden objects.*

agave [uh • gah' vay] or **century plant** or **maguey** [mah • gay'] a spiny evergreen related to sisal and commonly known as **mescal** that grows high in the desert hills of

North, Central, and South America. The leaves reach six feet in length. The spreading flower stalk can tower up to 40 feet. The **Aztec** gathered agave leaves to weave into thatch for roofs or to twist into rope or fiber for sewing, binding, and weaving. The **Pima** made burden baskets of twisted agave fiber woven around a **willow** hoop and supported with saguaro poles.

Agave had other uses. Its leaves were made into paper. The sweet juice of the agave heart was fermented into beer; the pulp was mixed with sunflower seeds, **piñon** nuts, or walnuts to make nut butter. The crown of the plant was seasoned with cattail pollen, baked in a stone pit, and eaten like an artichoke. Dried slices of agave served as snack food. The juice, which produces a white foam, was used by desert Indians as soap, shampoo, and healing lotion. [See also **basketry, mescal, pulque**.] *Because of its many uses, the agave was a sacred plant to the Pima and the Indians of Mexico.*

agave

a-gu-tuk [ah' goo • tuhk] or **aguduk** or **agoutak** or **akutaq** [ah' koo tak] a favorite **Eskimo** food made by pounding **caribou** fat with a small amount of fish oil or fish liver, sugar, snow, and berries, then whipping and chilling before serving. Because of its frothy texture and sweet flavor, a-gu-tuk is sometimes called Eskimo ice cream. [See also **bilberry**.] *The Inuit taught early Protestant missionaries how to make a-gu-tuk.*

agvik [ag' vihk] the right or bowhead whale, an Arctic mammal related to the gray whale and much prized by the Alaskan **Eskimo**. The agvik, a native of cold waters around Greenland and the Arctic, was the first sea mammal to be hunted commercially. Its **baleen**, or mouth tissue, as well as its bone, flesh, and oil, were so in demand that nineteenth century hunters almost killed off the species. [See also **baleen, harpoon**.] D. Timmons *For early Eskimos and Athapascan Indians, hunting the agvik required precision teamwork and the use of sharp harpoons.*

agvik

ahuacatl [ah' wah • caht'l'] or **alligator pear** the **Nahuatl** word for avocado, a bland, green or purple, pear-shaped vegetable-like fruit of a tall evergreen tree found

---

in tropical areas, including California, Florida, Hawaii, and Central and South America. Today, the greenish yellow avocado meat is mashed into a buttery pulp and mixed with pepper and flavorings to make guacamolé, a popular dip for tortilla chips. Some tribes used the oil extracted from the pulp to make soap and skin lotion. [See also **Nahuatl**.] *In the seventeenth century, the words* ahuacatl, cacahuatl, *and* tomatl *entered the English language as* avocado, chocolate, *and* tomato.

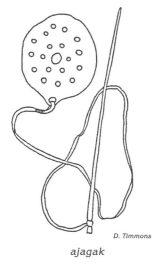

D. Timmons

ajagak

ajagak [aj' uh • gahk] a game for one or more played by **Eskimo** children in which a pierced disk of bone or wood is attached to a pin or bone sliver by a strip of hide from a bearded or ring seal. The player tosses the disk into the air and tries to catch it on the sharpened end of the pin. The disk has several holes, which vary in diameter and carry different values, with the narrowest earning the most points. The player with the highest score wins. [See also **ayahaaq**.] *Nalu felt that a simple game like ajagak was not appropriate for a girl her age.*

akicita [ah • kih • see' tuh] a **Sioux** society of camp police or peace officers similar to rural constables or military watch commanders. The akicita assigned tasks to **tribe** members when the group was on the move or when danger was near. Usually the akicita oversaw the picketing of pack animals and horses as well as the posting of sentinels. *To remind undisciplined braves of their duty to the tribe, the akicita tapped them with unstrung bows or tipped over their tepees, thus humiliating dawdlers in front of their peers.*

akutaq See **a-gu-tuk**.

Aleut [uh • loot' or al • ee • oot'] a tribe of sturdy fishers and hunters native to a string of foggy, windswept islands southwest of Alaska. As early as the seventeenth century, the Aleut, who are related to the **Inupiaq** or **Eskimos**, were exploited by Russian fur traders and were greatly reduced in number by enslavement and disease, particularly measles, smallpox, scarlet fever, tuberculosis, and influenza. Some Aleut sailors were impressed into the Russian navy and witnessed attacks against coastal villages and isolated islands. [See also **barabara, Beringia, Edward W. Nelson**.] *Aleut navigators carried whalebone carvings,* *seal-fur garments, and other trade goods as far south as the Catalina Islands and the California coast.*

Algonquin [al • gahng' kwihn] or **Algonquian** or **Algonkian** or **Algonkin** a massive nation of farmers, hunters, and fishers native to the Canadian plains and eastern North America, at one time reaching as far south as North Carolina, and including the **Penobscot, Narragansett, Pequot, Delaware, Shawnee, Kickapoo**, Miami, **Sauk, Fox, Ottawa, Blackfoot, Cheyenne, Nootka**, Nisquali, and Squamish. The Algonquin, ancestors of the **Ottawa**, migrated to the Great Lakes area around 2500 B.C. Algonquin **tribes**, noted for their extensive **tattoos** and conical hairstyles for men, were the first to encounter European explorers and settlers. For this reason, many early settlers and explorers assumed that all Native Americans were like the Algonquin. The most powerful Algonquin chiefs—**King Philip, Powhatan, Pontiac, Black Hawk**, and **Tecumseh**—could not halt the erosion of their power by the **Iroquois** and white settlers nor the destruction caused by European diseases. In New England alone, measles nearly exterminated native populations. Eventually, the tribe dispersed to hunting grounds around Lake Huron. Today, many Algonquin inhabit native reserves in Ontario and Quebec.

The term Algonquin also names the complex language spoken by these people, which encompasses 40-50 dialects. The influence of Algonquin dialects spread farther than any other Native American language—as far west as Montana, over most of Canada, and south to Texas and the upper reaches of Florida. Native Algonquin words common to English include *moose, squash, hominy, succotash, wigwam, tomahawk, papoose, squaw, wampum, Allegheny, Illinois, Connecticut, Chesapeake,* and *Massachusetts.* [See also **Black Hawk, Iroquois League, King Philip, Ottawa, Pocahontas, Pontiac, Powhatan, Tecumseh, Catherine Tekakwitha.**] *The smallest reservation in the United States is the Algonquin settlement in Trumbull, Connecticut.*

All-Father the spirit of permanence, as represented by rocks; the creator. Worship of the All-Father brought to native seekers of the forest and plains tribes a sense of oneness with the universe, which often seemed elusive and distant. The All-Father is akin to the Greek Zeus, the Roman Jupiter, or the Judeo-Christian Yahweh or Jehovah.

---

ih = sit; oh = soak; oo = soup; ow = sound; uh = such; y = side

[See also **Great Spirit, Manitou**.] *Crooked Knife withdrew to a cave, smoked the ritual pipe, and dreamed of Maheo, the Cheyenne All-Father.*

All-Mother   the earth spirit who served as a messenger between human beings and the **Great Spirit**, the lord of the universe. Symbolized by growing things, the All-Mother attended to all aspects of human life, particularly food. Respect for the All-Mother required worshippers to revere all living things, especially plants and animals that were used as food. [See also **Great Spirit, Manitou**.] *In his explanation of respect for the All-Mother, Chief Smohalla, a Wanapum priest, indignantly exclaimed that plowing the earth, mining ore, or harvesting grain was like knifing the goddess's bosom, digging up her bones, or cutting her hair.*

allotment   a government system of land allotment that tended to break up Indian communities and weaken native strengths. [See also **Dawes Act**.] *According to Wilson Rawls's* Where the Red Fern Grows *(New York: Bantam Books, 1961), his family's land was an allotment made to his Cherokee mother in the early years of Oklahoma's statehood.*

D. Timmons

amaguq

amaguq [am' uh • guhk]   the **Eskimo** word for wolf, the carnivorous hunting animal that supplied warm pelts for tunics, caps, and mittens and exotic trims for ceremonial costumes and ritual items, such as capes. The meat, which is stringy and tough, was rarely used for food. Wolf cubs were often domesticated as pets. They sometimes mated with dogs and sired unusually keen hunting animals, as immortalized in Jack London's adventure novel *White Fang* (Mahwah, N.J.: Watermill Press, 1980). The wiliness of the wolf, as well as its austere cry, made it a common **trickster** in folklore, stories, and songs. [See also **trickster**.] *On a bright winter's day, Takolik and Aqsuq hunted the amaguq together by tracking it through rabbit territory.*

amaranth [am' uh • ranth]   a sturdy reddish herb with fuzzy, scaly flower spikes. The amaranth is related to tumbleweed, tasselflower, Joseph's coat, coxcomb, and pigweed and is common to roadsides, river bottoms, and irrigated fields. Many Indians use amaranth seeds as snack food, cereal, and flour and as an ingredient in medicine. Mixed with **pinole**, the leaves are cooked like

*a = s**a**ck; ah = s**o**b; aw = s**au**ce; ay = s**a**fe; ee = s**ee**k; eh = s**e**t*

spinach. Dried seeds mixed with water are cooked like oatmeal. *Mata used a basket and stick to gather the dried, prickly heads from the amaranth stalks.*

amate [uh • mah' tay]   a textured brown paper made from the bark of the amate tree. The Otomi of Mexico peel amate bark, boil it, then stretch it out flat in overlapping strips, which are pounded into a single layer with stone mallets. The fibrous bark meshes into a coarse paper, which is dried, then painted with bright designs of flowers, animals, birds, and scenes of local festivals and Indian life. *At the Smithsonian Institution, workers pinned amate drawings onto a wall featuring artwork of the Otomi tribes.*

Amerindian or **Amerind**   native peoples of North, Central, and South America who share similar social, lingual, and cultural traits. In 1899, Major John Wesley Powell, a noted anthropologist and geologist who studied the **Hopi** and other tribes of the Colorado Plateau, coined the word Amerind, which refers to all native North American tribes, including Eskimo and Canadian tribes. In 1985, Joseph Greenberg amended the original definition by separating the 200 Amerind language families from Na-Déné and Eskimo-Aleut. [See also **Indian, tribe**.] *The term* Amerind *is useful to scholars who wish to differentiate between American Indians and natives of India.*

amouti [uh • moo' tee]   a **parka** with a fur-lined hood and strap designed to hold an infant. The purpose of the amouti's design was to share the warmth of mother and child and to prevent the baby from becoming chilled by strong winds or dampened by moisture. Suckling babies could nurse without being removed. Because the child was secure, the mother had both hands free. [See also **atigi, Eskimo, parka**.] *Mrs. Donovan bought a wolf-trimmed amouti from the Déné clerk at a general store in Yellowknife.*

Anasazi petroglyphs

Anasazi [ahn' uh • sah' zee]   an influential prehistoric **tribe** of wanderers, basket weavers, and cliff dwellers who inhabited parts of the American Southwest from 100 B.C. to A.D. 1400. Around A.D. 400, they colonized the banks of the San Juan and Virgin rivers and populated Glen Canyon of Colorado and the Grand Canyon. As shelter

---

ih = sit; oh = soak; oo = soup; ow = sound; uh = such; y = side

Canyon de Chelly

for 100 residents, between A.D. 1200 and 1276, they built the 114 rooms and 8 kivas of Spruce Tree House at Mesa Verde, Colorado. The ruins of this ancient condominium were rediscovered by ranchers in 1888. Similar architecture exists at Pueblo Bonito in Chaco Canyon, New Mexico, and Mummy Cave in Canyon de Chelly, Arizona. The Anasazi hunted with darts, **spears**, nets, and **snares**, grew **maize** and **squash**, lived in **pit houses**, wove sandals and rope from **yucca** and rushes, and pioneered the use of **adobe** in construction. The **Pueblo** and **Hopi** Indians are direct descendents of this tribe. [See also **adobe, kiva, mesa, pit house, pueblo, yucca**.] *Anasazi women, who kept flocks of wild turkeys on the terraces outside their adobe dwellings, wove blankets from the feathers.*

angatkuq [ang' uht • kuhk] or **angatkok** or **angakok** a medicine man or **shaman** of the **Eskimo**, who communicated with spirits by falling into trances. The angatkuq found lost objects and located herds of **caribou**, schools of fish, and other sources of food. At the age of seven, an apprentice was trained to beat the drum, chant, and imitate the adult angatkuq, who served as his teacher. At tribal gatherings, the angatkuq wore a carved ritual mask. *In order to hold back the winter, Oolak, angatkuq of his tribe, tried to trap the sun in a cat's cradle.*

Anishinabe [ah' nih • shih • nah' bay] original name of the Chippewa or **Ojibwa**. [See also **Ojibwa**.]

Antonio, Santana [an • toh' nee • oh san • ta' nuh] a twentieth-century Acoma potter who follows traditional methods of shaping, coloring, and firing under a heap of animal dung. Her methods have been studied by anthropologists, craft experts, and collectors. *Trained by a white teacher in native design, Santana Antonio uses the coil method of building a clay pot rather than the modern style of spinning a lump of clay on a potter's wheel.*

*a = s**a**ck; ah = s**o**b; aw = s**au**ce; ay = s**a**fe; ee = s**ee**k; eh = s**e**t*

Apache [uh • patch' ee]   a **tribe** of hunter-gatherers, kin of the ancient **Anasazi** and Fremont tribes. The Apache migrated from Canada and settled in the southwestern United States along Cataract Canyon of the Colorado River. Named The Enemy by the **Zuñi**, the Apache were divided into subgroups: Chiricahua, Jicarilla, **Kiowa**, Lipan, Mescalero, Tonto, Western, and the Fort Sill branch, which was itself later added to traditional groupings. The Apache were famous for their lightning-swift raids on Spanish and American settlers and took pride in their legendary leaders, **Geronimo**, **Cochise**, **Mangas Coloradas**, and Victorio. Today the Apache reside mainly in Oklahoma, New Mexico, and Oregon. [See also **Cochise, Geronimo, Mangas Coloradas**.] *A notable Apache physician and leader, Dr. Carlos Montezuma (1865-1923), published a progressive journal,* Wassaja, *that condemned reservation life and encouraged racial pride.*

Apache warrior

April, Nancy   See **Shawnawdithit**.

Apsaalooke   See **Crow**.

Arapaho [uh • rap' uh • hoh'] or **Arapahoe**   an agricultural **tribe** native to Minnesota, that migrated to the North American plains from Canada to Texas, pursued the buffalo, and developed into keen fighters against white settlers and competing Indian tribes. The Arapaho, who are divided into northern and southern branches and are related to the **Hidatsa**, joined with the **Cheyenne** in developing the **Sun Dance**, which became an integral part of their worship. Modern Arapaho tribes currently inhabit **reservations** in Oklahoma and Wyoming. *According to the Arapaho creation myth told by Lillian Toahty, a turtle, which was one of the first animals on Earth, dived to the bottom of the water and brought up enough earth for the gods to mold men, women, and buffalo.*

Arawak [a' ruh • wahk]   a peace-loving tribe of farmers, hunters, and fishers who were native to the Orinoco region of South America, displaced the Ciboney in Haiti around 300 B.C., populated St. Lucia around A.D. 200, and migrated to Jamaica around A.D. 1000. Evidence of their existence can be seen on the walls of the Hato Caves, Curaçao; Pie Corner, Barbados; and the Fountain on

---

*ih = si*t; *oh = so*a*k; oo = so*u*p; ow = so*u*nd; uh = s*u*ch; y = s*i*de*   **9**

Anguilla, where 500-year-old drawings are still visible. The **Taino**, relatives of the Arawak, were the first Native Americans whom Columbus met and described in his journals. Their chief, **Guacanagarì**, directed the unloading of the *Santa Maria*. In a letter dated March 14, 1493, Christopher Columbus noted that the Arawak were simple, honest, hospitable, and loving and that they respected a higher power. By 1550, the majority of the Arawak had either succumbed to cannibalistic **Caribs** or to European diseases, such as influenza, measles, smallpox, pneumonia, and scarlet fever. [See also **Martha, Brae, Carib, Ciboney, Taino.**] *The Arawak gave us the word* iguana, *a green, spiny-backed lizard.*

aronia See **chokeberry**.

Arrow See **Ouray**.

arrow a dart or **spear** shot from a **bow**. The arrowhead is a significant archaeological artifact because of what it tells about the date and lifestyle of a tribe. The earliest Indian arrowheads, which date from A.D. 500, were made entirely of wood or cane; the tip was merely sharpened and hardened over flame. Later, the Yurok fashioned arrow points out of **obsidian**, which is volcanic glass. Other types of points were fashioned from flaked ovals of stone, flint, shark teeth, snake fangs, fish scales and spines, the tail of the horseshoe crab, eagle claws, iron, brass, bronze, deer shank bone, antler points, quartzite, jasper, felsite, **chert**, argillite, or quartz. Arrowheads were triangular, diamond- or leaf-shaped, or notched to maintain a firmer lashing. The shafts were tapered and ranged from $\frac{1}{4}$-$\frac{1}{2}$ inch in diameter. They were made in one or two sections from varying lengths of reed, cane, or the straight stems of plants such

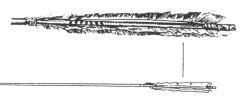

arrow with
stone head

as barberry, arrowweed, syringa, rosewood, greasewood, witch hazel, **serviceberry**, creosote bush, or dogwood. The shafts were straightened over heat, then planed with a sandstone and polished with horsetail fern. The butt end of the arrow was weighted with two or three long, narrow eagle or turkey feathers to guide the missile toward its target. The entire length averaged about 2 feet to accommodate the pull of the bow. Most arrows were marked by colored bands to indicate ownership. **Caribs** who attacked Columbus's crew fired poisoned arrows tipped with fishbone or shell. The **Timucua** tied moss to their arrow points, then lit the clumps and fired them at the roofs of enemy villages. [See also **arrow straightener, blowgun, bow, celt, chert, flaking, fletching, flint knapping, quiver, spear.**] *In arming himself for the hunt, James Paytiamo or Flaming Arrow of the Acoma Pueblo composed a verse telling how he would don moccasins and apron, paint his face and body, place yarn about his knee and an eagle feather in his hair, gather bow and arrows, and call to the deer.*

arrowroot See **coontie**.

arrow straightener a piece of wood formed into a lever or tool composed of a carved handle and an oval hole at the far end. The **arrow** maker placed a bent shaft in the hole, held it over a flame, and put pressure against the shaft by pressing down on the handle. This tedious task was essential to assure true aim. [See also **arrow.**] *Lone Eagle kept his arrow straightener close at hand as he inspected the quiver for damaged or irregular shafts.*

arrow straightener

arroyo [uh • roy' oh] the dry bed or channel of a creek or stream; a gully. Desert Indians sometimes utilized an arroyo as a pathway or direction finder. Modern scientists have utilized satellite photos of ancient arroyos to determine the location of long-lost desert tribes. [See also **barranca**.] *During flash floods, the arroyo can quickly fill with rainwater and runoff, which the watchful farmer diverts by digging side channels to connect with irrigation lines.*

ash cake an oval patty, pone, or loaf shaped from stiffened corn batter, which was sometimes mixed with cooked bean pulp. Ash cakes were placed on oak leaves on a hot stone, then covered with more leaves and hot coals and left to cook. Colonists who imitated ash cakes called their creations johnnycake or hoecake. [See also **maize, nokehick, piki**.] *Gray Squirrel's mother and aunts made enough ash cake to supply the villagers for the entire green corn ceremony.*

Assiniboin Indian

askootasquash See **squash**.

Assiniboin [uh • sin' uh • boin] or **Assiniboine** a **tribe** of buffalo hunters native to the plains stretching from Canada to the Missouri River. The Assiniboin, whose name means stone boilers, were proud people who revered members of their men's secret warrior society. Like other tribes, they suffered severe losses from epidemics of smallpox after their first encounters with white explorers. The Assiniboin observed firm rules regarding courtship, marriage, fair apportionment of work for women, and freedom to divorce. A man who mistreated his wife was labeled a disgrace and shunned by the tribe. [See also **Cree**.] *According to Assiniboin historian and writer James Larpenteur Long or First Boy, Tall Man encountered the first white man, named Lone White Man, who introduced them to the American custom of frying liver with onions.*

Athapascan [ath • uh • pas' kuhn] or **Athabascan** [ath • uh • pas' kuhn] or **Tena** [tay' nuh] a language group of nomadic tribes native to Canada and Alaska and extending to California and Mexico. The Athapascan, famous for their skill in hunting and fishing, are credited with inventing **quilling** and with originating the name Alaska, which means "great land." They successfully held off Russian exploration, but could not halt the intrusion of European gold prospectors into the Klondike. Athapascan tribes, whose members bear Mongoloid features, include the **Carrier**, Hupa, Kato, and Kutchin. [See also **Beringia, Carrier, Déné, Edward W. Nelson**] *To Koonah, a blind Athapascan sage, Mt. McKinley is known as Mt. Denali, or "High One," the seat of Sa, the solar medicine man and master of life.*

atigi [uh • tee' gee] a waterproof, windproof **parka** or knee-length, hooded, pullover jacket made of sealskin or **caribou** hide. The top portion of the atigi varied in style, sometimes including a **thong** fastener or a tight collar to protect the neck from cold wind or dampness. Layers of garments underneath helped hold in body heat, especially useful during outdoor chores and activities. [See also **amouti, parka**.] *Outside the door of the fisherman's hut in Point Hope, Alaska, one lone atigi hung from a nail.*

atlatl [aht' laht'l]   the **Nahuatl** word for a primitive-but-effective weighted wooden throwing stick or board from which a poised **spear** or dart was launched. The atlatl was designed 7,000 years ago by the Uto-Aztec. It was approximately 2 feet long and grooved; it had a raised knob, hook, **thong,** or finger grip at the end to allow the thrower increased speed and greater control of the weapon. [See also **flaking, spear**.] *The atlatl, which was counterbalanced with a stone, employed the basic laws of physics to extend the range and improve the accuracy and thrust of the ordinary hunting spear.*

atlatl with spear

atlih [aht' lee]   a game in which players guess the position of four sticks hidden by a blanket. *Throughout the blizzard, Jason and his pals sat by the fire and played atlih, keeping score with marks on the dirt floor of the hogan.*

atolli [ah • tohl' lee]   a hot cereal broth or porridge eaten by **Pueblo** Indians. It is made from coarsely ground **corn** and flavored with honey or pimiento peppers. **Aztec** families often sipped bowls of atolli for their morning meal. *Barbara White Cloud helped her three brothers hunt the saguaro cactus for beehives so that they could rob enough honey for their family's atolli.*

aungaak [awn' gak]   a feather or piece of bone used as a charm or good luck piece and fastened to an **Eskimo** child's clothing soon after birth. Shortly after the uaqti or midwife cleaned and dressed the infant, she protected it with an aungaak by tying the object about the baby's sleeve. As long as the aungaak remained in place, the child need fear no disease, accident, or evil spirit. [See also **i'noGo tied, medicine pendant**.] *Julie's great-grandmother reserved the honor of knotting the aungaak, raising her hands, and saying a prayer of protection over the infant.*

awl   a short, pointed piercing tool or punch made of bone, fang, tooth, horn, wood, or metal and employed in sewing or **quilling**. Native Americans punched holes or slits into hide, then laced the hides together with sinew,

bone awl

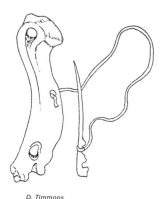

D. Timmons

ayahaaq

rawhide cord, **babiche**, or braided fiber. The awl was also useful in basket weaving because it could facilitate the tedious work of forcing bark strips or thin branches between the uprights of the loom without crimping or breaking the materials and could be used to tighten patterns, which sometimes required months in the making. [See also **babiche, basketry, coiling, quilling**.] *Like the quill needle, the awl was a precious tool to Indian seamstresses and basket weavers.*

ayahaaq [ay' uh • hahk]   an **Eskimo** skill game similar to **ajagak**. It features a short stick tied to a **thong** that ends in a pierced bone taken from a seal's flipper. The player swings the thong and tries to catch the bone by thrusting the stick through the hole. [See also **ajagak**.] *For Inuit children in Kotzebue, playing ayahaaq requires intense practice and much eye-hand coordination.*

Ayontwatha   See **Hiawatha**.

Aztec [az' tehk]   a pragmatic, literate **tribe** that in 1345 migrated to Lake Texcoco in the Valley of Mexico from the southwestern United States to avoid hostile migrants from the north. At the height of its power, the Aztec nation ruled from the Gulf of Mexico to the Pacific Ocean and spread its language, **Nahuatl**, over much of the Yucatan Peninsula. On the site of Mexico City, they developed a rich and influential slave-holding culture that cultivated **chinampas**, floating vegetable beds anchored by **willow** supports to the river bottom and filled with rich silt and plant matter. They grew **corn**, **cacao**, cotton, beans, **squash**, tomatoes, papayas, mangoes, and avocados and raised turkeys for food and trade.

The Aztec, who numbered 5 million at their height, were famous makers and builders of mounds, canals, skiffs, and bridges. They traded in rich stores of cocoa, macaw feathers, duck down, gold, ocelot and jaguar pelts, cotton, crystal, copper, rubber, amber, carnelian, and jade. One of their most esteemed chieftains was Montezuma I, who, from 1440 to 1468, ruled in the capital city of Tenochtitlán, which was then the sixth largest city in the world.

In the early sixteenth century, Hernán Cortés, a Spanish explorer in search of gold, conquered and destroyed their civilization. According to an eyewitness account, the Spanish violated a sacred rite. A conflict erupted on June 30, 1520. The Aztecs named the event "The Sad Night," when Cortés and his men fled at the cost of many lives. In May 1521, he returned to besiege Tenochtitlán anew. By August 13th, the Spanish were victorious. Cortés was granted the title of marquis and worked his holdings at Cuernavaca with the aid of 20,000 Aztec slaves. [See also **chinampa, huipilli, Huitzilopochtli, Montezuma II, Nahuatl, Olmec, pulque, tlachtli, Toltec, Tonalamatl**.] *Tourists still visit, climb, and photograph the pyramids of Mexico, a nation that is named for the Mexica or Aztec Indians.*

B

babiche [bah • beesh']   a leather, bark, or rawhide cord or string used to weave netting for **snowshoes**, hunting and gathering bags, **hammocks**, or fishnets. **Cree** and **Blackfoot** cut thin slices of buffalo hide into strong babiches, with which they tied their **leggings** and **parfleches** and rewove broken snowshoes. They also carried hanks of babiche to use in emergencies. The **Mandan** employed babiche in the weaving of gaming hoops, which were rolled on the ground and speared as a test of aim and control. One form of babiche was cut from rabbit pelts, curled into string with the fur on the outside, then woven to make warm blankets or cloaks. [See also **awl, bast, burden frame, chungke, lanyard, leggings, parfleche, sinew, snowshoe, spear, thong**.] *The Micmac of Nova Scotia relied on strong babiche for creels and fishnets.*

babiche with fur strip

baho [bah' hoh] or **paho**   a paddle-shaped **prayer stick** employed by desert tribes. The baho was marked with symbols and left near crops or water supplies to encourage the gods to be generous. It served as a directional signal to an object or place where divine intercession was needed. *Chole, his maize crop already withered in its first leaf, left the baho beside a gully that was cracked by three summers of drought.*

baleen [buh • leen']   thick bony plates in the mouths of toothless whales, used to filter small fish, krill, and plankton for food. Also called whalebone, baleen provided **Eskimo** artisans material for baskets, jewelry, and sled runners. The popularity of baleen caused European hunters to kill so many herds of gray whales that the species almost became extinct. [See also **agvik**.] *Kuliut used his snow knife to carve the frozen baleen into a ceremonial pipe stem.*

balsa   a lightweight raft shaped like a pointed boat and woven of **tule** rushes attached to a long driftwood frame. California Indians wove balsas for women to use in transporting branches, **amaranth** stalks, wild rice, and herbs across streams and lakes. Balsas waterlog after days in the water but quickly dry in the sun for later use. *While designing the Kon-Tiki to resemble the balsas used by the ancient Incas, Thor Heyerdahl visited Peruvian Indian villages in search of suitable materials.*

bandolier [ban' doh • leer'] or **bandoleer** a strap worn over the shoulder and across the chest. The bandolier, which often attached to a belt or sash, usually secured a pouch to the body or held cartridges. A bandolier could also be part of ritual or ceremonial dress, for instance marking the status of a **chief**, war leader, or **medicine man**. *White Dove worked quills into the shape of stars, which covered the outer edge of her husband's bandolier.*

barabara [buh • ra' buh • ruh] the traditional semi-subterranean Aleut sod hut. The barabara was built below ground so that residents could enter through a sunken foyer to keep out cold wind and foraging animals. If heavy rains weakened the outer surface, an application of new sod quickly repaired the damage. [See also **Aleut, igloo, innie.**] *Because of the availability of materials and the ease of construction, the ancient Aleut preferred single-family living in a barabara, or sod house.*

barbecue meat from an animal or fish that is roasted, whole or split, over hot coals or in a fire pit; a style of cooking that dates to Native Americans of the Caribbean. Today, barbecued meat, which in Jamaica and other Caribbean islands is called jerk meat, is tenderized and flavored by marinating, basting, or dipping it in acidic sauces made from tomato, onion, vinegar, brown sugar, pepper, and chopped chiles. Another method of altering flavor is varying the type and age of wood over which the meat is cooked. Currently, both a gathering at which barbecued meat is served and the pit on which the meat is roasted are referred to as barbecues. *A Carib barbecue pit is made deep to keep the coals hot.*

barranca [buh • rang' kuh] a deep gully or ditch. Barrancas were usually carved by wind or water into shale or other soft stone. Archaeologists often use the layered walls of the barranca to estimate the lengths of previous eras and the natural forces that affected them, such as floods, fires, or droughts. [See also **arroyo**.] *Tenaya's skittish Appaloosa had difficulty descending the barranca.*

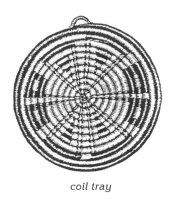

coil tray

basketry [bas' keht • ree]   the weaving or netting of reeds, straw, grass, or twigs into lightweight containers for a variety of uses. The style and purpose of baskets vary from **tribe** to tribe and depend heavily on the materials at hand. Common warp and weft supplies come from whole and split lengths of honeysuckle, **willow**, redbud, **tule**, hazel, sedge, **bear grass**, squaw bush, spiny rush, deer grass, pine, wheat straw, and **cattail**. The most common weaving methods are twining and **coiling**. The latter requires withes, or ties, to hold the coils in place. To keep a tight edge, the weaver uses an **awl** or punch to force withes between coils. The upper edge is finished with braiding. Baskets are often decorated with dyed grasses, animal hair, seedpods, or quills. [See also **agave, awl, coiling, Datsolali**.] *The Chumash coiled basket was bulbous with a narrow neck and flat bottom; in contrast, the Mission Indians' basketry had wide mouths with broader bases.*

bast   cord made from the inner fiber of the bark of hickory, walnut, basswood, or slippery elm used to tie **wigwam** poles, bedframes, **snowshoes**, and other handmade items. The external layer of the bark was stripped away and the inner layer coiled for storage. Bast was stored dry until it was needed. Then it was soaked overnight to make it pliant. [See also **babiche**.] *The Gay Head Indians stripped bast in a straight line from the bottom of a tree to the top.*

Battle of Little Big Horn or **Custer's Last Stand**   a major surprise engagement in Montana on June 25, 1876, when the combined forces of **Crazy Horse** and **Sitting Bull** wiped out three battalions of the 7th U.S. Cavalry led by General George Armstrong Custer, who died in the battle. The battle was preceded by unprovoked attacks on Indians at Sand Creek in 1864 and Washita River, Oklahoma, three years later. These two massacres by the American military created murderous tensions between **plains Indians** and the cavalry, which, under the guise of protecting settlers, decimated Indian tribes by murdering women, children, and the elderly.

a = sack; ah = sob; aw = sauce; ay = safe; ee = seek; eh = set

The Battle of Little Big Horn took place after the 1874 gold rush, which impelled greedy whites to seize Indian lands in the Black Hills. The Indian victory was short-lived; cavalry units, eager for revenge, relentlessly pursued plains Indians, crippling their defenses and wiping out women, children, horses, or sometimes entire villages. Cavalry units continued to exterminate tribes and push them onto undesirable lands. The end of the Indian domination of the Great Plains came at **Wounded Knee** in 1890. [See also **Black Kettle, Cheyenne, Chief Joseph, Crazy Horse, Crow, Gall, pictograph, Rain-in-the-Face, Sand Creek Massacre, Sitting Bull, Tashenamani, Wounded Knee**.] *According to Spotted Tail of the Brulé Tetons, the Battle of Little Big Horn*

> *was brought upon us by the children of the Great Father who came to take our land from us without price, and who, in our land, do a great many evil things. . . . This war—has come from robbery—from the stealing of our land.*

(Brown, Dee. *Bury My Heart at Wounded Knee.* New York: Henry Holt, 1970, 299.)

bayou [by' yoo]   a thick, slow-flowing, marshy creek that enters a larger body of water. Bayou country is navigable only by boats such as **pirogues**, which are paddled or poled. People who know how and where to look almost always succeed in hunting, fishing, and gathering in bayou country. Indians often moved to bayous to escape encroaching European settlers, who were wary of the dangers of quicksand, bayou fever, insects, and predators. [See also **chickee**.] *Choctaw and Koasati who lived in bayou country built chickees, which were summer houses on stilts to keep out alligators and snakes and to let cool waters flow under the floor.*

beading   a geometric or floral decoration made of beads applied to clothing and ceremonial objects, such as **coup sticks**, **cradleboards**, **wampum**, bridles, hair decorations, torques and chokers, chest armor, and **parfleches**. The **Olmec** and **Maya** created valuable beads from jade, gold, turquoise, pearl, and **abalone** shell. Northeastern Indians relied on **quilling** and homemade beads made from seeds, nuts, berries, teeth, beaks, talons, roots, clay, amber, shell, or stone until the nineteenth

beadwork breast ornament

century, when tribes began trading with whites for glass, china, or metal beads. Using sinew or plant fiber, bead workers fastened decorative beadwork onto strips for applique or sewed it directly onto garments, particularly headdresses, **moccasins**, parfleches, dresses, yokes, and shirts. The **Arapaho** were skilled at incorporating stories in their beadwork. Other tribes used beading to mark ceremonial dress, such as the headband of a **medicine man** or the tunic of a bride. Some notable examples of **Cheyenne** beadwork are housed in the Louvre Museum in Paris as models of crafts from the New World. [See also **abalone, quilling, wampum**.] *Lois Whitewater won tribal honors for beading a pair of leggings and matching moccasins.*

beaming a hide

beaming rubbing and pummeling a stretched elk, deer, or buffalo hide with a long, rounded mallet to work out tight spots. After a hide was beamed, it kept its shape in wet weather and remained supple and pliant. In most tribes, the tedious chore of beaming was considered women's work. [See also **braining, buckskin, flesher**.] *Little Elk sat on a low stool while beaming the hide her father brought back from the hunt.*

bean bread a kind of dumpling made from cornmeal, beans, and bean broth. The dough is shaped into a lump, wrapped in cornhusks, tied with thread, then cooked in boiling water. Variations of bean bread can be made by adding sweet potato, **squash**, seeds, or chestnuts to the batter. *Mattie served fresh bean bread with succotash and sallet.*

bearberry See **manzanita**.

bear grass See **camas**.

bear grease a sweet oil prized for cooking, hair and **bow** dressing, protection against insect bites, and treatment of scratches, scrapes, nicks, sunburn, and chapping. Bear grease was also used as a base for lotions and medicines, which were made by mixing the oil with powdered herbs, the ashes of **tobacco** or sweet grass, or other curatives. [See also **healing**.] *A gourd of bear grease proved handy to Gray Wolf and his fellow hunters, who accidentally uncovered a nest of yellow jackets.*

*a = s**a**ck; ah = s**o**b; aw = s**au**ce; ay = s**a**fe; ee = s**ee**k; eh = s**e**t*

berdache [buhr • dash'] a **plains Indian** who voluntarily abandoned the role of a brave by wearing women's clothing and accepting a servant's job or even aspiring to the role of **shaman** and applying love potions and officiating at ritual ceremonies. Women who wore men's clothes were called "manly hearts" and received a place of honor, especially if the change in their status was predicted in a dream. The existence of the berdache suggests that plains Indians were tolerant of nonconformity within the tribe. The berdache was not ridiculed, for he had seen his life's role in a vision on the day he achieved manhood. Thus, the choice was linked to the plan of the **Great Spirit**. [See also **winkte**.] *Limping Deer's decision to become a berdache was considered a suitable use for his talents as flute maker and adviser to young suitors.*

bergy bit [buhr' gee biht] the **Eskimo** term for a floating chunk from an iceberg. Because the submerged bit was edged with sharp points, it could easily wreck or sink a boat. [See also **floe**.] *Before launching a kayak, Jake scanned the bay for floes, bergy bits, and landfast ice.*

Beringia [beh • rihn' gee • uh] the land bridge that connected North America to Asia during the Pleistocene age. Dating to 90,000 B.C., this connector, which spanned the 56-mile Bering Strait between what are now Siberia and Alaska, was the route that Paleo-Siberians followed when they entered the Western Hemisphere between 50,000 B.C. and 10,000 B.C. Today, all that remains of the bridge is the Aleutian Islands. [See also **Aleut, Athapascan, Indian, subarctic Indians, Walum Olum**.] *Traveling the ice-free Rocky Mountain ridge on foot, early bands of human settlers moved from Beringia down the North American continent and into Central and South America, as far south as Tierra del Fuego.*

Big Black Bird Hawk See **Black Hawk**.

big knives an Indian name for white soldiers, who often affixed bayonets to the ends of their rifles and indiscriminately stabbed Indian dwellings, **cradleboards**, and bundles. The name connotes hate and fear for ruthless acts against women, children, and elderly tribe members. [See also **long knives**.] *Shadow reported the approach of big knives armed with cannon at the far end of the valley.*

---

ih = sit; oh = soak; oo = soup; ow = sound; uh = such; y = side　　**21**

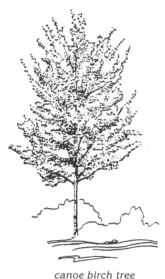
canoe birch tree

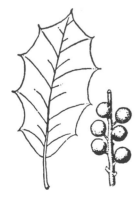
American holly

bilberry   the sweet blue fruit of a low, spreading plant native to the northern tundra. Bilberries could be eaten fresh or dried and stored for winter cooking. One important use of bilberries was the sweetening of **a-gu-tuk**, or **Eskimo** ice cream. [See also **a-gu-tuk**.] *Kopak and his baby brother picked bilberries and carried them to their mother.*

birch bark   the smooth bark of the birch tree, a hardwood common to eastern North America. Birch bark can be peeled from the trunk in large strips and used for a variety of purposes, including paper and bandages, or to make **canoes**, cups, pots, **mocucks**, and other containers. Because birch bark is waterproof, thin, and resistant to decay, it was a standard craft material for many tribes. Birch has a sweet sap, which was used as syrup and sweetener, and its oil has a wintergreen flavor. *Grandmother White Bear's birch-bark pan held the tree drippings, which she cooked into delicious brown sugar.*

Bird Girl   See **Sacagawea**.

black drink   a bitter ceremonial brew of ilex, yaupon, or dahoon holly leaves, which contain a great deal of caffeine. The leaves were parched over an open flame, then steeped in boiling water. Indulgence in the black drink, which was a part of both the **Green Corn Dance** and the **stomp dance**, caused the drinker to vomit and/or empty the bladder, thereby purifying the organs. **Huron** medicine men used a similar emetic drink to cleanse the soul of evil spirits; the **Creek** version was used in the ceremony conferring powers on a **medicine man**. Alabama ceremonial vessels were formed with round bottoms so that the container could not be set down until all the black drink was swallowed. [See also **busk, Green Corn Dance, ipecac, medicine man**.] *Pleasant Porter and other Creek tribesmen cleansed their bodies of disease and evil by swallowing large quantities of the black drink, then sitting in the close, steamy quarters of the sweat lodge.*

Black Drink Singer   See **Osceola**.

Black Elk or **Hehaka Sapa** [hee • hah' kuh sah' pah] (1863-1950)   an Oglala **Sioux** brave and relative of **Crazy Horse**. At the age of five, Black Elk experienced a vision that predicted his power as a healer and **medicine man**. In early youth he took part in an extensive tour of Europe with a Native American dance troupe. He dedicated his adult life to reviving Sioux traditions, although he lived to see them almost completely eroded by change. The autobiography of Black Elk (*Black Elk Speaks*) describes the prophet's dream of Sioux destiny. One prayer to the Great Spirit notes, "The good road and the road of difficulties you have made to cross; and where they cross, the place is holy. Day in and day out, forever, you are the life of things." (Collier, John. *Indians of the Americas.* New York: New American Library, 1947, 105.) [See also **Crazy Horse**.] *One of the strongest Native American voices condemning the destruction of his people, Black Elk said:*

> *When I look back now from this high hill of my old age, I can still see the butchered women and children lying heaped and scattered all along the crooked gulch as plain as when I saw them with eyes still young. And I can see that something else died there in the bloody mud. . . . A people's dream died there.*

(Brown, Dee. *Bury My Heart at Wounded Knee.* New York: Henry Holt, 1970, 446.)

Blackfoot a powerful, aggressive **tribe** of buffalo hunters native to the northwestern quadrant of North America. They migrated from their Canadian hunting grounds and became horse owners, like the **Crow**, **Cheyenne**, and **Sioux**. Confederates of the Bloods and Piegans, the Blackfeet were originally named "Siksika" for their **moccasins**, which they dyed black. Many of the modern Blackfeet, who have spread from Alberta, Canada, south into Montana, are ranchers and horse breeders. In 1914, a notable member of the Blackfoot nation, Red Fox James, rode 4,000 miles on horseback from Montana to the White House to support the celebration of American Indian Day, which was first celebrated the second Saturday in May in New York the next year. Much Blackfoot lore was preserved in 1920 in George Bird Grinnell's *Blackfoot Lodge Tales* (Lincoln: University of Nebraska Press, 1962). *White Quiver, the Blackfoot groom, gave a gift of horses to his bride's family.*

Black Hawk or **Black Sparrow Hawk** or **Big Black Bird Hawk** or **Makataimeshekiakiak** [may' kuh • ty' muh • shay' kee • ak • ee • ak] (1767-December 3, 1838) a **Sauk medicine man**, orator, and leader from Saukenuk, a village near Rock Island, Illinois. Black Hawk, who rejected peacemakers and fought for the British under **Tecumseh** during the War of 1812, belonged to a proud line of chiefs, including his father, grandfather, and great-grandfather. A man of honor and courage, Black Hawk contrasted with his rival, **Keokuk,** who gave in too easily to tricky white leaders. Following a miserable retreat from Wisconsin to the Mississippi River after his band was virtually wiped out at the Battle of Bad Axe on August 1, 1832, Black Hawk and White Cloud surrendered to the government in Prairie du Chien, Wisconsin. He served some months in prison, then retired from tribal duties, wrote an autobiography in 1833, and died in Oregon, Illinois. [See also **Keokuk, Tecumseh, Winnebago**.] *On his surrender on August 27, 1832, to white authorities at Prairie du Chien, Wisconsin, Black Hawk commented:*

Black Hawk drawn by George Catlin

> *I saw my evil day at hand. The sun rose dim on us in the morning, and at night it sank in a dark cloud, and looked like a ball of fire. That was the last sun that shone on Black Hawk. His heart is dead. . . . He is now a prisoner to the white man.*

(Bartlett, John. *Familiar Quotations.* Boston: Little Brown, 1980, 418.)

black Indian a person of mixed Native American and African American blood, such as the Brass Ankles of the Sea Islands, off the southeastern U.S. coast. Crispus Attucks, son of a Natick Indian mother and African father, was the first person to die in the Boston Massacre, a prelude to the American Revolution. Other famous black Indians were

- black **Cherokee** rodeo star **Bill Pickett**;

- Bessie Coleman, from the Oklahoma **Indian Territory**, who became the first black woman to receive an international pilot's license;

- pioneering black **Kiowa**, Diana Fletcher;

*a = s**a**ck; ah = s**o**b; aw = s**au**ce; ay = s**a**fe; ee = s**ee**k; eh = s**e**t*

- black **Sioux** Isaiah Dorman, army scout at the **Battle of Little Big Horn**;

- missionary John Stewart;

- black **Seminole** Chief John Horse, who defeated American troops at the Battle of Cheechebee in 1837 and helped negotiate the resettlement of his tribe at Fort Duncan and Fort Clark in 1870;

- Abraham, an African American adopted by the Seminole, who served as influential spokesman, interpreter, and ambassador during the Seminole wars;

- black **Ojibwa** sculptor Edmonia Lewis, who is best known for "Forever Free";

- the children of Seminole chief **Osceola** and his black wife, Morning Dew, the daughter of a runaway slave;

- the son of Chicago's founder, Jean du Sable, and his **Potawatomi** wife;

- 50 black Seminole army scouts, including John Ward, Adam Paine, Isaac Payne, and Pompey Factor.

[See also **Carib, gaucho, half-breed, Osceola, Bill Pickett.**] *Although not a black Indian by birth, Jim Beckwourth, noted fur trader for whom the Beckwourth Pass was named, was adopted by a Crow chief and earned the name "Bloody Arm" for his bravery in battle against Blackfeet.*

Black Kettle or **Motavato** [moh • tuh • vah' toh] (?-November 27, 1867)   a **Cheyenne** chief who was decorated by President Abraham Lincoln for service to his country. Much of Black Kettle's career comprised intense negotiations with opposing younger leaders, such as **Roman Nose**, who insisted that the white soldiers could be beaten and driven out of Indian lands. After signing a peace treaty with white authorities, Black Kettle was attacked by the outspoken racist Colonel John M. Chivington and the U.S. Cavalry at the **Sand Creek Massacre** of 1864. Black Kettle, his wife and son, and 200 others were killed and scalped by troops of General George Armstrong Custer at the Cheyenne Washita River camp in Oklahoma. [See also **Battle of Little Big Horn, Roman Nose**.] *Black Kettle, a skilled Cheyenne ambassador and peacemaker, earned a reputation for being fair, honest, and brave, as demonstrated by his speech before a council of whites and Cheyenne chiefs on September 28, 1864:*

> *We must live near the buffalo or starve. When we came here we came free, without any apprehension, to see you, and when I go home and tell my people that I have taken your hand, . . . they will feel well, and so will all the different tribes of Indians on the plains, after we have eaten and drunk with them.*

(Brown, Dee. *Bury My Heart at Wounded Knee.* New York: Henry Holt, 1970, 80.)

Black Sparrow Hawk   See **Black Hawk**.

blanket toss   a rough-and-tumble **Eskimo** game in which players hold the edges of a blanket and hoist a volunteer into the air until every participant has had a turn. The winner is the person who earns the most points for height of leaps, as well as turns and aspects of style and balance. *When players fail to land feet first, they lose the blanket toss game.*

blood feud   an escalating series of hostilities between **tribes**, beginning with an accident or argument involving individuals and gradually implicating more people on both sides seeking retaliation to defend clan or tribal honor. *Blood feuds sapped the strength of the Iroquois nation.*

blowgun   a hunting weapon common to Indians in Florida and Louisiana as well as in Central and South America. The blowgun was made from a light piece of cane, bamboo, elder stalk, reed, or hollowed ash limb 5-7 feet long. Users blew tufted darts through the blowgun at birds, snakes, lizards, and small animals. Lightweight and accurate up to 60 feet, blowguns were usually aimed at the eye of the prey. The use of blowguns was greatly enhanced by the application of fermented deer liver, venom, aconite, or other poison to the tip of the dart. [See also **arrow**.] *Muskhogean youth practiced marksmanship with bows, arrows, spears, tomahawks, and blowguns.*

blubber the thick layers of fat of a whale, seal, or other sea animal, which are cut away from the skin, then heated or pounded to extract valuable oil, which **Eskimos** burned in moss-wicked lamps for lighting and cooking. Indians of the Pacific Northwest traded the oil for other goods and kept the leftover meat to eat like bacon. [See also **flense, qulliq, seal-oil lamp**.] *Rain-Walker was amazed at the size of the animal from which the Chinooks cut chunks of blubber.*

Bodmer, Karl [bahd' muhr] (February 6, 1809-October 30, 1893) portrait artist and lithographer who captured animals, topography, and Indian culture in sketches and watercolors. Born in Zurich, Switzerland, Bodmer studied art in Paris before joining a scientific tour of the American West. From 1832 to 1834, he traveled up the Missouri River, producing keenly detailed pictures, which were collected and published in 1839. *One of Karl Bodmer's most famous portraits features a Hidatsa dog soldier.*

bogey See **booger**.

bois brule [boh • brool'] from the French for burned wood, a person of half-French, half-Indian parentage. [See also **half-breed**.] *The bois brule of eastern Canada, who were often trappers or fur traders, helped spread Catholicism among Indian tribes.*

bois d'arc [boh' dahrk] from the French for bow wood, a sturdy tree of the mulberry family, sometimes called Osage orange or orangewood, that produced flexible, lightweight wood favored by expert archers for bows. [See also **bow**.] *Shaping bois d'arc limbs over a slow flame takes time, skill, and patience.*

Osage orange

bola [boh' luh] or **bolas** a lightweight **snare** made of a string or piece of rawhide that is attached at each end to one or more pottery balls or stones. A hunter swings the string overhead, setting the weighted ends of the string in motion. When let loose, the bola wraps around the legs of an animal and causes it to fall. Bolas were common to Patagonia and Paraguay as well as to Alaska, where **Eskimos** used them for catching birds. [See also **gaucho**.] *By* *tangling the legs of the calf in a bola, the gaucho made quick work of branding.*

booger or **bogey** a menacing jester or clown. The **Cherokee** booger entertained at a winter ceremony by chasing women and girls, shoving men, and playing pranks on tribe members. Because they associated with the spirit world, boogers were thought to have the power to heal. *At Cullowhee Village, the local booger pretends to be crazy by wobbling, nodding his head, and making silly gestures.*

bow a rugged, serviceable weapon and hunting tool of Native American tribes. The wood of the bow, usually **bois d'arc**, **hickory**, ironwood, dogwood, mulberry, **willow**, aspen, **mesquite**, yew, juniper, witch hazel, or ash, was cut in 3–6-foot lengths and either split and separated from the inner core, or the bow was formed of laminated strips of hardwood. Another method of bow making was shaping segments of mountain goat horns that were held together with fish glue. The **Chinook** bowmaker, who formed his bow from a whale rib, added strength by gluing dried **sinew** to the arc. The finished bow, notched at each end and strung with bark, two-ply bear gut, squirrel hide, nettle fiber, or rawhide, was seasoned with **bear grease** or fish oil to prevent splitting. The waxed **bowstring**, about 4 inches shorter than the bow and hanging free when not in use, could be slipped over the frame in one quick motion. The grip, which was slightly thicker than the ends, was often wrapped in cord for ease of handling. The tough, springy bows of the **Nez Percé** were so prized by Europeans that they became valuable trade items. [See also **arrow, bois d'arc, sinew**.] *In a Spanish diary dating to 1528, an explorer notes that the Timucua used bows as thick as an arm that fired accurately from 200 paces.*

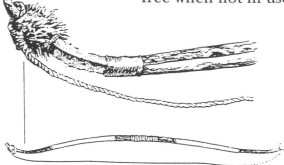

double-curved bow with fur end wrapping and sinew string

bowdrill a device used for carving, boring, or making fire. The bowdrill was fashioned from an arc of wood fastened at each end to a cord wrapped around a vertical stick. Twirling the stick rapidly by sawing back and forth on the bowdrill, the user made fine markings on ivory or whalebone or ignited a fire by grinding the end of the bowdrill in the socket of a piece of wood. [See also **firedrill, pump drill**.] *Jesse used his grandfather's bowdrill to kindle a spark, which he fed with dried moss, bits of bark, and shredded vines, encouraged with small puffs of air, then fanned into flame.*

bowstring   the cord that joins the two ends of a **bow**. Bowstrings were made from the **sinew** or gut of bears or buffalo, bark strips, rawhide, deer or squirrel hide, or nettle fibers. The bowstring was strengthened by the addition of a glue made from buffalo hooves or fish bones dissolved in boiling water. *Jake Bluehouse oiled buffalo sinew, then stretched and twisted it into a strong bowstring, which he carried in his backpack as a spare.*

Bozeman Trail   a passageway through the Rocky Mountains to the Montana gold mines. The trail was opened by John Bozeman in 1862. Traversing valuable buffalo grounds, the Bozeman Trail was to be guarded by a series of forts, thus cutting off **plains Indians** from their livelihood. **Sioux**, **Arapaho**, and **Cheyenne** chiefs, spearheaded by **Red Cloud**, fought so courageously for their rights that by late 1868, recurrent rebellion, climaxing in the 1866 battle with Captain William Fetterman's forces, forced government officials to abandon plans to complete the trail. [See also **Red Cloud**.] *With the advancement of the railroad, the Bozeman Trail faded into obscurity.*

bowdrill (above) and detail of stone drill point

Brae, Martha [bray] (*fl.* 1500-1510)   a legendary **Arawak** woman who in the sixteenth century chose suicide rather than betray tribal secrets to the invading Spanish. When pressed to disclose the location of a gold mine, Martha Brae leaped into a Jamaican stream, which her ghost is said to haunt. [See also **Arawak**.] *Today, the duppy of Martha Brae is said to hover over rafters, who enjoy the gently flowing waterway bearing her name.*

braining   the process of curing an untanned animal skin by applying the stewed brain of deer or buffalo to the dampened hide with a beamer or shaping tool made from the leg of a deer, then leaving the mixture overnight to be absorbed into the material. [See also **beaming,**

buckskin, flesher.] *Braining with buffalo brains was effective because the acidic paste quickly tanned and preserved hides.*

Brant, Joseph or **Thayendanegea** [tay' ihn • duh • nay' gyuh] (1742-November 24, 1807) a multilingual **Mohawk** war **chief**, diplomat, and Anglican missionary who founded Ohsweken (now Brantford, Ontario). The son of a **half-breed** mother and a Mohawk chief, Brant, the younger brother of **Molly Brant**, was born in **Ohio** and educated in a Lebanon, Connecticut, mission school. At the age of 13, he took part in the Battle of Lake George; he also fought in the Pontiac War in 1763. He traveled to England in 1775, rose to the rank of colonel in the British army, and translated a part of the New Testament and the *Book of Common Prayer* into Mohawk. At the age of 41, he governed the Six Nations Reserve near the Grand River in Ontario. He was succeeded by his son John. [See also **Iroquois, Mohawk**.] *While comparing systems of law among the Mohawk and whites, Joseph Brant commented, "Among us we have no prisons, we have no pompous parade of courts; we have no written laws."* (Pastron, Allen. *Great Indian Chiefs*. Santa Barbara, Calif.: Bellerophon, 1993, 19.)

Brant, Molly (*fl.* 1770s) the older sister of **Joseph Brant**, Molly was a mistress of Sir William Johnson, hero of the French and Indian War, trader, and Superintendent of Indian Affairs. While living at Johnson Hall, she impressed even the most sophisticated visitors with her beauty, grace, and intelligence. In 1777, Molly helped her brother and his **Seneca** allies, halt troops from Tryon County, New York, before they could stop the British and Indian siege at Fort Stanwix. *Both colonial patriot and Mohawk princess, Molly Brant epitomizes Native American women who tried to live in two worlds.*

breechclout or **breechcloth** a loincloth; among male desert and **plains Indians**, a single piece of leather, skin, or woven goods 1 foot wide in front and 4-6 feet long which passed between the legs and over a belt. The loose ends, sometimes fringed, stitched, or quilled, hung down as decoration. The **Inuit** version, which was made from sealskin, was a slender band resembling an athletic supporter. The breechclout served more as protection for the genitals than as a modesty shield. [See also **clout Indian, maxtli**.] *In warm weather, some tribes preferred simple breech-clouts to more complicated clothing.*

Bright Eyes or **Inshtatheamba** [insh' tah • thay • ahm' buh] or **Suzette La Flesche Picotte** (1854-May 26, 1903) an Omaha writer, lecturer, and social worker from Nebraska who aided the **Ponca** after a local tribe was forced to leave its **reservation** in South Dakota and go to **Indian Territory** in 1877. The daughter of Iron Eye, an Omaha **chief**, in childhood she demonstrated scholarly talents and was sent to eastern schools to earn a medical degree. Along with her brother Francis and her husband, editor Henry Tribbles, Bright Eyes conducted a public campaign to restore civil rights to dispossessed Poncas. As a result of her speeches in Boston, Philadelphia, New York, Washington, D.C., and England, she influenced the passage of the **Dawes Act**, which allowed Native Americans to own property. [See also **Dawes Act, Ponca**.] *Bright Eyes's husband wrote* Buckskin and Blanket Days *(Garden City, N.Y.: Doubleday, 1957), an account of his wife's dedication to bettering the lives of poor and dispossessed Native Americans.*

buckhorn a sharp scoring or piercing tool made of antler or bone honed to resemble an **awl**, punch, or icepick. The buckhorn was used to score or engrave metal or shell ornaments. [See also **ice chisel, pana, ulu**.] *On the opening day of the Amarillo rodeo, Billy Bowlegs wore a silver gorget, which was engraved with a buckhorn.*

buckskin a type of untanned suede leather made from deerskin, moose or elk hide, or the skin of smaller animals. Buckskin, which was softened by stretching, smoking, and kneading, was often dehaired, dyed, and decorated with fringe, beads, feathers, shells, or quills. Buckskin makes a serviceable waterproof cape that protects the wearer from wind and rough underbrush and remains soft and flexible even after many washings. Buckskin is also used to describe a horse that is yellowish tan with a dark mane and tail. [See also **beaming, braining**.] *Queen Edna Kash-kash, a Cayuga noblewoman living around 1900, displayed her status in the lavish decoration of her buckskin dress, which featured a beaded, feathered yoke.*

buckhorn awl

buffalo chips dried buffalo manure; dung. On the plains, where firewood was scarce, buffalo chips were the chief fuel for cooking fires. [See also **smoke signals**.] *Mattie and her little sisters did their part for each family meal by supplying buffalo chips to feed the cooking fire.*

buffalo dance a sacred ceremony in which the plains tribes honored the importance of the buffalo, which they considered a sacred animal. Dressed in buffalo heads, dancers imitated the movements of the herd as a way of thanking the gods for sending the buffalo, which was the tribe's major source of food, building and housing material, ceremonial garments, cooking containers, medicine, implements, toys, art and sewing supplies, clothing, and glue. *At the annual buffalo dance, Black Dove jostled to get a better view of the lead dancer.*

buffalo jump or **buffalo fall** a hunting method by which a whole **tribe**—rather than risk hunters' lives trying to shoot individual animals with **arrows** or stab them with lances—hooted, yelled, and waved branches, torches, and clackers to drive a herd of buffalo through a narrow path of boulders and over a cliff. The Plano culture of the Plainview, Texas, area (ca. 7,500-4,000 B.C.) may have developed the buffalo jump as an alternative to the lance. The Plano depended on bighorn bison to make **pemmican**, a preserved meat mixture packed in animal skins and intestines. To assure a successful hunt, Indians drew animal **pictographs** or carved **petroglyphs** and magic symbols on nearby cliffs. They also employed buffalo callers, who dressed in buffalo hides, snorted, and rolled on the ground to lure herds to their death. The killing of buffalo was done with great reverence; the Pawnee and **Blackfoot** method of killing them was a form of worship of the **Great Spirit**, who provided the animals to nurture life. [See also **deadfall, fire-surround, pemmican**.] *According to Old Fool Bull, the quickest and safest way to supply meat to a hungry tribe was with a buffalo jump.*

Buffalo Shields a secret **Kiowa** society of healers. The Buffalo Shields received deferential treatment for their kindness to the sick and injured. Their female counterpart, the Bear Women, were also revered for humane deeds. *Unlike the Dog Society and other ritual groups, the Buffalo Shields were believed to be adept at magic.*

Buffalo Soldiers   the first all-black U.S. Army troop, which served from the late 1860s until integration in 1952, so named because the soldiers' curly hair coated with dust reminded the Indians of a buffalo pelt. The Buffalo Soldiers fought in various Indian Wars, including the **Cheyenne** war (1867-1869), Red River war (1874-1875), **Apache** war (1875-1876), and **Sioux** war (1890-1891). Earning numerous citations and 24 medals of honor, these cavalry troops played an integral role in the settlement of the western United States. The Ninth and Tenth Regiments accompanied Teddy Roosevelt's Rough Riders to Cuba during the Spanish American War. *In September 1992, General Colin Powell dedicated Eddie Dixon's $850,000 Buffalo Soldier Monument at Fort Leavenworth, Kansas.*

buffalo stone   See **iniskim**.

bullboat   a cup-shaped boat made from buffalo skins stretched across a **willow** frame, seamed with **sinew**, and sealed with pitch or tallow. Bullboats could be poled or rowed by two paddlers and were frequently used for short trips, such as to ferry families and personal belongings over rivers and swift streams. To steady a bullboat, the builder left the buffalo tail intact and often attached a bit of wood to serve as a rudder. [See also **poling**.] *If paddled incorrectly, a bullboat merely spins around in the water.*

buffalo dance drawn by George Catlin

bull-roarer

bull-roarer a toy or ceremonial noisemaker made from a notched disc of wood, gourd, pottery, or bone attached to a long string, then swung about the head to produce a steady hum. Symbolizing the **thunderbird**, the hum of the bull-roarer summoned rain. [See also **thunderbird**.] *Dull Raven stood out as the best twirler of the bull-roarer.*

bundle keeper an honored tribe member chosen to inventory, preserve, and protect the tribe's sacred **medicine bundle**. [See also **cacique, medicine bundle**.] *When the bundle keeper died, council members asked the head woman of his clan to name a successor.*

burden frame a rack made of thin strips of **hickory** or basswood and carried on the back. The burden frame had a shelf at the bottom and was attached to the forehead by a burden strap, or **tumpline**, made of woven hemp, **babiche**, or animal hair. Various types of baskets and bags could be strapped to the frame for hauling vegetables, roots, berries, or stones to be used for cooking. [See also **babiche, tumpline**.] *Grace Whistling Bird trudged through the snowy field, keeping one hand on her burden frame to steady it.*

Bureau of Indian Affairs a federal department created in 1824 to resolve internal tribal problems and to smooth over difficulties between Native Americans and the U.S. government. Established as a part of the War Department, the Bureau of Indian Affairs became a division of the Department of the Interior in 1849. After Native Americans were granted citizenship in 1924, the Bureau of Indian Affairs continued to provide services to facilitate education, health, housing, and employment. *Often, council meetings between tribes and the U.S. Cavalry were mediated by members of the Bureau of Indian Affairs.*

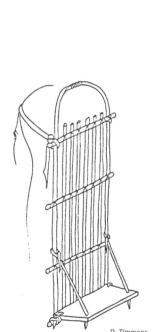

D. Timmons

burden frame

burial scaffold a raised platform built in a tree, on a rock ledge, or atop a wooden framework to support the remains of the dead, which were bundled in buffalo hides and secured with **babiche** or rawhide ropes. From this position, the spirit could free itself from the body and seek the wind and clouds. Women wept and wailed, supplying the only show of emotion associated with the ceremony honoring the departed. For great leaders, horses were sometimes killed and their heads and tails tied alongside the scaffold as symbols of honor and wealth. *The Blackfoot elders honored their family members who died of smallpox by placing them on a burial scaffold.*

busk or **posketa** [pahs • kay' tuh]   the **Creek's** four-day feast of green corn, for which tribe members purified their homes, clothes, bodies, and personal relationships. Following sweatbaths and purging black drinks, celebrants started a symbolic fire to roast the first corn of the harvest season, combining the equivalent of New Year's Day and Thanksgiving into one holiday. The celebration ended with more feasting, lacrosse, dancing, and games. [See also **black drink, Green Corn Dance**.] *The busk was so important to Creeks that they forgave all crimes, rekindled hearth fires, and replaced old clothing.*

butterbean game   a favorite indoor sport of the **Cherokee**. Players put six butterbean halves in a flat basket and tossed them in the air, catching them in the basket. Scoring depended on how the bean halves landed. If all landed on their flat sides, the player earned six points. Six halves on their round sides earned four points. *The players of the butterbean game were often two teams, men against women, who blackened with soot the faces of members of the losing team.*

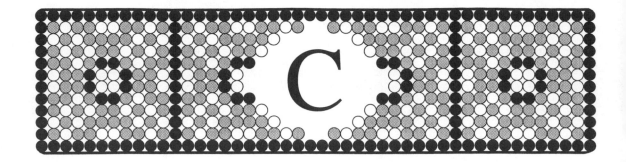

cabin court an open-ended summer version of the **Muskhogean hot house** or men's club, composed of four cabins where men gathered to worship and conduct business. One segment of the cabin court housed holy objects and was guarded by the **medicine man** or **shaman**, called the Beloved Man. [See also **hot house, kiva**.] *Muskhogean men met at the cabin court to discuss the growing problem of slave catchers, who carried off African American wives and adopted children.*

cacao [kuh • kow'] a tropical evergreen tree that produces a pod from which cocoa beans are extracted, fermented, dried, roasted, and made into cocoa, chocolate, and cocoa butter. Cacao beans became so valuable that the **Aztec** used them as money. [See also **chocólatl**.] *Central American Indians anticipated the refreshing taste of a frothy cup of cacao, flavored with honey and spices.*

cache [kash] a hidden supply of food or other goods, such as harnesses, extra clothing, or tools; a root cellar. In the tundra, a cache functioned as a deep-freeze, keeping fresh meat and fish until they were needed. The **Eskimo** weighted their caches with stones to prevent foxes and other predators from stealing food. **Plains Indians** dug meat pits with an **adze** made from the shoulder blade of buffalo, then lined the walls with moss, grass, or **willow** limbs and hides. Topping the pit with a bark roof and replacing dirt and sod over the cache, the diggers sealed in meat odors and kept out hungry animals and thieves. They built similar caches over stores of **corn**, heaping ash and litter over the spot to deceive their enemies. The Kutchin built their caches on tall platforms, which kept food safe from prowling and climbing animals. *Oto hunters concealed a portion of their fresh venison in a cache dug in the hillside and lined with bear grass.*

D. Timmons

cache

*a = s**a**ck; ah = s**o**b; aw = s**au**ce; ay = s**a**fe; ee = s**ee**k; eh = s**e**t*

cacique [kuh • seek'] the chief priest and magistrate of a town or **pueblo** who repaired, cleaned, and supplied the **kiva**; inventoried ceremonial objects; organized worship and initiation rites; and arranged for rain dances and other seasonal rituals. [See also **bundle keeper, chief, mingo, sachem**.] *Lone Lost Moon willingly served his term as cacique, which brought honor to him and his family.*

cactli [kak' tlee] sandals made of rawhide or **yucca** fiber. Unlike the **moccasins** of forest Indians, **Aztec** cactli had a heel and tied on with straps or laces. [See also **huarache, yucca**.] *Tashquent told stories about how his Pima grandmother made cactli for the whole family.*

calmecac [kal' muh • kak] an **Aztec** school for upper-class boys. Because education was reserved for only a few, attendance brought great honor and prestige to graduates, who studied hard to achieve high positions in the military or priesthood. *In the calmecac, children learned about the Aztec calendar by studying the Codex Barbonicus.*

chief holding a calumet

calumet [kal' yuh • meht] a special ceremonial pipe, made of reed, clay, stone, or wood, used in religious rituals to bring rain or good luck to the tribe or bind friendships and alliances; a peace pipe. The calumet was almost a yard long and featured extensive beadwork, **quilling**, horsehair, feathers, and carving. Some were shaped like animals or mythic figures. Devout tribesmen believed that smoke from the bowl drifted to the four winds and brought peace. Because it was a holy object, the calumet was often used as a flag of truce or a badge of safe conduct for ambassadors traveling on official business to neighboring tribes. [See also **medicine pipe, peace pipe, pipe bag**.] *Janey Corn Woman formed a long ceremonial cornhusk cigar, the Southwest version of the Algonquin calumet.*

camas [kahm' uhs] or **camass** or **bear grass** a coarse plant of the lily family that is native to both Atlantic and Pacific coasts and grows in boggy grassland and produces a purplish blue flower; also called wild hyacinth, pommes des prairies, bear grass, or sweet flag. In harvesting camas, Indian women used a dibble, or digging stick, to unearth the edible starchy bulbs, which they dried, pounded into small loaves, or steamed and ate fresh with huckleberries or blackberries as a major portion of their diet and as an aid to digestion. The Kalispel **tribe** of Idaho took its name from the camas plant, which they used as a valuable trade item. Camas root was used by the **Cherokee** as a soap for washing blankets and as a poison to stun fish. Any location with a stand of camas was precious to the tribe. [See also **squamash**.] *When the shiny black seeds appeared on the camas plant, Ada knew that it was time to organize a digging party.*

camisa [kuh • meez' uh]   a long-sleeved blouse, tunic, or shirt worn either belted or loose by females in southwestern tribes. The camisa topped a long skirt, usually composed of tiers of cloth shirred or gathered for fullness. *Rosa's camisa matched the red stripe in her belt and sash.*

candlefish or **eulachon** [yew' luh • k'n]   a short, slender silver fish of the smelt family that flourishes in the sea, then migrates to the rivers of the West Coast, from California to Alaska. The **Nootka** caught candlefish in **weirs** or baskets, then dried and strung them on a wick for use as candles. Candlefish oil, which was stored in cedar boxes, served as a food preservative, seasoning, and medicine. *Karana regretted that predatory animals stole her winter supply of candlefish.*

Caniba   See **Carib**.

canoe   a narrow, lightweight boat, sometimes 18 feet long and less than 2 feet wide, that is propelled by a single paddler or by 4-10 rowers kneeling in place. Making canoes from cedar or spruce ribs and three pieces of birch or linden bark, northeastern forest Indians shaped the pieces and stored them in water. As crafters formed the body, they used **sinew** or split cedar root to stitch the bottom piece to two side panels, weighting the outer layer with rocks and caulking with spruce gum or pine pitch mixed with soot. Ribs and gunwales gave shape to the finished boat.

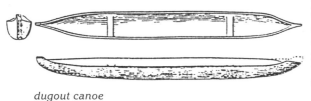

dugout canoe

Women completed the external work by stitching the ends together and sealing them with heated gum. Then

*a = s**a**ck; ah = s**o**b; aw = s**au**ce; ay = s**a**fe; ee = s**ee**k; eh = s**e**t*

men inserted the ribs under the rails and stretched the covering to fit. The Beothuk of Nova Scotia added a raised crosspiece at the center to facilitate portage. In contrast to this style of building canoes, the Chumash of southern California split driftwood into planks, drilled holes in the edges, then lashed them together with strong cord or sinew and fastened them to a framework. To keep out seepage, they sealed the inner side with tar or asphaltum. [See also **dugout, kayak, pirogue, portage, umiak**.] *Traveling by canoe is the best way to see the Chattahoochee River.*

Careta [cah • ray' tuh] (?-1514)   a chief of the Darién tribe, which inhabited the area around Cueva, Panama, at the time of European discovery. Leading 2,000 natives, Careta met Vasco Balboa, an Italian explorer, in September 1513. Balboa captured Careta by night and extracted Careta's promise to supply provisions for Balboa's expeditionary forces. Careta, eager to ally himself with Balboa, gave him his daughter as wife. Because of Careta's expert advice, Balboa made a useful alliance with local chiefs and built ships out of a bitter native timber that was resistant to sea worms. *Careta introduced Balboa to Chief Comogre and Comogre's son Carlos, who knew the location of a vein of gold.*

Carib [kuh • reeb'] or **Caniba** [kah' nee • bah]   an oceangoing **tribe** native to Central America, the northeastern shore of South America, and the Amazon Valley. The Carib are noted for keeping female slaves and for decking themselves in bright parrot feathers and red paint before attacking other tribes. The Carib, who migrated to the West Indies around A.D. 1000, proved so challenging to Columbus's sailors in 1493 that he gave up hope of landing on Dominica, Martinique, and Guadeloupe. Later, French and British settlers were similarly repulsed, and they left the natives in peace until 1795, when the English drove them out. Some Caribs chose to hurl themselves off the limestone cliffs of Martinique rather than accept European domination. Grenada, St. Kitts, St. Lucia, and St. Barts shared a similar history, with the French ousting the Caribs in the 1650s. Many surviving Caribs settled on the reservation near Rosalie, Dominica, and interbred with Africans, producing a tribe of **black Indians**. [See also **Arawak, black Indian, petroglyph**.] *The Arawak tribes complained to Christopher Columbus about the treachery of the cannibalistic Carib warriors.*

---

ih = sit; oh = soak; oo = soup; ow = sound; uh = such; y = side

caribou [kar' uh • boo'] a large migrating deer that supplies the needs of the **Chipewyan** and Naskapi tribes of northern Canada as well as the Caribou Eskimo, who live on the Barren Grounds west of Hudson Bay in northern Canada. These hunters use every part of the animal for food, clothing, housing materials, cooking fat, utensils, and oil for heating and lighting. A favorite recipe is broiled caribou head, which is suspended over a fire and **barbecued** for a whole day. [See also **tuttu**.] *Naskapi and Chipewyan hunters trick caribou herds with stone decoys, which scare the animals away from the trail toward blinds where the hunters are hiding.*

D. Timmons

caribou

Carlisle Indian School a Native American vocational and academic training center in Carlisle, Pennsylvania, founded by General R. H. Pratt in 1882 to force Indian students to give up their native culture. Jim Thorpe (May 28, 1888-March 28, 1953), one of the outstanding athletes to graduate from the Carlisle Indian School, was an All-American track star who won awards for the decathlon and pentathlon at the 1912 Olympic games. Dr. Carlos Montezuma, an Apache physician, practiced medicine at the Carlisle Indian School. *Graves on the Carlisle Indian School grounds reveal the names of deceased Apache, Ponca, Cheyenne, and Sioux students, such as Ada Foxcatcher, William Snake, Nannie Little Robe, and Dennis, son of Blue Tomahawk.*

Carrier a **tribe** of hunters and fishers native to British Columbia. Their name derived from an early custom requiring women to carry the ashes of their dead husbands on their backs for a three-year mourning period or until her immediate family could distribute an acceptable amount of furs, foodstuffs, or other wealth at a **potlatch**. The Carrier subsist mainly on salmon, which they dry for food and skin to make **moccasins** and clothing. [See also **Athapascan, potlatch**.] *Bernadette Carey passes along Carrier lore and heritage to Ronald, her only son.*

*a = s**a**ck; ah = s**o**b; aw = s**au**ce; ay = s**a**fe; ee = s**ee**k; eh = s**e**t*

cassava See **manioc**.

Catawba [kuh • taw' buh] a large **tribe** of hunters and fishers native to the Carolinas and kin to the Cherokee. The Catawba were famous for their pottery. Utilizing certain native clays they fashioned bowls, jars, jugs, and crocks, which they glazed with taupe, brown, and gray finishes and fired in hillside ovens. Native crafts spawned a major industry carried on by European potters, who copied their methods. Today, to obtain authentic colors and textures, a handful of North Carolina potters have returned to the old methods of mixing clay and firing crockery in woodstoves rather than electric kilns. *On August 29, 1754, King Haglar, a Catawba chief, rebuked English colonists for making ale and liquor, which made some of his people so sick that they died.*

Catlin, George (July 26, 1796-December 28, 1872) an American artist who captured on canvas and in his journals the culture and philosophy of American Indian tribes, particularly the **Mandan**. A native of Wilkes Barre, Pennsylvania, Catlin studied law, then chose art, particularly depictions of Native American life, as his life's work. After circulating his paintings, writings, and artifacts in the United States, England, and France, he resumed painting Indians, journeying from Central America up the Pacific Coast. [See also **Tenkswatawa**.] *George Catlin remarked,*

George Catlin

> *I love a people who have always made me welcome to the best they had . . . who are honest without laws, who have no jails and no poor-house . . . who never take the name of God in vain . . . who worship God without a Bible . . . who are free from religious animosities . . . who have never raised a hand against me, or stolen my property . . . who never fought a battle with white men except on their own ground . . . and oh! how I love a people who don't live for the love of money.*

(McCracken, Harold. *George Catlin and the Old Frontier.* New York: Dial Press, 1959, 14.)

catlinite [kat' lih • nyt] a soft reddish stone quarried by many tribes from mines located in neutral territory in Minnesota. Henry Wadsworth Longfellow mentions catlinite in his epic poem *The Song of Hiawatha* (New York:

Dial Press, 1983). The word *catlinite* honors painter George Catlin, who had samples of the stone tested in an eastern laboratory. Because it was easy to carve, catlinite was used to make bowls and stems of pipes or **calumets**. In 1937, residents of Pipestone, a city in southwest Minnesota, created the Pipestone National Monument to protect 282 acres where catlinite was once quarried. [See also **medicine pipe, steatite**.] *Tall Wolf used a crooked knife to carve the outline of his pipestem in catlinite.*

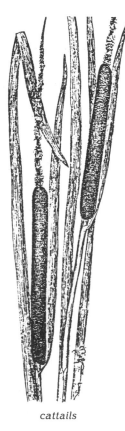

cattails

cat's-cradle a popular **Eskimo, Navaho**, and **Zuñi** game in which the player intertwines a circle of string or rawhide into various figures across the fingers. *Irvana taught her small son to wrap a thong about his outstretched thumbs and form a cat's-cradle.*

cattail a common water reed that grows in marshes or along streams. It has a furry brown spike and straplike green leaves. In the green stage, cattail shoots are used as salad or boiled, seasoned with wild onion or ginger, and eaten like asparagus. Sprouts and tender stalks are eaten raw. If cattails are picked in summer, pollen and fiber from the brown stems can be used to thicken pancake batter, soup, stew, or gravy; they can also be used in makeup and ceremonial skin decoration. The tubers can be eaten raw or cooked like potatoes; the leaves make a tea or fiber for weaving mats, baskets, and roofs; the down serves as soft pillow stuffing. Cattails were also used to make torch lights, lining for **cradleboards**, chewing gum, and a ceremonial powder for **Apache** puberty rites. [See also **tule**.] *Because the Narragansett Indians depended on cattails as raw material, they protected the waterways on which the cattails grew.*

caucus [kaw' kuhs] a closed discussion; a private meeting. In many tribes, a caucus not only included women but featured female advisers, whose advice carried great weight with chiefs and elders. [See also **palaver, powwow**.] *Liota's role in the caucus was to introduce the main speaker and to help answer questions.*

cayenne [ky • ehn'] a hot pepper that Indians of the Southwest and Mexico ground into powder, which they added to hot drinks to cure fever. Cayenne stimulates the body, producing a sensation of warmth and well-being. *Kito kept a rawhide bag of cayenne powder in his travel kit so he would have seasoning for the rabbits he cooked over open fires.*

Cayuga [cah • yoo' guh]   another name for the **Iroquois** or the People of the Swampy Land. [See also **Iroquois**.] *In a remorseful address to the New York Historical Society in May 1847, Cayuga orator Peter Wilson lamented that his tribe did not stop Europeans from taking charge of tribal lands.*

Cayuse [ki' yoos]   a **tribe** of Pacific Coast Indians famous for breeding and training a wild, sturdy desert pony called a cayuse. The Cayuse met peacefully with the Lewis and Clark expedition in 1804 but came to grief for kidnapping Presbyterian missionaries and their families who, in 1847, spread an epidemic of measles. Joined by the Palouse, the Cayuse, led by Chief Tilokaikt and his aide, Tomahas, eluded pursuing white soldiers for two years, then surrendered in 1849. *Arthur Iron Hook declared that the horse he bought was an Appaloosa, not a paint or a cayuse.*

celt [sehlt]   a polished stone blade for an ax or **tomahawk** that, when sharpened, was capable of killing a grizzly bear. Archaeologists date settlements of prehistoric forest Indians by the style of celts, arrowheads, and other stone artifacts. [See also **arrow, tomahawk**.] *The celt found near the burial mound linked the sunken settlement with tribes crossing Beringia in search of better hunting grounds.*

century plant   See **agave**.

chaparral [shap' uh • rehl']   a thicket of shrubs and small trees. Because the chaparral grows into a dense tangle, it is the natural habitat of many low-growing plants, birds, amphibians, and small animals. *Walini located the lost lamb near the edge of the chaparral.*

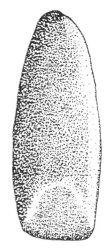

stone celt

chaps [shaps *or* chaps]   wide, flexible leggings that are joined or laced together and belted over pants to protect the legs, particularly for horseback riding in rough terrain. Chaps are handy because they can be removed in hot weather. They are easy to replace when torn or scratched by cactus thorns or briars. [See also **leggings**.] *Cudjo made and fringed several pairs of chaps and sold them at the Wednesday market.*

char   a small, bony sea or freshwater fish of the trout family that Indians netted and dried for winter food. Because they have few scales, char are a favorite of Arctic **Eskimos** and Indians living from Alaska to northern California. *Lona split and boned enough char to roast over the open flame for her two children.*

Charbonneau, Jean Baptiste [shahr • bohn • noh' zhahn bah • teest'] (February 11, 1805-1866)   famous trapper and guide; the son of Sacagawea and her French Canadian husband, Toussaint Charbonneau. Born of mixed **Shoshone** and French ancestry in a **Mandan** camp at the beginning of the **Lewis and Clark expedition**, Charbonneau, nicknamed Pompey or Pompe, remained in his mother's **cradleboard** for the duration of the journey. Afterwards, Clark provided for Charbonneau's education at a Catholic school. From 1823 to 1829, Charbonneau traveled Europe and North Africa, returning to the Rocky Mountains to trap for the American Fur Company and guide American soldiers through Indian country. In 1866, on his way to California, at the Owyhee River, near Oregon, Jean Baptiste Charbonneau died and was buried. [See also **Lewis and Clark expedition, Sacagawea**.] *Pompey's Tower, a sandstone butte east of Billings, Montana, is named for Jean Baptiste Charbonneau.*

charqui   See **jerky**.

chemuck [shay' muhk]   mush or hot cereal made from acorns, which was cooked in baskets with hot stones or was boiled in clay pots. Making chemuck was tedious because **acorn** meal had to be washed to remove its bitter flavor. Chemuck was often flavored with berries or honey. [See also **acorn, coontie, sofkee**.] *The Pomo and Pacific tribes near Yosemite favored meals of chemuck.*

*a = s**a**ck; ah = s**o**b; aw = s**au**ce; ay = s**a**fe; ee = s**ee**k; eh = s**e**t*

Cherokee [cher' uh • kee]   an influential Indian nation of the **Iroquois** language group, native to Kentucky, Virginia, West Virginia, North and South Carolina, Georgia, Alabama, and Tennessee. The Cherokee, who probably originated around the Great Lakes, numbered about 20,000 and occupied 40,000 square miles of land before white settlers came. Cherokees learned to farm and to live in log cabins, and they gave important leadership roles to female chiefs or **sachems**. Women's status eroded after Echota, the capital of the Carolina piedmont tribes, was visited in 1540 by de Soto.

The Cherokee were uprooted by President Andrew Jackson. They were condemned to a long journey known as the **Trail of Tears** and were resettled in Oklahoma in 1838. Respected for their strength of character, they were able to adapt to rapid cultural changes. In Oklahoma they formed schools and started small businesses, such as blacksmith shops, ferries, trading posts, tanneries, and mills, and they printed their own newspaper in the Cherokee language. **Sequoyah**, Dennis Bushyhead, **Nancy Ward**, Junaluska, **John Ross**, **Wilma Mankiller**, **Corn Tassel**, and William Keeler are noted members of the Cherokee nation. Today their tribal members number more than 100,000, forming the second largest Native American nation. [See also **Corn Tassel, Wilma Mankiller, John Ross, Sequoyah, Shawnee, Trail of Tears, Tsali, Nancy Ward**.] *"The Lone Wild Bird," a Cherokee call to worship in the Presbyterian hymnal, petitions the Great Spirit to rest in the human heart.*

*Little Robe,
Cheyenne chief*

chert [churt]   a grainy, flintlike quartz rock that Indians used to fashion tools and weapons, such as arrowheads and **tomahawks**, and later to strike sparks for building fires. Chert was so important to Native American travelers that pieces were often kept handy in a buckskin pouch tied about the waist or suspended from a **lanyard** about the neck. [See also **arrow, flint knapping**.] *Archaeologists recognize the importance of chert to early tool makers.*

Cheyenne [shy • an']   a nomadic **tribe** of western **Algonquin** buffalo hunters native to the Great Lakes area who migrated to the western plains. Named for their practice of painting their bodies with earth pigments, the Cheyenne developed a sophisticated governing board for their

10 **clans**, each of which elected four chiefs to serve 10-year terms as lawmakers. The Cheyenne met the **Lewis and Clark expedition** in 1804. Later encounters with Europeans brought plagues of smallpox, cholera, measles, tuberculosis, scarlet fever, and flu, as reported in 1849 by Cheyenne trader George Bent.

From the mid-1800s until the **Battle of Little Big Horn**, the Cheyenne teamed with **Comanches**, **Kiowas**, and **Apaches** against the U.S. Cavalry and white settlers. Their revolt reached a high point after the **Sand Creek Massacre** and concluded in the defeat of General George Armstrong Custer. The Cheyenne admired bravery, like that displayed by Buffalo Calf Road Woman, who in 1876 rescued her brother from the thick of the Battle of the Rosebud after his horse had been killed. Led by **Dull Knife**, the Cheyenne attempted to escape white authorities in 1878, but failed to recover their former independence. In November 1992, Ben Nighthorse Campbell, a Cheyenne from Colorado, was the first Native American elected to the U.S. senate since 1929. [See also **Battle of Little Big Horn, Dull Knife, Roman Nose, Sand Creek Massacre, Sweet Medicine chief**.] *As demonstrated by a Cheyenne myth told by Mary Little Bear Inkanish in* The Plains Indian Mythology *(New York: Meridian, 1985), the owl is a ghost that returns to Earth to complete a task or satisfy a hunger it knew when it was alive.*

George Bent

Chickasaw [chihk' uh • saw']   a native **tribe** of Alabama, Georgia, Kentucky, Tennessee, and Mississippi; a member tribe of the **Muskhogean** nation. The Chickasaw fought Hernando de Soto's expedition in 1541 and joined with the **Natchez** against the French. The Chickasaw, who succeeded during the pre-Civil War era in farming, lumbering, and milling, became town dwellers and lived in well-constructed log homes. By 1835, however, the Chickasaw were forced to join the **Creek**, **Cherokee**, and **Choctaw** in exile to the West. Their removal along the **Trail of Tears** was led by Chief Levi Colbert. By 1855, most Chickasaw had withdrawn to **reservations** in Oklahoma. [See also **Trail of Tears**.] *The Chickasaw welcomed runaway slaves and intermarried with black refugees.*

chickee [chih' kee] or **chiki**   an open, wall-less dwelling or pavilion. The chickee was made of a framework of cypress sticks, a raised platform, and a roof thatched from

a = sack; ah = sob; aw = sauce; ay = safe; ee = seek; eh = set

cabbage palm; an attic space was used for storage. For the **Seminole**, the chickee offered a practical solution to hot, muggy weather and the menace of the snakes, alligators, and ground insects common to swamps and **bayous**. Furniture consisted of a few mats and **hammocks**. The area under the chickee was reserved for watchdogs and domestic animals. [See also **bayou, ramada**.] *The chickee suits the lifestyle of Native Americans who live in subtropical heat.*

Seminole chickee

chicle [chihk' lee] or **chictle** a reddish-brown gum resin extracted from the coagulated sap or latex of the sapodilla tree, a tropical evergreen native to Central America. The **Maya** used the wood of the tree to make rot-proof beams. *People who chew gum owe their treat to chicle, a chewy sap that native children of the Yucatan Peninsula chewed centuries ago.*

chief a high-ranking tribal leader or adviser. The concept of chief, which is not comparable to the idea of a military commander in chief, could apply to any leader of spiritual, political, or military matters. Even the interpreter was given the title Talking Chief. To the **Yuma**, the highest-ranking tribe member was called the Brave Man; among the **Seneca**, the godiont was a female chief who assisted the **false faces** in superintending the healing of the sick. Some **tribes**, such as the **Paiute**, gave no power to their chiefs, whom they called talkers. **Plains Indians** established town vegetable plots reserved specifically for their chiefs. The **miko**, the ruling chief of the **Creek** nation, attained great prestige and was borne on a litter to high-level meetings. Alongside the miko sat a council of Beloved Men, made up of veterans retired from active service who became his advisers. [See also **cacique, false face, miko, mingo, nantan, sachem, sagamore**.] *Osceola served as the Seminole war chief, Chief Joseph as chief of the Nez Percé, Sitting Bull as Sioux chief, and Wilma Mankiller as the elected chief of the Cherokee.*

Chief Joseph or **Thunder-Rolling-in-the-Mountains** or **Heinmot Tooyalaket** [hyn' maht too' yuh • lah' kiht] (1840-September 21, 1904) the brilliant, eloquent camp **chief** of the **Nez Percé** during a crucial period of their history. Chief Joseph, the son of Old Joseph, a **Cayuse** chief, and a Nez Percé mother, was born in Wallawa

Chief Joseph

Valley, Washington, was educated at a mission school, and became chief in 1871. After gold was discovered in Oregon, he refused to allow white settlers to dispossess his tribe. He was then forced into a disastrous winter retreat, which took him and his 750 followers along a 1,300-mile mountain trail and over the Missouri River, crossing Idaho, Wyoming, and Montana.

On October 13, 1877, with only 47 healthy braves to guard his people, he was apprehended in the Bear Paw Mountains 30 miles from the Canadian border while awaiting rescue by **Sitting Bull's Sioux**. Joseph's small group resettled on an Idaho **reservation**. After many futile journeys to Washington, D.C., to intercede for his dispossessed tribe, he and 150 of his strongest warriors were imprisoned in Kansas, where five of his children died of disease. The tribe was exiled from the main body of the Nez Percé to the Colville reservation in Washington, where Joseph despaired and died. [See also **Battle of Little Big Horn, Nez Percé, Sitting Bull**.] *A memorable phrase in American history are the decisive words of Chief Joseph: "I will fight no more forever."* (Bartlett, John. *Familiar Quotations*. Boston: Little, Brown, 1980, 642.)

chiki   See **chickee**.

Chilkat [chihl' kaht] a **tribe** of hunters and fishers native to the Canadian Northwest from Cape Fox to Yakutat Bay, Alaska, and members of the **Tlingit** language group. The Chilkat are famous for weaving elaborate cedar-bark and goat-hair blankets, which are prized as ceremonial robes. The blankets are formed as a rectangle with a vee cut out of one edge. The Chilkat blanket, as well as aprons, **leggings**, and shirts, are fringed and feature yellow, white, black, and blue-green natural **dyes**, yarn, and painted designs of wild animals, supernatural beings, or geometric or imaginary shapes. *Only Chilkat men are permitted to draw the whale, bear, or other natural* *shapes on a blanket; women complete the designs by adding details, some of which show top, side, bottom, and inside views of a single object.*

chinampa [chee • nahm' puh]   an artificial vegetable or flower garden plot made by staking out a small terrace in shallow water and filling it with rich black mud from the lake bottom. The chinampa was portable and could be poled to market like a raft. The **Aztec** extended their gardens by adding chinampas, which were framed with pilings, vines, and woven reed mats. [See also **Aztec, poling**.] *On Chole's chinampas he and his family grew chili peppers, tomatoes, squash, and corn.*

chinampa

Chinook [shih • nook'] or **Flathead** a populous **tribe** of fishers, trappers, and traders native to the Pacific Northwest. The Chinook were described in 1805 in the journals of Lewis and Clark, particularly for their custom of flattening infants' heads by binding stones to their foreheads shortly after birth. Contact with the Hudson Bay Company and European settlers destroyed Chinook trading alliances and nearly wiped out the people by introducing diseases that reduced their population in the early twentieth century to 100. [See also **Comcomly**.] *The languages of many Pacific Northwest tribes are loosely referred to as Chinook.*

chinquapin [cheeng' kuh • pihn] a native chestnut that grows on a shrub or small tree. Covered by a spiny bur, the edible nut of the chinquapin requires a two-year growing period. Eastern Indians prized chinquapin wood for weather-resistant posts. **Cherokee** healers blew dried chinquapin leaves on patients to cure headache, chills, sweating, and fever blisters. [See also **healing**.] *Visitors to the Tuscarora camp were introduced to the chinquapin, which cooks ground to a powder and used to thicken and flavor squirrel stew.*

Chippewa [chihp' puh • wah]   See **Ojibwa**.

---

chocólatl [chahk' uh • lat'l'] or **cacahuatl** a frothy, bitter drink common to the **Maya** and **Aztec**. Chocólatl is made from ground roasted **cacao** seeds mixed with sugar, cinnamon, and vanilla. Hernán Cortés carried the drink to Spain, from which it spread to all of Europe. The **Nahuatl** term in English is *chocolate*. [See also **cacao**.] *Montezuma demanded a ready supply of chocólatl for festivals, ceremonies, and daily use.*

Choctaw [chahk' taw] a prosperous **tribe** of farmers and stock breeders native to Mississippi, Louisiana, and Alabama and a member tribe of the **Muskhogean** nation. The Choctaw, who were known for hunting with **bows** and **blowguns**, were also famous for wearing their hair long and for drying the bodies of their dead on scaffolds, then cleaning the bones and piling them in burial mounds. Their homes, built of palmetto fronds attached to a gabled framework, derive from natural materials suited to a semitropical climate. Their language is said to have originated the slang word *okay*.

Most Choctaws were forced into Oklahoma during the 1830s by the U.S. government, which yielded to pressure from advancing waves of white settlers. Today their tribal headquarters is in southeastern Oklahoma. A large group of Choctaws, known as Mississippi Choctaws, managed to escape removal; they form a large group near Philadelphia, Mississippi. *One of the most famous contemporary Choctaw leaders was Oklahoma Congressman William Stigler.*

chokeberry or **aronia** [uh • row' nyuh] a common, low-growing deciduous shrub related to the rose. Chokeberry shrubs produce bitter berries that grow in clusters of 20 to 25 and range in color from yellowish-red to purple to black. The berry is made into jelly, sauce, and wine or is used to flavor **pemmican** or stew. *Myesa worked a handful of dried chokeberries into the pemmican she was packing into a casing.*

chukuviki [choo • koo' vee • kee] a tapered loaf formed of coarse cornmeal, wrapped in cornhusks, and baked. Chukuviki, which is baked in a hive-shaped oven called a **horno**, is a **Hopi** delicacy. *Rosa's grandmother rounded the chukuviki with a wooden paddle, then slid it onto the grate.*

a = sack; ah = sob; aw = sauce; ay = safe; ee = seek; eh = set

chungke [chung' kee] or **chunky** or **chunkey** a hoop-and-pole game played by several Indian tribes. The rules of the game require players to throw a pole to the spot where a hoop or chungke stone will stop rolling. A variation of the game requires players to spear a hoop netted from **babiche**. Also, a rectangular courtyard with a sand floor surrounded by dirt bleachers in the center of a **Muskhogean** village, where children played and women worked. Whole communities gathered in the chungke yard for rituals and dancing. [See also **babiche, hoop-and-pole game**.] *Lana's village turned out for the long-awaited chungke tournament.*

Ciboney [see • bow' nee] or **Siboney** a small, prehistoric **tribe** of gatherers, fishers, and nomadic hunters that settled St. Vincent Island around 4300 B.C., then migrated to Cuba and Haiti, leaving their former home to the **Arawak**. Like other Caribbean tribes, the Ciboney subsisted on island birds, wild plants, and shellfish. [See also **Arawak**.] *When Christopher Columbus landed in Cuba, he found petroglyphs and other remnants of an ancient Ciboney civilization.*

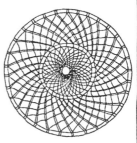
D. Timmons

chungke pole and hoop

clan a Native American group that claims descent from a common ancestor, often represented by a clan totem. All members of the clan are related, by their fathers or mothers, and must marry outside the kinship group. For matrilineal tribes, such as the **Iroquois**, the clan mother served as head of her people and spoke before the group during political meetings and at pre-election caucuses. [See also **totem**.] *Chief Joseph was related on his mother's side to a Nez Percé clan.*

clout Indian a rude slang term for a person, usually male, who keeps to traditional ways and avoids associating with white society. Being a clout Indian meant wearing the draped **breechclout** rather than pants or **leggings**. The absence of leg coverings caused outsiders to sneer that the clout Indian was uncivilized and therefore inferior or dangerous. [See also **breechclout, maxtli**.] *Wearing a breechclout and living in the wild, Roe imagined himself a clout Indian.*

club a clump of hair or ponytail pulled to the nape of the neck and tied or bound with **buckskin**, **babiche**, snakeskin, **yucca** fiber, or wool. To make their hair shine and keep it in place, Indians combed in **bear grease**, then wrapped the hair tightly to keep it neat. On the trail, clubbed hair prevented telltale bits of hair from catching in overhanging twigs and giving away the hiding place or trail of a traveling band. *Flying Squirrel made a quick club of her hair to keep it out of her way while she cooked sofkee.*

coca a shrub native to Central and South America yielding a leaf that Indians dried, powdered, and used as local anesthetic. Because of its medicinal value, coca—not to be confused with **cacao** or chocolate—was used as a trade item or a form of money. *Fernando, Christopher Columbus's brother, reported seeing Panamanian Indians chewing coca leaves.*

Cochise [koh • chees'] (1812-June 8, 1874) a **chief** of the Chiricahua **Apache** born in New Mexico and named for an ancient native **tribe** that lived in the southwestern United States. He supported peace until 1861, when he was wrongly accused of kidnapping a white settler's child and his people were tricked by repeated broken promises guaranteeing them possession of their land. In September 1861, the embittered Cochise, with his lieutenant, **Geronimo**, and his father-in-law, **Mangas Coloradas** of the Mimbrano Apache, took revenge by ambushing and killing many whites before agreeing to end their warfare and live on a **reservation**. After his death, reverent friends, led by Cochise's son Taza, carried the chief's body to a hidden burial site in the mountains of New Mexico. [See also **Apache, Geronimo, Mangas Coloradas**.] *Describing the arrival of settlers, Cochise asked,*

> *When I was young I walked all over this country, east and west, and saw no other people than the Apaches. After many summers I walked again and found another race of people had come to take it. How is it?*

(Brown, Dee. *Bury My Heart at Wounded Knee.* New York: Henry Holt, 1970, 209-210.)

code talkers Native Americans who served as soldiers during World War II and used native languages to pass highly important military secrets over radios to one another. The terms they created for grenades, dive bombers, tanks, machine guns, battleships, and ground and amphibious operations baffled enemy cryptographers who were never able to break their code. Because of the skill and ingenuity of the code talkers, American forces were able to win many battles, one of which was Iwo Jima. [See also **Navaho**.] *Distinguished tribesman, Peter MacDonald (December 16, 1928-), served with the Marines during World War II as one of its 400 renowned Navaho and Comanche code talkers.*

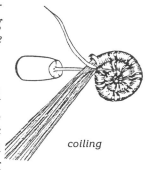

coiling weaving or twisting grasses into a thick rope and then coiling or spiraling the rope to form a plaque, basket, or other container. To achieve a tight fit, the coiler used an **awl**, needle, or punch to join the coils with withes to form baskets, storage vessels, mats, and cooking pots. Coiled baskets were waterproofed with resin or pitch. [See also **awl, basketry**.] *Mata dipped the end of the grass rope into water, then formed the first curve of a coil basket.*

coiling

coil pot a container made by rolling clay between the palms into a long rope, then coiling the rope into the shape of a pot or bowl. The finished form is dampened with water and smoothed with a stone paddle to the desired shape, then fired in an oven before being decorated with colored powder, ash, or paint. To give added strength, the coil pot is baked a second time at high heat. *North Carolina Cherokee sold their coil pots near Oconaluftee Village.*

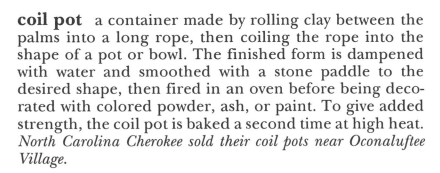

coil pots

comalli [koh • mahl' lee] or **comal** [koh • mahl']   a flat clay cooking slab on which **Aztec** women baked tortillas, which were filled with chopped tomato, onion, and meat, rolled, dipped into hot-pepper sauce, and eaten with the fingers, much as burritos are eaten. Many comalli were pierced at one end to form a drain so that juices would not collect on the surface. *Around the comalli, hungry men congregated, waiting for Malinalli to bake the tortillas.*

Comanche [kuh • man' chee]   a **tribe** of nomadic hunters, horse breeders, and traders native to the midwestern plains, whose name, Komanteia, given them by the **Ute**, means one who wishes to fight me. The Comanche, who

---

ih = sit; oh = soak; oo = soup; ow = sound; uh = such; y = side

allied themselves with the **Kiowa**, were famous for their skillful handling of horses. By the age of five, most Comanche children owned a horse or pony and practiced snatching heavy objects from the ground as they galloped past. Young braves honed their riding techniques, particularly the trick of clinging to the side of the horse and riding into battle unseen. *In 1867, as white troops increased pressure on the Comanche, Chief Ten Bears asserted proudly,*

> *I was born upon the prairie, where the wind blew free and there was nothing to break the light of the sun. I was born where there were no enclosures and where everything drew a free breath. I want to die there and not within walls.*

(Brown, Dee. *Bury My Heart at Wounded Knee.* New York: Henry Holt, 1970, 242.)

By 1910, after lengthy battles with U.S. Cavalry, the Comanche, who were relocated to an Oklahoma **reservation**, had shrunk to fewer than one-tenth their earlier number. [See also **Quanah Parker**.] *LaDonna Harris, the Comanche wife of Senator Fred R. Harris, describes herself first as a Comanche, second as an Indian, and third, an American.*

Comanche warrior drawn by George Catlin

Comcomly [kahm • kahm' lee] (1765?-1830) a Chinook **chief** who supplied food and canoes to Lewis and Clark in 1805. He offered his daughter as a wife to Duncan McDougal, who served as the U.S. representative to the newly acquired Louisiana Purchase. [See also **Chinook, Lewis and Clark expedition**.] *A flamboyant leader, Comcomly liked pomp and fuss at his official appearances.*

contrary [kahn' treh • ree] a plains brave who, because of some personal misfortune, chose to live backward, doing the opposite of what is expected, for example, saying goodbye for hello, laughing at solemn occasions, or washing with dirt. These men were fierce warriors, especially when others withdrew or gave up. [See also **booger, heyoka, plains Indians**.] *Because of his upside-down behavior, the contrary amused fellow tribe members by clowning and posturing.*

*a = s**a**ck; ah = s**o**b; aw = s**au**ce; ay = s**a**fe; ee = s**ee**k; eh = s**e**t*

coontie [koon' tee]   a woody plant favored by the Seminole for its roots, which they dried and pounded into a flour called arrowroot. Coontie flour was useful to Seminole cooks, who made it into puddings, cereals, and breads for babies, the elderly, invalids, and other sick people. [See also **chemuck, sofkee**.] *Light Stream's bag of coontie was soon emptied after her tribe adopted sick and injured runaway slaves.*

Coowescoowe   See **John Ross**.

copper   a metal trinket, crest, shield, or sun symbol given in a **potlatch** ceremony. Some coppers were destroyed as a demonstration of wealth. Others obtained great worth by the number of times they changed hands. [See also **giveaway, potlatch**.] *The Chilkat treasured a ceremonial copper that their chief had received as a gift.*

cording   a type of string made from rolling and twisting the bark of basswood, tulip popular, or linden trees. Fibers were boiled with wood ash to add strength, then split and massaged or pulled through a bone to lighten and toughen them. In the final stage, cording was rolled against the thigh, then used for craft items, such as combs. [See also **lanyard, milkweed**.] *Rhoda's aunt, Spring Blossom, taught the class how Canadian Indians made cording and cut babiche.*

comb fastened together
with cording

corn   See **maize**.

Cornplanter or **John O'Bail** or **Abeel** [ah' beel] (1732-February 18, 1836)   **Seneca** chief who challenged European settlers, at one point changing his allegiance from Britain to America. Born in Conewaugus, New York, to a Dutch trader and Indian mother, Cornplanter, a brother of the prophet **Handsome Lake**, participated in British raids in western New York. His role in negotiating treaties between 1784 and 1802, by which large areas were conceded to the United States, made him so unpopular with his tribe that for a time his life was in danger. He accepted land from Pennsylvania, where he farmed and raised cattle, but near the end of his life, he grew disillusioned with the weakening of Native American culture. [See also **Handsome Lake, Seneca**.] *Cornplanter proved his pragmatism* by his formal request of whites, *"We ask you to teach us to plow and to grind corn; and above all, teach our children to read and write."* (Pastron, Allen. *Great Indian Chiefs.* Santa Barbara, Calif.: Bellerophon, 1993, 20.)

Corn Tassel or **Onitositah** [oh' nee • toh' see • tuh] (?-1788) **Cherokee** orator. Because of Corn Tassel's skill in diplomacy and public speaking, Oconastota, a Cherokee elder, in 1777 deferred to Corn Tassel, who addressed an American commissioner concerning land apportionment on Long Island, New York. A stocky, round-faced man, Corn Tassel succeeded in clarifying the Cherokee position. Eleven years later, Corn Tassel, Abram, and other tribal dignitaries who signed the treaty were murdered by Kirk, a white man who ignored their truce flag. [See also **Cherokee**.] *In an impassioned call for separatism, Corn Tassel noted that the Great God of Nature made whites and Indians different, but did not intend for Indians to be slaves.*

council lodge   the meeting place of a tribe's elders and wise leaders. About 50 feet in diameter, the council lodge housed meetings of warriors who had proved themselves worthy. Their major task was the political business of the assembled tribes and the settling of territorial disputes. [See also **hot house**.] *In the council lodge, the smoking of the calumet encouraged unity.*

coup [koo]   a military honor won by a formal touch on an enemy or corpse or by the theft of an enemy's horse. Coup was counted when a witness attested that a warrior touched a body with a ceremonial wand called a **coup stick**. The purpose of counting coup was to extend the ritual act by bringing the warrior in contact with the enemy. As a sign of honor, counting coup was a more meaningful act than scalping, which involved dishonoring a corpse. A **Sioux** brave who was wounded while counting coup was given an eagle feather to wear as a token of courage. The feather, the equivalent of a war medal, might be dyed, split, stripped, notched, or shaped to indicate symbolically whether the person was wounded, had lost a horse, or had wounded or killed his enemy. [See also **coup stick**.] *Gray Wolf risked capture so that he could count coup.*

a = sack; ah = sob; aw = sauce; ay = safe; ee = seek; eh = set

coup stick [koo stihk] a ceremonial wand, stick, or rattle with which a warrior tapped an enemy. Because of its ritual use, the coup stick became an integral part of each fighter's war dress and was used for honorable, ceremonial purposes. In the absence of a coup stick, the warrior could use a **bow** or **spear**. [See also **coup**.] *Nekomis attached a quilled band to Swift Runner's coup stick, which he inherited from his father.*

coyote [ky' oht *or* ky • yoht' ee] an animal of the dog family that is related to the wolf; a prairie wolf. The coyote, valued for its wisdom, was originally called coyotl in the **Nahuatl** language. It was often the subject of tribal folklore, as in the Brulé **Sioux** story, Old Man Coyote and His Mother-in-Law or the **Shoshone** tale, Old Man Coyote and Buffalo Power. [See also **trickster**.] *In recognition of their son's sharp eye, the Aztec family named him Son of Coyote.*

D. Timmons

coyote

cradleboard a flat piece of wood to which an infant was strapped, with arms straight at its sides. The cradleboard made it convenient to carry or tend an infant until the child was capable of walking. Many cradleboards sported a wicker visor or awning to protect the child from sun and rain; rattles; protective charms, such as a pouch containing the child's umbilical cord; **abalone** shells; and other amusing pendants hung from the top to jingle and entertain the child. A small shelf of wood or **saguaro** rib at the bottom served as a foot prop. Inside, soft padding of felt, **cattail** down, fur pelts, cotton, or moss kept the child dry by absorbing body wastes.

The cradleboard could be suspended from a wall peg, tree limb, **lodge pole**, or **travois**, or it could be hung by a strap or **tumpline** from the mother's forehead, shoulders, or a saddle horn. Two horns at the top could offset a jolt or cushion a fall in case of accidents. The ancient **Anasazi** method of supporting the infant's head by securely tying it to the cradleboard is thought to have caused the distinctive flattening on the back of the skull. [See also **tumpline**.] *Sacagawea padded Jean Baptiste's cradleboard with soft pelts.*

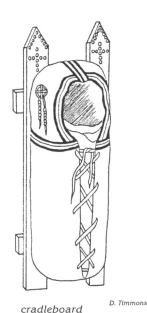

cradleboard

D. Timmons

Crazy Horse or **Curly** or **Tashunka Witko** [ta • shuhn' kuh wiht' koh] (1842-September 5, 1877) a chief of the Oglala **Sioux** and native of the Black Hills in South Dakota.

Crazy Horse, whose father bore the same name, followed a boyhood vision in which he saw himself unharmed in battle. In 1876, he joined **Sitting Bull**; they led 2,000 braves against U.S. Army troops at the Battle of Rosebud in Montana and to greater fame at the **Battle of Little Big Horn** in Montana.

Refusing to sell Indian lands, an act he called a sacrilege, Crazy Horse was imprisoned. He died on the **reservation**, stabbed in the back by a Sioux sentry. In 1940, Chief Henry Standing Bear invited Korczak Ziolkowski to carve a statue honoring Crazy Horse. Begun in 1948, the 563-foot mounted figure rises out of the sacred Black Hills, where workers continue adding details. [See also **Battle of Little Big Horn, Black Elk, Gall**.] *Shortly before his death at age 35, Crazy Horse reflected that the Sioux dependence on the buffalo for food and hides for tepees had been replaced by a life of idleness on government reservations.*

Cree [kree]   a nomadic **tribe** of hunter-gatherers, trappers, fishers, and horse breeders native to the Hudson Bay, who distinguished themselves by extensive tattooing. One notable scout, Ochagah, led Pierre Gaultier de Varennes and his son across the North American plains over a 16-year period (1727-1743). The Cree, who allied themselves with the **Assiniboin**, suffered from smallpox and scarlet-fever epidemics. They intermarried with French settlers to produce a distinct métis or **half-breed** culture. [See also **Assiniboin, half-breed, Poundmaker**.] *Buffy Sainte Marie, a Cree folk singer, composer, and popular performer during the 1960s and 1970s, learned from her parents that history books and movies do not always tell the truth about Native Americans.*

Creek   a flourshing confederacy of farmers and town dwellers native to the **Muskhogean** nation, which settled Alabama and Georgia. The Creek were famous for decorating themselves with body paint and **tattoos**. Divided into the Red Stick, or Upper Creeks, and the White Stick, or Lower Creeks, the nation as a whole was known for their democratic government, which was headed by a **miko**, or **chief**. During the War of 1812, Chief Little Warrior led a Creek strike force against settlers of the Ohio River in an effort to secure native hunting grounds. By the late 1830s, the Creek, who once inhabited 50 towns, gave up their lands to the United States and moved to a **reservation** in Oklahoma. [See also **Muskhogean**.] *In a pointed speech to his people in 1829, Chief Speckled Snake warned that negotiations with the U.S. president always concluded with a relocation of the Creek at a distance from white settlers.*

crooked knife   a standard utility knife or gouge with a beveled edge, used for shaving wooden bowls, **dugouts**, masks, cups, or snowshoe frames. The Chipewyan made crooked knives from wood or antler handles fitted with curved metal blades. *Louisa's mother fleshed the moose hide with deft strokes of her crooked knife, then cut the tanned hide into moccasins.*

crooked knife

Crow or **Absaroke** [ab' suh • roh' kee] or **Apsaalooke** [ap' suh • loo' kee]   a nomadic **tribe** of **plains Indians** native to Wyoming, Montana, and North and South Dakota whom their rivals, the **Cheyenne**, named bird people. Unlike the **Hidatsa**, their relatives, the Crow raised only one crop, **tobacco**, which they used in religious rituals. In 1805, during the tribe's first recorded acknowledgment by explorers, Chief Arapoosh met Lewis and Clark. In 1880, Chief Plenty Coups and five delegates visited Washington to discuss the building of a railroad on Crow land. Regretting that the **Battle of Little Big Horn** led to the end of the Indian dominance of the plains, Plenty Coups commented that the Crow were like birds with broken wings. Following a period of epidemics, the Crow population stabilized. Today, most Crows live on **reservations** in Montana. [See also **Battle of Little Big Horn, Hidatsa**.] *Pretty Shield, a Crow living near the Missouri River around 1860, describes how Chief Walks-with-the-Moon shared tobacco with white visitors but refused to let them live with the tribe.*

crow   a decorative bustle worn by **dog soldiers** and dancers of plains tribes. The crow consisted of a rawhide frame covered with an eagle's skin and decorated with bone pendants, feathers, fangs, and other items that symbolized military accomplishments. [See also **dog soldier**.] *Tied to the wearer's back, a crow was meant to hang down to the back of the knees.*

Cuna [koo' nuh] a native **tribe** of farmers, hunters, fishers, and traders inhabiting 50 of the 400 San Blas Islands and sections of the Panama mainland on the Atlantic side. The Cuna first met Europeans in 1913, when two Protestant missionaries settled among them, yet today they live much as they did in prehistoric times and maintain their isolation from outsiders. The Cuna are famous for their unique method of quilting colored cloth into patterns called molas. *In a matriarchal system like that of the Cuna, the husband lives with the wife's family and fells a tree as a symbolic gift to the bride's mother.*

Curly See **Crazy Horse**.

Custer's Last Stand See **Battle of Little Big Horn**.

a = sack; ah = sob; aw = sauce; ay = safe; ee = seek; eh = set

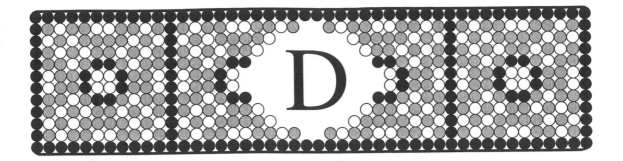

Dakota [duh • ko' tuh] a major division of the **Sioux** nation. See **Sioux**. *The largest Sioux language group are the Dakota.*

dance house a gathering point for **Eskimos** during the off-season, where they eat, dance to the beat of a drum, celebrate, and tell stories. Because of the extreme heat in the dance house, participants wear light garments. Visitors to the dance house settle their arguments by beating drums and calling out insults. *Kipu found the dance house filled with his relatives, who had come long distances to enjoy a family feast.*

Datsolali [daht' soh • lah' lee] (1831-1926) a **Washo** artisan famous for her traditional style of basket making. Born in Carson Valley, Nevada, Datsolali bore two children to her first husband, Assu. In 1895, to rescue her family from hunger, she broke a **Paiute** law banning Washo artisans from selling their wares. One of her baskets sold for $10,000. Datsolali's baskets, some of which required a year to make, are among the few signed exhibits by Native American artists in museums and private collections. [See also **basketry**.] *Like other Native American women, Datsolali was recognized for peaceful skills.*

Dawes Act or **General Allotment Act** a law passed in 1887 to abolish reservations by alloting to individual Indians a piece of **reservation** land, usually 160 acres. The act authorized the U.S. government to purchase the remaining acres for non-Indian use. Some land was sold to the public; other acreage was given away. The U.S. government still holds many allotments in trust for individual Indians. The Dawes Act had a major impact in Oklahoma, where only one tribe, the **Osage**, out of 36 tribes, still maintains a small reservation. Few Indians ever farmed or lived on allotted lands. [See also **allotment,**

Bright Eyes, Indian Removal Act, Indian Territory.] *Wilson Rawls's* Where the Red Fern Grows *(New York: Bantam, 1961), which is set in the years following Oklahoma's achievement of statehood, recalls his family's cabin on land allotted to his mother, a Cherokee.*

deadfall

deadfall a baited log that was lightly propped so that an animal would take the bait, which was daubed with fish oil, liver, or other fragrant meat, then knock out the props and be killed or trapped by the falling weight. [See also **snare**.] *Woods Indians preferred a deadfall to a fire-surround, which could get out of control and destroy a village.*

death dirge the plaintive ritual song or chant sung by an Indian who is about to die. The death dirge often calls on the **Great Spirit** to accept the dying person's spirit into the next world. *Rock Climber's death dirge was filled with longing for his former homeland.*

de Brébeuf, Father Jean [duh bray' burhf zhahn] (1593-1649) a French Jesuit missionary and translator from Normandy who lived among the **Hurons** outside Fort Ste. Marie, Ontario, near the modern town of Midland. During his evangelical mission to the tribe, he emphasized the Christmas story, which he recorded in his *Huron Carol*, which is still sung in Huron, French, and English. [See also **Huron**, *Huron Carol*.] *Times were hard for the Huron after Father de Brébeuf was killed in an Iroquois raid, but the people remembered the priest's kindness and continued to sing his Christmas carol.*

D. Timmons
deer decoy

deer decoy a dried deer head with attached ribs and hide beneath which a hunter hid while creeping close to his prey and imitating the noises and movements of deer, such as rubbing antlers against a tree. The deer decoy proved beneficial to **Tuscarora** hunters, who obtained not only venison but also skins for clothing and for trading with other tribes. *An English settler's diary entry describes the Native American hunter's deer decoy, which was a deer hide worn like a mask during the hours when deer came to the water to drink and could be easily shot.*

deer song a ritual chant sung by **Cherokee** hunters to thank the **Great Spirit** for the deer they killed. The deer song was sung with reverence and promised that the hunter violated nature only to provide food or skins for the tribe. Often, the singing accompanied the eating of organ meats, particularly the heart or liver, which transferred the animal's strength to the hunter. *Sam burned bone fragments in the sacred fire, over which he sang the deer song, which he had learned from his grandfather.*

Deganawida [day • gah' nuh • wee' duh] or **Dekanawi-dah** or **Degandawida** (ca. 16th century) legendary **Iroquois shaman** and prophet who was adopted by the **Mohawk**. In 1570, Deganawida foretold an era of peace, which he envisioned as a giant spruce tree with five main roots, symbolizing five Indian nations, and a top reaching to the sky. Acting on his vision, he established a coalition of tribes known as the Iroquois League. Said to be born of a virgin in Kingston, Ontario, and impeded by a stutter, he took **Hiawatha** as his disciple and spokesman. Deganawida prophesied the union of Five Nations. As a gesture of concession, he planted the Tree of Peace on Lake Onondaga and topped it with an eagle, symbol of shelter and protection for all tribes seeking refuge. In 1880, three centuries after Deganawida and Hiawatha, Seth Newhouse, a **Seneca** writer, drew up a written version of the constitution governing the Iroquois League. [See also **Hiawatha, Iroquois League, Mohawk, shaman**.] *The code of the Iroquois League read:*

> *I, Deganawida, and the Confederated Chiefs, now uproot the tallest pine tree, and into the cavity thereby made we cast all weapons of war. Into the depths of the earth, deep down into the under-earth currents of water flowing to unknown regions, we cast all weapons of strife. We bury them from sight and we plant again the tree. Thus shall the Great Peace be established.*

(Collier, John. *Indians of the Americas.* New York: Signet, 1947.)

Delaware [del' uh • wayr] or **Leni-Lenape** [leh' nee • leh nah' pay] a powerful and established agricultural nation native to the Delaware Valley. The Delaware became the parent **tribe** of the **Mohican, Shawnee, Ojibwa**, and Nanticoke. The Delaware, who called themselves the Leni-Lenape or real men, worked in close-knit communities to prepare land for planting. They shared equally the produce they raised. In cycles of 15 years, they deserted their towns for more promising fields in a new location. In 1682, they attacked Dutch settlers; the hostilities concluded that year with a treaty between William Penn and Chief **Tammany**, which was commemorated in a **wampum** belt showing an Indian grasping the hand of a white man. By 1720, the Delaware and their allies, the **Huron** and **Shawnee**, moved west to the Ohio Valley.

In 1787 Chief Pachgantschilias complained that, because the Delaware could not be enslaved, the whites killed them. As Pachgantschilias warned, by 1800, the Delaware, their tribal unity destroyed, settled in Oklahoma and Kansas. All that remain of them in the East are place names such as Susquehanna and Muncy. [See also **doll dance, Mingo, Tammany, Walum Olum, wampum.**] *Morning Star took pride in the Walum Olum, a Delaware history presented in pictographic form.*

dentalium shell

Déné [dihn' eh]   a nomadic **Athapascan tribe** of hunters and trappers native to the Northwest Territory, Canada. The Déné battled the **Inuit**, their northern neighbors, for hunting privileges in the **caribou**-rich **tundra**. The population center of the Déné is the city of Yellowknife. [See also **Athapascan, Inuit, tundra.**] *In his new home, Bernadette's son Ronald, a full-blooded Carrier, has made friends with Déné children.*

dentalia [dehn • tay' lee • uh]   toothed mollusk shells that were strung on a rope or rawhide cord and used by California Indians as money. In contrast to forest Indians, who strung shells into **wampum**, Yuroks amassed wealth through the gathering of dentalia. [See also **otekoa, quahog, wampum.**] *Ishi took a special interest in displays at the San Francisco anthropological museum, which featured dentalia, basketry, ritual items, clothing, and hunting weapons.*

D. Timmons
dew cloth inside a teepe

dew cloth   an inner curtain hung from the inside of a **tepee** to the ground to keep out dampness and wind. Reaching to heights of 6 feet or more, the dew cloth often displayed **pictographs**, beadwork, and **quilling**. [See also **tepee.**] *Singing Bird painted the dew cloth with exploits of her father's ancestors and relatives.*

dibble   See **digging stick**.

Diggers a derisive term applied by nineteenth-century European settlers to desert Indians. Because desert Indians grubbed out **pit houses** and eked a tenuous living from any natural food source, they were named Diggers. According to explorer John C. Fremont's 1843 diary, Digger Indians grubbed out roots, seeds, grass, and other plants, even insects and worms. A decade later, about 10,000 Digger children were kidnapped and used as forced labor in the United States and Mexico. *Mormons won the respect of Digger Indians, whom they accepted as a Lost Tribe of Israel.*

digging stick a sharpened stick used by desert Indians for plowing, planting, weeding, and cultivating crops; a dibble. To gain leverage, the user pushed down on a knot or stump, which was left on one end of the stick as a grip or handle. *For ease of maintenance and harvest, primitive farmers did not plow; they mounded earth over dead fish or other natural fertilizer, punched holes in the top of the mound with a digging stick, and planted several bean, squash, corn, or melon seeds close together.*

dip net a net of woven bark, **sinew**, **babiche**, or braided skin that attached to a lightweight oval frame ending in a handle or grip. Indians used dip nets for removing fish from **weirs** or scooping up migrating fish from backwaters, spawning grounds, poisoned coves, or illuminated areas during light-fishing. The job of managing the dip net often fell to children or elderly tribal members. [See also **fish poison, weir**.] *With his dip net, Lanny captured enough bluefish for his family's dinner with a few left over for smoking.*

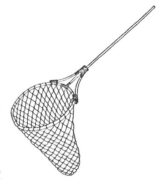

dip net for salmon

dog rope a 10-foot band of leather or rawhide tied to a picket; a fixed leash. One of four chief **dog soldiers** fastened himself in the center of a battlefield by attaching a dog rope from his shoulder to a peg in the ground or spearing it with his lance. Use of the dog rope indicated that the soldier was willing to fight to the death. [See also **dog soldier, trailer**.] *The Cheyenne dog rope was decorated with symbols of courage and strength.*

dog soldier or **kit foxes** or **Strong Heart Society** a member of the tribal police, a **plains Indian** military society of dedicated warriors who took an oath to fight to the death. **Kiowa** dog soldiers, who were trained from boyhood in advancing stages of bravery, wore red or black sashes and distinctive ornaments to mark their importance. The **Hidatsa** dog soldiers adorned their heads with turkey, eagle, and magpie feathers. Their courage inspired less aggressive soldiers to rededicate themselves to battle, even when threatened with death or capture. The dog soldiers were defeated for the last time in 1875 during the **Sand Creek Massacre**. [See also **crow, dog rope**.] *Chief Tall Bull's dog soldiers defended their camp on the Platte River, Kansas, in July 1869.*

female corn doll

dog travois   See **travois**.

doll dance   an annual **Delaware** ceremony in which sacred corn dolls carved from wood are removed from their husk wrappings and fitted with new garments. As part of the religious ritual, dancers place the redressed images on sticks and carry them around the assembled group. [See also **Delaware**.] *The doll dance ends with a traditional feast of venison, corn cakes, and fresh berries.*

Dorset [dohr' seht]   an extinct, nomadic tribe of **Eskimo** hunters and fishers native to Cape Dorset, Baffin Island, and extending to Greenland from 800 B.C. to A.D. 1200. The Dorset lived in semi-subterranean houses, met as a group in meeting halls, and traveled on small hand-pulled sleds. In summer, they pitched skin tents, which enabled them to move easily where game and fish were plentiful. Archaeologists have located a few implements, harpoon points, moss lamps, **ulus**, and bone or ivory buttons, charms, and ornaments that establish what little is known of Dorset culture. [See also **barabara, igloo, ulu**.] *Viking journals record meetings with the coastal Dorset tribes.*

D. Timmons

double ball

double ball   a game enjoyed by **plains Indian** women. The rules involved the tossing of a game piece made of two stuffed rawhide balls connected by a string. Players caught the double ball on a stick and hurled it toward a goal. *Elk Woman's skill at double ball earned her a reputation for swiftness and accuracy.*

a = sack; ah = sob; aw = sauce; ay = safe; ee = seek; eh = set

drum dance   an informal **Eskimo** get-together at which individual or pairs of singers beat on the drum and chanted about their hunting adventures. Each round concluded with a refrain, which everybody sang. The drum, shaped like a tambourine and extending up to 3 feet in diameter, was made of bone topped with skin. Each village had at least a few people who remembered the words to all traditional songs. *At the drum dance, Nasarlulik sang of his first whaling trip to Baffin Bay, where his village gathered enough blubber to feed them well all winter.*

duck not yet   an Eskimo delicacy. Gatherers select duck eggs shortly before they hatch, hard boil them, and eat the tender ducklings. [See also **kittiwake**.] *Duck not yet is an Aleut favorite.*

dugout   the world's first boat, the dugout was a heavy wooden **canoe** made by peeling the bark from a stout cedar, cypress, or pine trunk, flattening the bottom with a plane or **adze**, then burning out the heart. Shell, metal, or bone scrapers smoothed out the charred remnants, then builders heated water in the hollow and molded the frame by forcing crossbars between the sides as stretchers. More ornate than **Nootka** designs, the **Haida** dugout was 2 inches thick and was first seasoned, then painted or carved; it often sported a decorative tribal or **clan** insignia or staff on either or both ends. A dugout could be poled or paddled through swamps, **bayous**, or shallows or even fitted with mast and sail for ocean voyages. Its weight made it unsuitable for lengthy **portage**. A good dugout was a family heirloom, treasured by succeeding generations as a symbol of wealth and tradition. [See also **adze, canoe, pirogue, poling, portage**.] *Julie considered the wearying task of hollowing out the great cypress log to make a dugout, which would be her principal form of water transportation.*

D. Timmons

Haida dugout

Dull Knife (?-1883)   a **Cheyenne** leader who, in 1878, when he was in his fifties, tried to rescue his people from their Oklahoma **reservation**. A second escape from Fort Robinson, Nebraska, to the Black Hills of South Dakota ended in disaster for some of the group, although Dull

---

ih = sit; oh = soak; oo = soup; ow = sound; uh = such; y = side   **67**

Knife eluded his captors. He pretended to surrender his band's guns; in reality, he disassembled them and stored the parts under stoves, in flooring, and among jewelry and decorations. [See also **Cheyenne**.] *In a defiant stand against aggressors, Dull Knife proclaimed that it is better to die fighting than to die of illness.*

duma [doo' muh]   a flat, polished baking stone that was greased, then heated over a **mesquite** fire. **Hopi** cooks dropped a dollop of corn batter on the duma. The batter quickly spread and cooked into lacy **piki** bread. [See also **piki, pone**.] *A traditional Hopi cook seasoned a new duma with cottonseed oil and piñon sap.*

dye   coloring made from plants and minerals that could be used on garments, utensils, baskets, and human skin. Native Americans colored their **buckskin** garments and their cane splits and vines for weaving by smoking them over cedar fires for a rich brown tone or over new cedar wood for a lighter shade of tan. For a blackened finish, artisans smoked materials over a pine fire, which they covered with green branches and leaves. Other natural sources produced bright shades. Following are sources of various colors:

Black: wild grapes, guaco seeds, bee plant, soot, sulfur mud, hemlock boiled in saltwater, butternut, California-blackberry juice, elderberry stems, honey-mesquite root gum, **manzanita** wood, mistletoe leaves, poison-oak juice, valley-oak bark, iris roots, or charcoal.

Blue: duck manure, copper salts, indigo, coast-blue larkspur, or cactus flowers.

Brown: black-walnut hulls, indigo bush stems, staghorn-sumac berries, canaigre roots, dock, ratany, or coneflower.

Gold: lily-of-the-valley leaves.

Green: pond scum, Indian tea, or juniper.

cactus

a = sack; ah = sob; aw = sauce; ay = safe; ee = seek; eh = set

Magenta: bilberry juice.

Orange: oak bark, onion skin, mulberry, or bloodroot.

Purple: huckleberries, blueberries, or grapes.

Red: peach or alder bark, buffalo berry, mahogany root, achiote, hematite, grass soaked in urine, tickseed, redbud stems, alder bark, cinnabar, bedstraw root, fishhook cactus, dock, brazilwood, or iron-oxide paint pots.

Rose: hemlock, blackberries, **prickly pear**, and madder.

bloodroot

Tan: white or red oak leaves and gall, mormon-tea leaves and twigs, or black-willow bark.

Turquoise: a mix of hemlock, iron oxide, and urine.

White: clay or **willow**.

Yellow: buffalo gall, chamiso, rabbit brush, moss, yellow-root, apple bark, broom sedge, marigold, barberry root, buttercup, oregon-grape roots, parsnip leaves, creek-nettle roots, leather root, sunflower seeds, Spanish needles, wolf moss, curly-dock roots, dandelion blossoms, or sea blite.

Adding ash, alum, or urine to dye helped to set the color. For paint brushes, Indians used **willow** limbs, strands of **yucca**, splintered cottonwood sticks, antelope hair, **cattails**, or splintered buffalo bone. [See also **paint pot, quilling**.] *The addition of soot or ash to base colors produced a deeper shade of dye; mixing with animal glue helped the colors stick to the surface.*

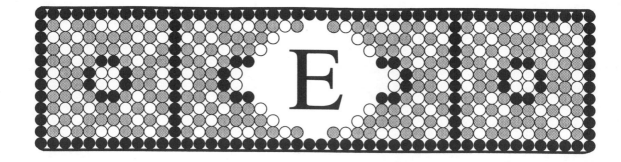

Eagle   See **Quanah Parker**.

ear pull   an **Eskimo** endurance game in which players fasten ties to each other's ears and tug. The person who pulls the string from the other player's ear wins the game. *After a few rounds of ear pull, the children of the MacKenzie River Valley were ready for the annual winter feast.*

Eastman, Charles Alexander or **Ohiyesa** [oh' hee • yay' suh] or **the Pitiful Last** (1858-January 8, 1939)   Santee **Sioux** writer and physician who served the Pine Ridge agency as a medical doctor and organized YMCA, Camp Fire Girl, and Boy Scout groups. Born in Redwood Falls, Minnesota, Eastman, whose mother died at his birth, fled north with his tribe from rampaging whites. The tribe resettled at Fort Ellis, Manitoba, Canada, where Eastman remained uneducated until the age of 15. His phenomenal academic progress led him to Dartmouth College and Boston University, where he completed a medical degree at the age of 32 and married poet Elaine Goodale. Eastman, author of *Soul of the Indian* (Lincoln: University of Nebraska Press, 1980), *Indian Boyhood* (Williamstown, Mass.: Corner House, 1975), and *From the Deep Woods to Civilization* (Lincoln: University of Nebraska Press, 1977), served as Washington spokesperson for the Sioux and as a member of the **Bureau of Indian Affairs**. He was one of an official party to examine Indian corpses at the site of the **Wounded Knee** massacre. [See also **Rain-in-the-Face, Sioux, Wounded Knee**.] *In his memoirs, Eastman, fascinated by the scientific minds of white people, marveled that they divided the day into hours, like the months of the year.*

effigy mound [ehf' fuh • gee mownd]   See **mound**.

---

a = sack; ah = sob; aw = sauce; ay = safe; ee = seek; eh = set

Erie [ihr' ee]   a populous agricultural **tribe** nicknamed panther people or cat people. The Erie were native to Ohio and were famed for their skillful archers. After joining the **Huron** in a catastrophic territorial war with the **Iroquois** in 1656, most of the Erie were enslaved or absorbed into other tribes, particularly the **Seneca** and **Onandaga**. *One theory of the Erie tribe's disappearance suggests that survivors migrated south and took the name Black Minqua.*

Eskimo [es' kuh • moh] or **Esquimau**, pl. **Esquimaux** or **Esquimawes**   a general term for tribes native to an Arctic and subarctic expanse of 5,000 miles, including the northernmost reaches of Canada, Siberia, Alaska, and Greenland, where more than half of their number live. Racially, Eskimos bear more resemblance to their Siberian ancestors than to American Indians. The **Algonquin** word Eskimo, once an insult, means eaters of raw meat. Today, Eskimos prefer to be called **Inupiaq**. Following encounters with white explorers in 1790, many Eskimos died of tuberculosis; an epidemic of typhus repeated the pattern in 1902. [See also **amouti, igloo, Inuit, Inuk, Inupiaq, Thule**.] *From 1889 to 1892, Dr. Wilfred Grenfell, a British physician, used his skills to improve the health and hygiene of the Eskimos of Labrador.*

eulachon   See **candlefish**.

false face or **wooden face**   a member of a secret **Seneca**, **Mohawk**, or **Onandaga** society who put on an expressive basswood mask that was carved from a living tree, hollowed out, and painted red and black. False faces assembled beside sick people to sprinkle ashes on their heads, dance, and pray for their recovery. During epidemics, false faces, summoned through dreams or visions, moved from lodge to lodge, shaking their mud-turtle rattles, blowing hot ash on the sick through a hollow tube, and making noises to scare off evil spirits. The original false face, a fallen god, was punished for bragging by the **Great Spirit**, who sentenced him to a life of serving the sick. Survivors of serious illness, including women, automatically become members of the secret society. [See also **chief, healing, husk faces**.] *All the efforts of the false faces could not stop the scarlet fever epidemic from reaching Winter Blossom's lodge.*

firedrill   a pointed stick or **yucca** or cottonwood root that fit a groove in a board and was used to start a fire. When the stick was twirled between the palms of the firemaker's hands, the stone point made friction in the groove. This motion produced enough spark to ignite a bit of moss, dry leaf, bark, dried mushroom, feather, rotted wood, buffalo dung, or rush. A quicker method of starting a fire was the use of a **bow**, the string of which was wrapped about the firedrill to make it twirl faster. According to **Arapaho** legend, an ingenious tribe member discovered that he could strike certain stones together to make a spark and ignite tinder, thus avoiding the hard work of the firedrill. [See also **bowdrill**.] *Colani ignited a ceremonial fire using the firedrill, which hung on the wall of the medicine man's hut.*

firedrill

fire-lighting   a method of hunting geese or ducks by layering clay on the bottom of a canoe, then building a

*a = s**a**ck; ah = s**o**b; aw = s**au**ce; ay = s**a**fe; ee = s**ee**k; eh = s**e**t*

fire on the clay. The hunter, hidden by the flames, could maneuver close to the birds, which associated the sight of fire with the reflection of the moon on the water. [See also **jack-lighting**.] *North Carolina outlawed fire-lighting in 1777.*

fire-surround a hunting method used by eastern and **plains Indians** by which a large party of hunters set fire to the perimeter of a circle of brush and grass extending over several miles. As the smoke and flame drove animals toward the center, hunters pursued and shot, speared, or clubbed them. [See also **buffalo jump, deadfall, rabbit drive, savanna**.] *Tom Taylor joined the next village in a fire-surround, from which his tribe netted deer, rabbits, and squirrels.*

fish fall See **weir**.

fish poison a toxic solution that stunned or stupefied fish so that they would float to the surface to be caught by hand or in a net. Indians used plants such as soap plant, smartweed, turkey mullein, dove weed, and California buckeye as fish poison. [See also **dip net, harpoon, weir**.] *Fish poison deprived the fish of oxygen and therefore did no harm to the meat, which was safe to eat.*

Five Civilized Tribes an informal union of the **Seminole**, **Cherokee**, **Chickasaw**, **Choctaw**, and **Creek tribes**, who populated Georgia, Alabama, and Mississippi. The Five Civilized Tribes adopted European farming methods, ginned cotton, ground corn and wheat, attended missionary schools, published newspapers, and acquired business skills. Under the **Indian Removal Act**, between 1832 and 1839 these Native Americans were forced to settle on **reservations** in Oklahoma. [See also **league, Muskhogean**.] *In Oklahoma, the Five Civilized Tribes evolved similar cultures based on their former lifestyles.*

Five Nations See **Iroquois League**.

flaking breaking off thin chips from the edge of a stone tool or weapon to make a sharp edge. Flaking, which was done with a sharp piece of bone, flint, **chert**, **obsidian**, or horn, is a skill that most Indians have valued from

flaking flint with a bone chipper

prehistoric times. Flaking patterns help to identify the culture that produced an object.

- The 2-4-inch Sandia point, associated with settlers of New Mexico's Sandia Mountains from 25,000 B.C. to 10,000 B.C., is flaked irregularly and ends in a rounded bulge on one side.

- The Clovis or Llano point, a common mammoth or mastodon bone artifact found throughout New Mexico, is a narrow projectile, 1-5 inches long, with fluted edges and a channel carved vertically on each side.

- The Folsom or Lindenmeier point, common to Folsom, New Mexico, and Lindenmeier, Colorado, resembles a fern leaf with narrow fluting about the edge and horizontal grooves covering the body of the projectile. This point was inserted in a wooden lance shaft and may have been used with the **atlatl**.

- The Old Cordilleran, or Cascade, point, was common among settlers of the Columbia River Valley, Washington, from 9,000 B.C. to 5,000 B.C., who preferred a narrow, unfluted projectile shaped like a willow leaf.

[See also **arrow, atlatl, flint knapping, harpoon, obsidian, spear**.] *The job of flaking requires hard, downward strokes and careful padding to prevent injuries to the hand and legs.*

Flathead See **Chinook**.

flense [flehnz] to strip **blubber** from a whale carcass; to flay. [See also **blubber**.] *The small bone tool used to flense blubber is called a flensing knife.*

flesher a sharp tool, made from the shin bone of a deer or buffalo, used to remove fat, meat, and membrane from the underside of a hide. After fleshing, the hide was **brained** and **beamed** to make it suitable for use as clothing, tent cover, or **parfleche**. [See also **beaming, braining**.] *In ancient times, people used a flesher to clean a hide and make it usable as cloth.*

fletching the feathered end of an **arrow**. The person who made arrows, called the fletcher, fashioned each arrow's fletching from a single turkey wing or goose feathers and lashed it into place with fine **sinew**. The purpose of adding parallel feathers to arrows was to keep the rear of the arrow in line with the point. A well-fletched arrow was built to withstand buffeting and to be reused. The style of fletching varied so distinctly from group to group that a tribe could be identified by its arrow. [See also **arrow**.] *Artifacts, including Paiute and Miwok fletching, have been found in Yosemite National Park.*

fletching

flint knapping chipping the edges of a piece of flint to create a sharp edge or point. [See **arrow, chert, flaking**.] *Little Wolf carried a scar on his thigh from a slip of his hand during flint knapping.*

floe a floating sheet of ice. [See also **bergy bit**.] *Ice floes jammed the harbor, making travel difficult for Fina until the spring thaw.*

Four Corners the mountainous territory where Utah, Arizona, New Mexico, and Colorado join. Four Corners was the site of several historic events, particularly the **Pueblo** defeat of Hispanic settlers, who fled south to Juarez, Mexico, in 1680, and the resettlement of **Navahos** in the fall of 1868, when tribesmen migrated on foot to Canyon de Chelly. *The Canyon de Chelly National Monument in Arizona preserves Anasazi cliff dwellings which were once common in the Four Corners region.*

Fox or **Mesquakie** [mehs • kwa' kee] an **Algonquin tribe** native to the Great Lakes region and supportive of the British. Renamed the Fox by white settlers, they referred to themselves as Mesquakie, or red earth people. Their resistance to the French fur trade helped to keep France from claiming Wisconsin, but continual struggle greatly reduced the Fox population. The Fox were related to the **Kickapoo** and **Sauk**, who lost territory during the War of 1812. By resilience and perseverence, the Fox retained their identity, traditions, and uniqueness, even after removal to **reservations** in Kansas and Iowa by the mid-1800s. In 1867, Chief Chekuskuk was maneuvered into signing away tribal lands on the Mississippi River and

Missouri River in exchange for the services of a doctor and a manual labor school. [See also **Keokuk**.] *Portrait painter George Catlin immortalized Keokuk, a Fox chieftain.*

Francis, Milly Hayo (1802-1848) a Creek-Seminole princess from western Florida who in 1817 begged her father, Chief Hillis Hadjo (also known as Josiah Francis), not to kill Captain Duncan McKrimmon, a captive militiaman from Georgia who was condemned to burn at the stake. Only after she vowed to join him in the ritual execution did the chief free McKrimmon. Within months, Hillis was executed. McKrimmon reciprocated for Milly's brave deed by rescuing her, her sister, and mother from starvation. At McKrimmon's proposal of marriage, Milly declined and returned to her village, where she died of tuberculosis at the age of 46. Her story, like that of Pocahontas pleading with Powhatan for the life of Captain John Smith, has passed into Native American lore as a type of Romeo-and-Juliet romance. [See also **Pocahontas, Powhatan, Seminole**.] *After he gained his freedom, Duncan McKrimmon offered to marry Milly, but she preferred a Seminole husband.*

a = s**a**ck; *ah* = s**o**b; *aw* = s**au**ce; *ay* = s**a**fe; *ee* = s**ee**k; *eh* = s**e**t

Gall or **Pizi** [pee' zee] (1840-December 5,1894) an orphaned Oglala **Sioux**, Gall was born near Moreau River in South Dakota. According to tradition, he earned his name in boyhood by devouring the gall of a wild animal. The adopted brother of **Sitting Bull** and pupil of **Crazy Horse**, Gall led a band of Hunkpapa Sioux rebels and in 1876 served as a key leader at the **Battle of Little Big Horn**. From his retreat in Canada, he broke with Sitting Bull and surrendered himself and his 300 followers to government troops in 1880; he then became a farmer. In 1889, after adjusting to white ways, he served as a judge at the Standing Rock Reservation. [See also **Battle of Little Big Horn, Crazy Horse, Sitting Bull**.] *An opponent of the Ghost Dance, Gall believed that the old life was ended and that the white man's culture was the only alternative.*

Gall

Ganeagaono See **Mohawk**.

Ganiodaio See **Handsome Lake**.

gaucho [gow' choh] a nomadic frontier horseman or cowboy of the South American plains, usually a mestizo, or **half-breed**, of mixed Hispanic, black, and Indian heritage. Some European communities rejected the gaucho as too wild, too unmannerly for polite company. As a result, the gaucho, armed with **bolas**, was forced to take whatever jobs were available in the outback, usually herding. He became a romanticized, mythic figure in song and folktale, as in José Hernández's poem *Martin Fierro.* [See also **black Indian, bola, pampas**.] *Gauchos, who were Indian herders in Peru, developed techniques of breeding and breaking fine riding horses.*

gauntlet a course lined by two facing rows of Indian villagers armed with whips, rocks, and clubs who struck

---

an individual forced to run the narrow path between them; an ordeal. Often women and children increased the humiliation of the gauntlet by yelling insults. Successfully running the gauntlet proved courage and could save a captive from execution. *Santela faced the gauntlet, then quickly ran the distance without flinching or crying out.*

General Allotment Act   See **Dawes Act**.

Geronimo [juh • rah' nih • moh'] or **Goyathlay** [goh • yath' lay] or **One Who Yawns** (1829-February 17, 1909) a **medicine man**, grandson of Chief Mahko, and **chief** of the Chiricahua **Apache** in southeastern Arizona. As **Cochise**'s lieutenant, Geronimo led raids from the Mexican mountains into southern Arizona, earning media attention for his swiftness and daring. In 1858, Geronimo swore revenge on Mexican soldiers who murdered his mother, wife, and three children. He preferred guerrilla tactics to full-scale battles and frequently eluded search teams by clever tricks, such as setting up fake camps. Often apprehended, he earned a reputation for frequent escapes. He, **Mangas Coloradas**, and the rest of the Chiricahua band were placed on the San Carlos reservation in 1883 and kept in leg irons. Along with his cousin, Jason Betzinez, and half-brother, White Horse, Geronimo escaped and renewed his effort. He was recaptured in 1886, imprisoned and forced to do hard labor at Fort Marion, Florida, and remanded to Fort Sill, Oklahoma. In his old age, he farmed and wrote an autobiography. [See also **Apache, Cochise, Mangas Coloradas**.] *In 1877, addressing President Ulysses S. Grant from Fort Sill, Oklahoma, Geronimo said:*

> *[Arizona] is my land, my home, my father's land, to which I now ask to be allowed to return. I want to spend my last days there, and be buried among those mountains. If this could be I might die in peace, feeling that my people, placed in their native homes, would increase in numbers, rather than diminish as at present, and that our name would not become extinct.*

(Bartlett, John. *Familiar Quotations.* Boston: Little, Brown, 1980, 603.)

Ghost Dance   a ceremony of unity and brotherly love begun by **Gray Hair** in 1869 in Nevada. In 1888, the dance was encouraged by **Wovoka**, a **Paiute medicine man**, who received a spirit message while he was delirious with fever. He used his supernatural powers to call back the buffalo and summon dead warriors to help Indians rid their land of white settlers. Unaccompanied singers, painted with red, white, and black body paint, hummed a woeful dirge and shuffled slowly in a clockwise movement for four days without food or water as they communed with spirits and worked themselves into ecstasy. At times the dancers sank into ecstasy and envisioned the coming of an earthly paradise. A magical shirt was believed to protect each ghost dancer from bullets. Two years after Wovoka's religious movement began, it spread to the **Washo**, Tillamook, Klamath, Wintun, and **Pomo**. The U.S. Cavalry ended the cult by massacring ghost dancers at **Wounded Knee**, South Dakota. [See also **Gray Hair, Wananikwe, Wounded Knee, Wovoka**.] *Frederic Remington's drawings of the Ghost Dance, which appeared in* Harper's Weekly *in 1890, depict the participants' religious fervor.*

ghost trail an invisible pathway to the afterlife, where spirits encountered the homes of their ancestors. *The soles of Crooked Foot's moccasins were beaded with religious symbols so that he might find his way along the ghost trail.*

giveaway a plains tradition of the **Crow**, Lakota **Sioux**, **Blackfoot**, and **Kiowa**, similar to a **potlatch**, by which a **tribe** rewards a young student or graduate with gifts. The gifts are usually practical, such as fabric, clothing, blankets, cash, or livestock. The giveaway is organized by a caller, or master of ceremonies, who announces the reason for

Oglala Sioux Ghost Dance drawn by Frederic Remington

ih = sit; oh = soak; oo = soup; ow = sound; uh = such; y = side

the occasion and arranges a dance to celebrate the event. The **Yupik** perform a similar ceremony at the Messenger Feast. [See also **copper, Kwakiutl, potlatch**.] *At the Kiowa giveaway, the sound of the drum echoed far into the night.*

giviak [gihv' ee • uhk]   an **Inuit** delicacy composed of small birds stuffed into a sealskin and buried under stones for several months. *At the end of summer, Matt's father unearthed the giviak and served it to the visiting family.*

gluckaston [glook' uhs • t'n]   a favorite stew of the **Kwakiutl** made from seaweed and corn. *Mark sampled the steaming pot of gluckaston and found it surprisingly good.*

gorge   an inch-long stick or bone sharpened on each end and attached to a fish line. When the gorge is baited, it entices a fish to swallow it and impale itself on the line. *Crowmocker honed the gorge with a stone before tying it to his fish line.*

shell gorget

gorget [gohr' jeht]   a disk of conch shell, slate, or pottery pierced in two places and worn on a **thong** about the throat as decoration or protective armor. *Gorgets found in a Cherokee burial ground featured a pattern of three rattlesnakes.*

gourd   a vine of the cucumber, **squash**, and **pumpkin** family that produces odd-shaped fruit varying in color from yellow and orange to dark green and white; also, the fruit of this vine. Native Americans used dried gourds or calabashes as pots, dishes, utensils, and storage containers, which they plugged with corncob stoppers. Central and South American Indians used the hollow-bottle gourd to make musical instruments. The loofah gourd supplies a complex inner fiber that is dried and used as a washcloth or scrubber. *Cherokee cooks used tender gourds in early spring vegetable dishes and toasted the seeds for snacks or used them to make jewelry and ceremonial adornments.*

gourd vine and fruits

a = **s**a**c**k; ah = **s**o**b**; aw = **sau**c**e**; ay = **s**a**f**e; ee = **s**ee**k**; eh = **s**e**t**

Goyathlay   See **Geronimo**.

Gray Hair   a Paviotso brave who created a revival movement in Nebraska around 1869. From information learned in a vision, Gray Hair prophesied the coming of a messiah who would restore the dead to life and turn Earth into a paradise where all would live in harmony. [See also **Ghost Dance, Wananikwe, Wovoka**.] *Gray Hair's concept of God demonstrates the influence of Christian missionaries.*

Great Mystery   the Indian term for religion or an understanding of the ways of nature. [See also **medicine feast, Great Spirit**.] *Young men studied the Great Mystery by drinking the black drink, sitting in a sweat lodge, and thinking about their place in the universe.*

Great Spirit   the English name for the Indian god of the universe, an animistic deity who revealed his divinity through nature. Whether he was known as the Great Spirit, the **All-Father**, or **Manitou**, the Indian deity was reverenced at all levels of society. Norman Russell, **Cherokee** poet and botanist, explained the importance of the Great Spirit and the oneness with the Earth that resulted from his worship as an outgrowth of the Native American way of life. [See also **All-Father, All-Mother, Manitou, Orenda, Wakan Tanka**.] *At the Council of Vincennes on August 14, 1810, Tecumseh exclaimed, "The Great Spirit is my father! The earth is my mother—and on her bosom I will recline."* (Bartlett, John. *Familiar Quotations*. Boston: Little Brown, 1980, 419.)

Green Corn Dance   a week-long secret ceremony in **Seminole** culture held in midsummer, during which court cases were tried, divorces granted, contracts and treaties settled, marriages conducted, and teenage male initiates given new names. The Green Corn Dance, which marked the Seminole New Year, began with the relighting of the fire, a ritual that served as a renewal of faith, a time when people sought healing of the body and spirit by rinsing the skin in ash, bathing, and drinking a cleansing drink. Concluding with games and folk dancing, celebrants told stories and played musical instruments. A similar rite held in late summer among the **Iroquois** featured speeches, worship, dancing, and gambling. [See

ih = sit; oh = soak; oo = soup; ow = sound; uh = such; y = side

also **black drink, busk, maize, Seminole**.] *Creek visitors were allowed to take part in the Green Corn Dance, which was held in the chungke court.*

Gros Ventre See **Hidatsa**.

ground cloth a hide used by native hunters and travelers to protect their bodies from contact with moist cold. During the march into exile known as the **Trail of Tears**, many elderly **Choctaw** and some of the children became ill because they did not have enough ground cloths to keep out the chill of the swamp. *Daniel Light Feather spread the ground cloth carefully over the tufts of buffalo grass.*

guacamolé See **ahuacatl**.

Guacanagarì [gwah' kuh • nah • gah' ree] (*fl.* 1490s) **Taino cacique** or chieftain who on December 24, 1492, invited Christopher Columbus to visit his village of Marien, near present-day Cap-Haïtien, Haiti. Guacanagarì's gift of a gold belt buckle ended speculation about whether the expedition would find riches. On Columbus's second voyage to the Caribbean, Guacanagarì claimed to have been wounded while protecting the Spanish settlement of Navidad. *Guacanagarì helped the European sailors salvage wood, tools, stores, and personal possessions from the wreck of the Santa Maria.*

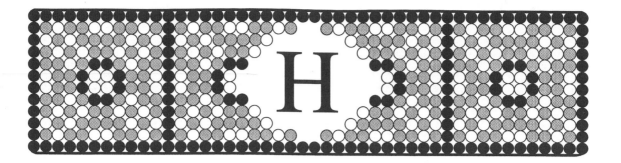

Haida [hy' dah] or **Kaigani** [kay • gah' nee] a **tribe** of fishers and traders native to Prince of Wales Island, Alaska, south to Queen Charlotte Islands, British Columbia. The Haida are famed for their skills in woodcraft and for their customs of tattooing faces and bodies, wearing conical cedar-bark hats, practicing slavery and polygamy, and living in towns rather than tribal communities. The early Haida built boats and rectangular, plank-sided multifamily dwellings, which they decorated with ancestral designs. [See also **dugout, potlatch, totem**.] *Many British Columbia canning factories are staffed with Haida workers.*

half-breed a person of mixed parentage, usually Indian and white but also Indian and Hispanic or Indian and black. The Spanish and French terms equivalent to half-breed are *mestizo* or *métis*. The term, often used as an insult, has denigrated whole tribes of disadvantaged and landless people, particularly the Lumbee, Chickahominy, Mattaponi, and Pamunkey. A few half-breeds, such as Jean Pere, who explored the Hudson Bay and Lake Superior in 1660, earned the respect of both parent nations. Another, the son of Jean du Sable, the African American founder of Chicago, had an Indian mother. Others, like Peter McQueen and William Weatherford, chose to make a stand against white supremacy by siding with their **Creek** relatives. [See also **black Indian, bois brule, Cree, Ouray**.] *Lottie grew up with the understanding that half-breeds like her could expect racial discrimination and constant ridicule.*

hamatsa [huh • maht' suh] a carefully staged native dance and magic show of the **Kwakiutl**, performed by a sacred male hermit during the winter ceremony. The coveted position of hamatsa, or cannibal dancer, which was extended to members of an exclusive dance society, carried much prestige. Young male members, crowned with sacred red-cedar bark, endured a ritual kidnapping and pretended to eat human flesh as proof of their spiritual awakening. As the dance progressed, initiates gradually returned from frenzy to normalcy. *With a mixture of dread and anticipation, Lota looked forward to the annual appearance of Owl Man, who performed the hamatsa for her tribe.*

hammock a rectangular piece of net or canvas stretched between two points and used as a bed, baby crib or carrier, seat, or shroud. The **Cuna** Indians of the San Blas Islands wrap their dead in a hammock. Ranging from 5-15 feet, hammocks traditionally have been woven from pita string, liana, palm leaves, **willow** cord, cotton, iris shoots, **Indian hemp**, **agave**, **mescal**, grapevine, and **yucca** fibers. *The traditional Taino hammock, which Christopher Columbus described in a log entry following his visit to San Salvador, resembles the weaving in the Cahuilla baby carrier.*

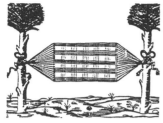

hammock

hand game a game in which the player hides a small object, such as a fruit pit, gumball, bone, stone, bean, ball, or piece of wood in the palm of one hand. Other players try to guess which hand holds the object. A variation of this game requires two objects, one plain and one marked. *Cheyenne gamblers bet heavily on who would win the hand game.*

decorated bones used in hand games

Handsome Lake or **Ganiodaio** [gan' ee • oh • dy' oh] (1735-1815) **Seneca shaman** and seer who founded an influential cult and taught a philosophy known as the Good Message, which tribal storytellers in New York and Canada memorized and recited as learning material for the young. Born in Conawagas near Avon, New York, Handsome Lake suffered from alcoholism and failing health until the age of 64, when he received a vision urging him to lead his people back to traditional values, such as prayer, meditation, family, and charity. Handsome Lake, who was the brother of **Cornplanter** and uncle of **Red Jacket**, encouraged the Seneca to remain firm in the old ways by avoiding the white race and abstaining from alcohol. He particularly revered children and forbade others from striking them. [See also **Cornplanter, Red Jacket, Seneca**.] *One significant change in tribal life under Handsome Lake's management was a lessening of* *matriarchal authority as Seneca women came under the power of their husbands.*

harpoon a long **spear** or javelin that bears a pointed hook at one end; the hook is made from sharpened bone, iron, or flaked stone. Smaller versions, used by New England tribes to catch eels, small fish, lobsters, and frogs, were relatively plain and contained only shaft and sharpened pronged head. On more complicated harpoons, a sharpened crosspin, or toggle, jutted inward to tighten the hold on the catch.

    Eskimos and other native fishers speared their catch with precision and often affixed a detachable point to the harpoon shaft by a long **sinew** to assure its safe return. To hasten the death of a whale, they tipped their harpoons in extract of monkshood root, a powerful poison. The **Nootka** made a distinctive harpoon with a sharpened shell banked by bone spurs. Each harpoon was attached to sealskin buoys that kept the whale carcass afloat for easy retrieval. Some modern harpoons incorporate an explosive charge or electrical shock in the point, thereby assuring a greater rate of kill. [See also **agvik, fish poison, flaking, leister**.] *Kapugen showed his skill by plunging the harpoon deep into the fish's side.*

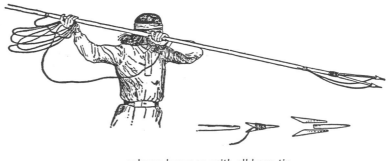

salmon harpoon with elkhorn tip

hatali [hah • tah' lee] a **Navaho** singer-healer; a **medicine man** or **shaman**. The hatali chants and gestures while surrounding the patient with geometric arrangements of colored sand depicting religious symbols. [See also **medicine man, sand painting, shaman**.] *The hatali believes that disease is caused by supernatural forces and can be healed only by a holy person.*

hatchet a small ax with a one- or two-headed blade that was sometimes decorated with feathers and **wampum** and stuck in a ceremonial post in time of war. If a war council chose not to accept a challenge, members buried the war

---

ih = sit; oh = soak; oo = soup; ow = sound; uh = such; y = side

hatchet in a special place to show their unwillingness to fight. From this act comes the American saying, to bury the hatchet, or end a quarrel. [See also **pipe tomahawk, tomahawk**.] *Jody found the hatchet useful as he searched for kindling.*

healing Healing was a serious undertaking for every native tribe, particularly after contact with Europeans spread fearfully dangerous diseases, such as tuberculosis, measles, scarlet fever, and diphtheria. Native American healers depended on good health practices, mineral baths, and ritual preparations to procure strength and long life. They invoked supernatural power, or **medicine**, as a spiritual relief of pain or cure for insanity.

Practitioners also used common potions. They carefully mixed dosages of elixirs, ointments, poultices, ash, and other healing drugs and tonics made from common plants, trees, and shrubs, and even badger fat, which was said to cure baldness. Some of these common herbs and barks, such as wormwood, cowbane, curare, and cascara sagrada, are extremely toxic and can be used as poisons, depending on the strength and amount of the dosage. The extensive list of Native American curative herbs includes the following:

- agrimony, the burs of which can be boiled in a tea to cure diarrhea and fever. A tea of agrimony root served as a tonic or cure for pox.

- allspice, a stimulant and cure for excess menstrual bleeding.

- aloe, the root of which can be chewed as a cure for diarrhea, liver ailment, and worms.

- alumroot, the root of which is an astringent to cure colic, excessive menstrual flow, hemorrhage, ulcers, thrush, dysentery, and sores.

- angelica, a root tonic to cure fever, colds, nervousness, colic, and sore throat.

- anise, which is boiled in a drink to cure bronchitis.

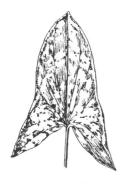

arrowhead

*a = s**a**ck; ah = s**o**b; aw = s**au**ce; ay = s**a**fe; ee = s**ee**k; eh = s**e**t*

- apple, the inner bark of which is boiled into tea to cure laryngitis, gallstones, and hemorrhoids.

- arbutus, which is used to make a tea to cure indigestion and kidney disease.

- arrowhead, the leaves of which are made into a strong tea to cure fevers in infants.

- asafoetida, of which the gum or resin from the roots cures spasms, cramps, colic, whooping cough, asthma, and worms.

- asparagus, which is made into a tea to cure rickets.

- aster, which is made into a tea to cure fever, bronchitis, and diarrhea. The roots can be crushed into a poultice for sprains and swellings.

- azalea, the twigs of which can be boiled to yield an ointment to cure rheumatism.

- balm, which is made into a stimulant, tonic, and cure for cold, fever, and chills.

- basswood, the bark of which can be boiled with cornmeal to make a poultice to cure boils or a tea to cure dysentery, snakebite, heartburn, nausea, cough, consumption, or hangover.

- bearberry, which is made into a tea for sprains or kidney and venereal diseases.

- **bear grass**, which is boiled into a tea to treat diabetes. The root may be crushed with fat to make a salve for sores.

- beech, the nuts of which are chewed to cure worms.

- beggar's lice, the root of which is crushed with **bear grease** to make an ointment for tumors. It may also be boiled to make a tea to cure itch, to improve memory, or as a love charm.

- bellflower, the root of which is simmered to cure diarrhea or to make a poultice for boils.

- benne, the leaves and seeds of which are made into tea to cure diarrhea, dysentery, or cholera.

- bittersweet, the bark of which makes a tea to settle the stomach. The root can be chewed as a cure for coughs; the leaves make a tea to cure colic or ulcers.

- black ash, the bark of which makes a tea to cure liver and stomach ailments.

- black cohosh or squawroot, which is made into tea for cramps, rheumatism, snakebite, or sleeplessness.

- blackberry, the root and leaves of which can be boiled to make a tea to cure bladder infection, diarrhea, malaise, sore throat, hemorrhoids, and rheumatism.

- blackgum, the inner bark of which may be boiled into a tea to cure kidney disease, diarrhea, and inflamed eyes.

- bloodroot, which may be boiled to make cough syrup or medicine for pneumonia and croup. As a wash, it cures ulcers, sores, and ringworm.

- bluebell, the leaves of which may be boiled to make a cure for whooping cough and consumption.

- boneset, the leaves and stalks of which can be boiled into a tea to cure pneumonia, sores, fever, chills, colds, sore throat, and flu.

- broom sedge, which is boiled into a tea to cure frostbite, itch, sores, and diarrhea.

- buckeye, which may be crushed into a poultice to ease rheumatism, sprains, swelling, tumors, and infection. Buckeye tea cures indigestion, fainting, bleeding, colic, sores, rheumatism, and hemorrhoids.

blackberry

*a = s**a**ck; ah = s**o**b; aw = s**au**ce; ay = s**a**fe; ee = s**ee**k; eh = s**e**t*

- buckthorn, the bark and fruit of which may be boiled into a tea to cure itch, sores, burns, cuts, and inflamed eyes.

- buckwheat, the heads and leaves of which may be boiled into a tea to cure headache and upset stomach.

- burdock, the root and seeds of which make a tea for purifying the blood and curing venereal diseases, leg ulcers, scurvy, and rheumatism.

- butterfly bush, the roots and seeds of which are a laxative, emetic, or lung medicine. The roots may be boiled into a tea to cure heart disease.

- calabazilla, the roots of which may be chewed into a paste to be applied to sores. It is also the basis of soap and shampoo.

- camphor tree, which provides sweating medicine for fever, flu, colds, nervous diseases, headache, fainting, colic, cramps, and worms.

- cardinal flower, the root of which serves as an emetic and expectorant and which cures stomach upset, worms, pain, fever, nosebleed, rheumatism, headache, swelling, sores, croup, and syphilis.

- cascara sagrada, the bark of which is a strong laxative and the berries an emetic.

- castor beans, which can be crushed to make a poultice to cure boils and boiled into a purgative tea.

- catnip, which is made into tea to cure hysteria, worms, spasm, colic, swelling, boils, and fever.

- cereus, a night-blooming cactus, the tubers of which are boiled into a tea or sucked for juice to cure diabetes.

- chamomile, one of the prize herbs for making tea to cure hysteria, colic, vomiting, ulcers, and swelling.

- cherry, the bark of which is boiled into tea to cure fever, chills, flu, labor pains, cough, colds, measles, thrush, laryngitis, swelling, jaundice, sores, ulcers, and bloody discharge.

- chestnut, the leaves of which may be boiled to make a tea to cure heart disease, bleeding, sores, inflamed navel, coughs, and typhoid.

- chickweed, the roots and stems of which may be boiled into a tea to cure worms.

- chicory, the roots of which are steeped to make a nerve tonic.

- chinaberry, the root and bark of which may be simmered into a tea for worms and ringworm.

- chinchona, or Peruvian bark (now called **quinine**), to cure malaria, impotence, and malaise.

- cinquefoil, the roots of which may be boiled into mouthwash or a cure for thrush, fever, weakness, and dysentery. Athletes ate cinquefoil roots and bathed in root tea to improve their strength and stamina.

- clematis, a vine that gives an extract used as liniment for cuts and sores, itch, rheumatism, ulcers, palsy, and venereal disease.

- clover, which is made into a tea to cure fever and kidney disease.

- cocklebur, the roots of which may be chewed to cure cramps, snakebite, and croup.

- comfrey, which is boiled into a mild tea to cure hemorrhaging, dysentery, gonorrhea, heartburn, sprains, and bruises.

- coneflower, the root of which cures earache. A tea made from coneflower root cures diarrhea, snakebite, worms, and swelling.

cocklebur

a = sack; ah = sob; aw = sauce; ay = safe; ee = seek; eh = set

- cornflower, which is used to cure snakebite.

- cowbane, a toxic plant the roots of which cause sterility.

- crabapple, the bark of which may be boiled into tea to cure gallstones, mouth sores, hemorrhoids, and asthma.

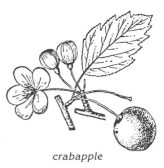

crabapple

- creosote, an oil obtained from various woods that is used to cure coughs, tuberculosis, and pneumonia; to draw out poisons and prevent infections and body odor; to relieve rheumatism; and to heal wounds and impetigo. Steam formed as the creosote boils in water treats headache and stomach cramps.

- croton, the stems and leaves of which can be boiled into a tea to induce abortion or can be used in poultices to cure earache.

- crowfoot, which may be made into tea for gargling or curing thrush, sleeplessness, and abscess.

- curare, a South American vine, the juice of which serves as a muscle relaxant.

- dandelion, the roots of which may be made into tea as a blood tonic or cure for toothache and nervousness.

- digitalis, which controls an irregular heartbeat and eases fluid in the lungs.

- dock, the roots of which may be bruised for poultices to cure sores, ulcers, tumors, skin disease, and itch. Dock tea cures dysentery, colic, ringworm, sore throat, and constipation in humans; it cures stomach disease in horses.

- dogbane, which cures mange in dogs.

- dogwood, the bark, leaves, and roots of which may be made into tea to cure backache, fever, colic,

dogwood

worms, measles, chicken pox, diarrhea, laryngitis, headache, poison, flu, and ulcers.

- elder, the bark of which makes a tea to cure heartburn, swelling, skin disease, burns, rheumatism, boils, infection, and fever.

- elderberry, the juice of which is drunk hot to reduce fever or cure cold, sore throat, or stomachache.

- fairywand, a lily that prevents miscarriage, relieves pain, treats uterine disease, stimulates the bladder, and prevents vomiting.

- fennel, a cure for colic and intestinal gas.

- garlic, which may be eaten as a stimulant, diuretic, expectorant, cathartic, or a cure for scurvy, swelling, asthma, deafness, worms, colic, and croup.

- ginseng, the roots of which may be boiled into a potion to heal wounds and cure shortness of breath, nervousness, headache, thrush, gout, rheumatism, pox, liver ailments, breast pain, hives, cough, fainting, tuberculosis, and colic.

- goldenrod, the roots of which make a tea to cure cold, cough, nervousness, measles, nerve pain, mouth sores, and tuberculosis.

- goldenseal, the root of which treats sores, swelling, hemorrhaging, tumors, weakness, upset stomach, and eye disease.

- ground ivy, the stems and leaves of which make a tea to cure hives, measles, and colds.

- hemlock, the stem tips of which may be boiled into tea to cure kidney disease, itching armpits, and diarrhea.

- hepatica, which cures swollen breasts, liver ailments, constipation, and indigestion.

- **hickory**, which cures colds, sore mouth, and cuts.

*a = s*a*ck; ah = s*o*b; aw = s*au*ce; ay = s*a*fe; ee = s*ee*k; eh = s*e*t*

- horsemint, the leaves of which may be crushed into a poultice to cure headache, colds, nausea, colic, flatulence, hysteria, nosebleed, measles, flu, heart trouble, and restlessness.

- Indian pink, which is a cure for worms.

- Indian pipe, the roots of which may be crushed to cure convulsions, sore eyes, bunions, and warts.

- indigo, which may be made into a tea to cure toothache, swelling, and vomiting.

- ironweed, the roots of which may be boiled into a tea to cure loose teeth, stomach ulcers, and hemorrhaging.

- jalap, a Mexican vine used as a laxative.

- jimson, the leaves of which may be made into tea to cure constipation or smoked to cure asthma. A poultice of jimson leaves cures boils and toothache and is also used as a painkiller for simple surgery, such as thorn removal, or the setting of bones.

jimson

- **juniper**, the needles of which can be used to make a tea that cures colds, stomachache, kidney disease, and gas pains.

- kelp, a treatment for sores, rheumatism, and diseases of the mucous membranes.

- lichen, which is ground to a powder and sprinkled lightly on the bites of snakes, poisonous spiders, or scorpions.

- licorice, a cure for asthma, cough, and hoarseness.

- lotebush, the roots of which are boiled into tea to use as eyewash or hair conditioner.

- lousewort, to put in dog beds to kill lice.

- lupine, the leaves and seeds of which can be boiled into a tea to cure diseased bladders.

- mistletoe, which is dried and powdered to cure headache, high blood pressure, infected eyes, stomachache, and lovesickness.

- mormon tea, the leaves of which are dried and powdered and administered as a cure for syphilis, boils, or bleeding sores.

- mullein, which may be rubbed on the skin to cure a rash or made into tea to cure swelling, mumps, sores, swollen glands, and coughs.

- nettle, the roots of which are placed around a baby's neck to ease teething; the seeds are made into tea to cure goiter.

- nightshade, the leaves of which are scored and rubbed on boils, ulcers, and hemorrhoids. Nightshade tea stops the pain of childbirth.

- onion, which is fried and placed on the chest to cure colds and croup. Onion juice cures hives, colds, sore throat, liver disease, and nervousness.

- pennyroyal, which may be made into a tea to cure fever, toothache, menstrual problems, headache, and colds.

- pine, the sap of which may be made into syrup to cure cough, bronchitis, rheumatism, venereal disease, swollen breasts, arthritis, fever, shortness of breath, constipation, worms, hysteria, colic, gout, weak back, consumption, ringworm, bruises, sores, ulcers, measles, and diarrhea. The ashes of burned pine boughs were used to cleanse a home after a death.

- plaintain, the leaves of which may be scalded and placed on burns, insect bites, headache, or swelling.

- pokeweed, the roots and berries of which may be made into tea to cure rheumatism, fever, ulcers, swellings, tumors, eczema, and arthritis.

- poplar, the buds of which produce a juice that cures sores, colic, rheumatism, venereal disease, cholera, fractures, and toothache.

- poppy, which relieves sleeplessness, pain, cramps, and spasms.

- prairie clover, the blossoms of which cure sore throat.

- prickly ash, or toothache plant, which is used as a poultice for sores, venereal diseases, rheumatism, swollen joints, and sluggish circulation.

- **pumpkin**, the seeds of which cure kidney diease, menstrual problems, worms, swelling, and burns. Softened pumpkin seeds are used as a facial cream.

- ragweed, the leaves of which can be rubbed directly on insect bites, poison ivy, or other skin eruptions.

- red alder, the bark of which makes a tea to control high blood pressure, the pain of childbirth, swelling, sprains, skin disease, jaundice, cough, thrush, toothache, hemorrhoids, and kidney disease.

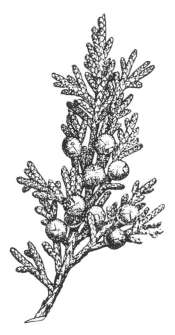

red cedar

- red cedar, which is made into tea to cure colds, measles, worms, itch, swelling, and rheumatism.

- redbud roots, the bark of which may be made into tea to clean teeth, gums, and breath and to cure whooping cough.

- red ocher, which is mixed with oil for sunburn ointment.

- **sage**, the branches of which are boiled to make a tea to cure fever, asthma, nervousness, coughs, and colds. Sage is also used in making shampoo and deodorant.

- sagebrush, the leaves of which can be brewed into a tea to cure colds, sore eyes, and fever. Galls are burned on sores to cauterize them or to relieve rheumatism.

- saguaro or giant cactus, used to bring milk to the breasts.

- **sassafras**, the roots and bark of which may be made into tea to cure coughs, soothe sore throats and stomachaches, and aid in weight loss. English settlers valued sassafras as a cure for syphilis.

- skunk cabbage, used as a birth control agent.

- slippery elm, a major herbal cure for burns, colic, heartburn, dysentery, quinsy, cold, cough, bronchitis, consumption, sore breasts, and sore eyes.

- smartweed, which may be made into tea to cure stomach cramps, diarrhea, swelling, and pain. It is also useful to prevent thumb sucking in children and to poison fish.

- snakeroot, the roots of which increase appetite and cure snakebite, toothache, whooping cough, colic, backache, swelling, and muscle aches.

- snow on the mountain, used to make tea to help nursing mothers make milk.

- soapweed, used to ease difficult births or to abort.

- spikenard, the roots and berries of which may be made into tea to cure backache, cough, asthma, broken bones, intestinal gas, cuts, and the pain of childbirth.

- sweetflag, the roots of which may be chewed to cure kidney disease, fever, muscle cramps, colic, swelling, worms, headache, sore throat, colds, diarrhea, spasms, and hernias.

- sweetgum, the resin of which cures nervousness, diarrhea, dysentery, sores, ulcers, itch, and swelling. It may also be used for chewing gum.

sassafras

*a = s**a**ck; ah = s**o**b; aw = s**au**ce; ay = s**a**fe; ee = s**ee**k; eh = s**e**t*

- toadflax, the roots of which are simmered to make a tea to cure kidney disease, cuts, or sores.

- trembling aspen, the bark of which makes a tea or syrup for cough, cold, worms, sores, arthritis, and weakness.

- **tule**, which is ground into a ritual powder that is also a stimulating tonic.

- white alder, the inner bark of which is used to purge the stomach, ease diarrhea, and cure fever.

- white oak, which makes an astringent tea useful for diarrhea, hemorrhoids, sores, poison ivy, and insect bites.

- wild ginger, which eases intestinal gas, breaks fever, stimulates the appetite, and cures boils and menstrual distress.

- wild potato, which is mashed and made into a poultice to cure boils and swellings.

- **willow**, the inner bark is used to break fever; control pain; and treat rheumatism, nausea, and malaria. It was also used in shampoo to brighten hair.

- witch hazel, the bark of which may be steeped to make a tea to bathe sores, sprains, and scratches and to cure tuberculosis.

- wormwood or artemisia, which is boiled as a bitter tonic.

- yellowroot, the roots of which make a tea for colds, mouthwash, ulcers, upset stomach, and the pain of childbirth.

- yerba-mansa, a creeping root used in poultices and tea to cure sore throat, fatigue, syphilis, and rash.

[See also **bear grease, chinquapin, dye, false face, heyoka, husk faces, ipecac, juniper, kachina, manzanita, mayapple, medicine man, milkweed, pokeberry, pumpkin,**

toadflax

quinine, sage, sand painting, shaman, tobacco, toloache, tule, willow.] *In many tribes, healing was accompanied by dancing or pantomimes in which the chief healer appeared behind a mask and performed ceremonial curing in silence or while chanting or praying.*

Hehaka Sapa   See **Black Elk**.

Heinmot Tooyalaket   See **Chief Joseph**.

He Makes Rivers   See **Hiawatha**.

herbs   See **healing**.

herring rake   a paddle with spiked teeth along one edge used to snare herring. As the rower paddled into a school of herring, the spikes stabbed the fish, which the rower flipped into the boat. *Nootka villagers were expert with the herring rake.*

He Who Combs   See **Hiawatha**.

heyoka [hay • yoh' kuh]   a brave who had a vision of thunder or who spoke directly to the spirit that guarded warriors. Common to plains tribes, a heyoka, or **contrary**, acted opposite to what was expected, for instance, by wearing his clothing inside out or covering up with blankets in the heat of summer. His hair was long on one side and shaved on the other; he sat on his horse facing the tail. His words said the opposite of his meaning. Tribe members admired and respected the heyoka, who was a combination of clown, spiritual leader, and healer. If the heyoka wanted to return to normalcy, he had to undergo the ordeal of reaching into a kettle of boiling dog meat and retrieving the head. [See also **contrary, healing, koshare, medicine man, plains Indians, witkowin, yucca**.] *The Sioux visionary heard a great clap of thunder and was changed into a heyoka by the experience.*

Hiawatha [hy' uh • wah' thuh] or **Ayontwatha** [a' yahnt • wah' thuh] or **He Who Combs** or **He Makes Rivers** (*fl.* 1550-1570)   a semilegendary Onandaga brave and orator from New York State who taught his people medicine, agriculture, art, and navigation. Influenced by the prophet **Deganawida**, Hiawatha, who served as the prophet's spokesman, tried to end the perpetual warfare between his nation and the **Mohawk, Seneca, Oneida, Onandaga**, and **Cayuga**. The resulting peace council, which grew to include the **Tuscarora**, became the **Iroquois League**. [See also **Deganawida, Iroquois League, Mohawk**.] *Hiawatha the statesman is often confused with a fictional character by the same name in Henry Wadsworth Longfellow's American epic,* The Song of Hiawatha *(New York: Dial Press, 1983).*

hickory a Native American hardwood tree that was used as an astringent, medicine, detergent; its wood was used to make **blowgun** darts, **arrow** shafts, tool handles, barrel hoops, chair bottoms, and baskets. Indians also used the edible hickory nuts in cooking and made dye from the outer husks. [See also **dye, healing, jerky**.] *As she colored pieces of woven cotton, Roan found her hands turning dark brown with hickory stains.*

hickory

Hidatsa [hih • daht' suh] or **Gros Ventre** [groh • vahn' truh] a native **tribe** of hunters and stock breeders, also called the Gros Ventre, or the Big Belly, of South Saskatchewan River. In 1867, while battling the **Crow, Cree**, and **Assiniboin**, the Hidatsa and their allies, the **Blackfoot**, were defeated. Their population shrank even further from epidemics of smallpox and scarlet fever. The Piegan name for the Gros Ventre means gut people, but they prefer the chalk people. *A famous 1908 painting by Charles M. Russell of the visit of the Lewis and Clark expedition to a Hidatsa village shows Chief Le Borgne rubbing his fingers over the chest of York, who was the first black man the Hidatsa had seen.*

Hobomak [hoh' boh • mak] (?-1640?) a trusted **Wampanoag** adviser and ambassador. Dispatched by Chief **Massasoit** to accompany **Squanto** on a diplomatic mission to the Pilgrims of Plymouth, Massachusetts, Hobomak later became a Christian and served Miles Standish as staff adviser. [See also **Squanto**.] *Hobomak left the Wampanoag tribe and lived among English settlers.*

Hodesaunee See **Iroquois League**.

hogan [hoh' gahn] a one-room **Navaho** residence made of mud, brush, gravel, and pine logs assembled horizontally into a beehive 6 feet high. The hogan, which is meant to blend in with nature, has one door, no windows, a rounded roof, and a single smoke hole. Furniture is usually limited to sheepskin beds. [See also **lean-to, roundhouse**.] *Navahos frequently build their hogans with eight sides.*

Hohokam [hoh • hoh' kahm] a prehistoric **tribe** of farmers, traders, and artisans who migrated from Mexico to south-central Arizona around 300 B.C. and thrived until A.D. 1450. Their name means the ones who have gone. Although game and wild plants were scarce, the Hohokam thrived because they lived in harmony with nature. They raised **corn**, beans, tomatoes, **squash**, cotton, and **tobacco** on terraces watered by a network of canals. In addition, they built temple mounds, ball courts, and multifamily dwellings that blended with their surroundings. Their craftwork was marked by clay figures, copper bells, stone palettes, iron mirrors, and patterned shells etched with fermented saguaro cactus juice. [See also **mound, Pima**.] *The Hohokam, who are ancestors of the Pima and Papago, built Snaketown, their cultural center, on the fork of the Gila River outside what is now Phoenix, where an irrigation canal and watchtower remain as examples of their expertise.*

hogan

holy dog See **horse**.

hominy [hahm' uh • nee] a common cereal grain; dried **corn** kernels that were soaked and boiled for an hour with the ash of blackjack or scrub oak. This process loosened the hulls, which were removed by rubbing kernels between the palms of the hands or twirling, **Mohawk** fashion, in a hulling bag or pouch. Hominy had to be rinsed repeatedly to remove the taste of ash; then it was cooked with seasoning, such as a soup bone, herbs, or vegetables or served plain with milk. Dried hominy was pounded into grits. The **Cherokee** also fermented hominy to make a strong drink. [See also **maize**.] *Hominy, which is still a staple in the South, makes a hearty, nourishing food for children and adults.*

*a = **sa**ck; ah = s**o**b; aw = s**au**ce; ay = s**a**fe; ee = s**ee**k; eh = s**e**t*

hominy grits [hahm' uh • nee grihts'] the coarse, bland residue sifted from dried hominy and cooked separately as a hot cereal or used as a thickener for soup or stew. Cooked grits can be baked with a seasoned topping, such as bacon bits or parsley. *From local Indians, southern cooks learned to appreciate hominy grits.*

hooch a slang term for poor-quality whiskey. *The Hoochinoo of southeast Alaska originated the term* hooch.

hoop-and-pole game See **chungke**. *The Pawnee credit the mythic figure of Moon Woman as the giver of the hoop-and-pole game.*

hoosegow [hoos' gow] a slang term for jail, prison, or stockade. *In Hollywood westerns, wrongdoers are locked in the hoosegow.*

Hopi [hoh' pee] or **Hopitu** [hoh' pee • too] a tribe of desert farmers native to Arizona and parts of the Southwest whose name means peace-lovers. In 1540, Hopi scouts guided Pedro de Továr, a scout for Francisco de Coronado, to the Grand Canyon and Colorado River. The Hopi, who succeeded the ancient **Anasazi**, built **pueblos** in remote canyons, where they battled drought as they eked a living from **corn**, bean, and **squash** gardens and raised cotton for weaving.

Their numerous festivals, involving **kachina** dolls and live snakes, sought help from the gods for a good harvest. The Hopi village of Oraibi, Arizona, is the oldest North American settlement still in use. Today, Hopi artisans of northeastern Arizona decorate their pottery with traditional earthtone designs. [See also **kachina, kiva, Nampeyo, petroglyph, Snake Dance**.] *In his eighties, Dan Katchongva, or White Cloud Above Horizon, philosopher and sachem to the Hopi of Hotevilla, Arizona, spoke before a congressional hearing in 1955 about the messiah his tribe had long awaited.*

horno [hor' noh] a beehive-shaped outdoor adobe oven common to Indians of the Southwest. This knee-high oven helps to keep dwellings cool by keeping heat and steam outdoors. [See also **adobe**.] *Women of the San Ildefonso tribe baked their corn loaves in hornos.*

horse or **spirit dog** or **holy dog**   the **plains Indians'** chief mode of transportation. Coronado introduced horses to the continent in 1541, but they were not available for breeding until the arrival of Juan de Oñate to the Chama and Rio Grande rivers in 1598. Prior to the arrival of the horse, the largest domesticated animal owned by plains tribes was a type of dog, a short-haired pack animal similar to a boxer. The introduction of a large work animal greatly changed the lives of the nomads of the plains, enabling them to acquire more food, to travel farther, and to live in larger **tepees**, which they loaded on large **travois** for horses to pull. Owners kept their mounts tied to their tepees and painted them with brightly colored symbols to protect them in battle. **Crow** Indians adorned their horses with beaded and feathered stirrups, saddles, rosettes, and neckpieces. *The great riders of the plains—the Sioux, Cheyenne, Crow, Arapaho, and Comanche— elevated the horse or spirit dog to godlike status.*

Frederic Remington sketch of plains Indian on a horse

horse effigy [hors ehf' fih • jih]   a carving of a horse on the end of a stick, which a person would take along on a **horse raid** as a good luck piece. *On his way out of the village, Matahe gripped the reins with one hand and his horse effigy with the other.*

horse raid   a secretive venture, often by night, to obtain horses, which served as evidence of wealth and social position. The horse raid was often conducted by a group of young men seeking to establish themselves among older tribe members so that they could bargain for wives. For the **plains Indians,** the horse raid was a proof of manhood, a challenge to the skill and stealth of the raider. It often involved the use of horse medicine, a magic spell or incantation that enabled a warrior to sneak up on an enemy camp and steal horses without being detected. *Mink Woman concentrated on creating the strongest horse medicine to protect braves who would take part in the horse raid.*

hot house   a circular building with a cone roof in the center of a **Muskhogean** village, where men gathered to worship and conduct business. The inner wall of the hot house was edged by a two-tiered platform, where members lolled, sat, or slept. [See also **cabin court, council lodge, kiva, longhouse.**] *A steady hum of voices arose from* *the hot house, where Abra's father conferred with the other men of the village.*

housewife an embroidered tote bag, sewing kit, or carryall used by **Eskimo** women to store needles, **sinew**, feathers, down, and wool. *A Yupik housewife often displayed intricate beadwork depicting an animal.*

huaca [hwah' cuh] a stone altar. Incan sun temples were surrounded by a series of community huacas, each serving a neighborhood and staffed by priestesses, seers, and keepers of the sacrificial animals. [See also **Inca**.] *In honor of the gods, local priests kept the huaca swept clean of ash and residue.*

huarache [hwuh • rahch' ay] or **hueracho** [hwuh • rah' choh] a flexible, air-cooled, woven leather sandal worn by desert Indians of the Southwest. Without huaraches, desert runners and hunters risked stone bruises, scorpion bites, and serious puncture wounds from cactus thorns. [See also **cactli**.] *Ida sat near the fire and cut long slits in a piece of leather to make huaraches for her oldest son.*

huipilli [hwee • pee' lee] a long overblouse or tunic with holes cut out for head and arms. **Aztec** women wore the huipilli either sashed or loose over layers of skirts. [See also **Aztec**.] *Moon Woman's huipilli was dyed with blossoms picked from cactus and wildflowers.*

Huitzilopochtli [wee' tsee • loh • pock' tlee] the **Aztec** god of sun and war, who was called "the hummingbird wizard" and was said to draw strength from the hearts taken from human sacrifices. [See also **Aztec**.] *Huitzilopochtli, who promised the Aztec a glorious future and dominance over their enemies, sent his followers to locate a new homeland at Tenochtitlán.*

huka [hoo' kuh] an adoption ceremony described by Afraid-of-Soldier, a **Sioux** historian, in *Winter Count* (Minneapolis, Minn.: Thueson, 1966). Begun in 1805, this ritual involved the **shaman** swishing of a horsetail over candidates for tribal adoption. The rite included ceremonial songs. [See also **hunka**.] *According to Ben Kindle's* *account of Sioux oral history, the huka became an official part of Oglala practice.*

hunka [hoon' kuh]   an adopted brother. Wealthy **Sioux** brought honor to themselves and their families by adopting likely young men, particularly orphans or deprived children. The adoption ceremony required a **medicine man** to tie the adoptee and his sponsor together with a **thong**, symbolizing that their lives and destinies were joined. [See also **huka**.] *Sitting Bull took a captive of the Assiniboin as his hunka.*

Huron [yoo' rahn] or **Wyandot** [wy' uhn • daht] or **Wyandotte**   a **tribe** of farmers, traders, and hunters belonging to the **Iroquois** nation and inhabiting Ontario and parts of the north central plains states. French traders called the tribe Huron, the French word for *ruffian.* Tribe members referred to themselves as Wendat, Wendate, Wyandot, or Wyandotte. One tribesman, Donnaconna, accompanied Jacques Cartier on his explorations and, in 1542, traveled with him to France. French cartographer Samuel de Champlain encountered Huron in 1615. As early as 1634, Huron guides assisted Jean Nicolet in exploring the Great Lakes region, but their association led to a devastating smallpox epidemic the following year; within five years, the epidemic halved the Huron population. During this period, Jesuit priests ministered to the Indians near Midland, Ontario. By the beginning of the War of 1812, the Hurons realized that the white settlers could not be defeated. A realistic Huron orator, Between-the-Logs, warned his fellow braves that a single defeat of the American army would not halt successive waves of settlers, who would one day supplant them. To protect their interests, the Hurons developed a northwestern fur, produce, and **tobacco** trade circle, which they covered by canoe. They were superstitious about dreams and ghosts, avoided mentioning death, and carefully protected the graves of their ancestors. In 1843, the Huron of Ohio were removed by government agents to Kansas; currently they live on Oklahoma reservations. [See also **Father Jean de Brébeuf,** *Huron Carol.*] *Today's grand chief of the Huron-Wendate, Max Gros-Louis, takes pride in the 2,000 tribe members living in Quebec.*

a = sack; ah = sob; aw = sauce; ay = safe; ee = seek; eh = set

Huron Carol Beginning in the seventeenth century with the work of **Father Jean de Brébeuf**, many religious groups, including early Catholic missionaries, tried to Christianize the Huron. From 1816 to 1823, a **black Indian,** John Stewart, joined Jonathan Pointer, a former slave, along the Upper Sandusky River, 70 miles north of Columbus, Ohio, to minister to the **Huron**. Out of this evangelistic era came a Christmas carol that blends the story of Christ with the Huron deity **Manitou**. [See also **Father Jean de Brébeuf, Manitou**.] *The Huron Carol was sung for a century in the Huron language before being translated into French and English.*

hurricane [huhr' rih • k'n]   the **Carib** word for violent and often destructive storms common to the Caribbean. *One of Columbus's greatest disasters was the loss of ships during the hurricane of October 1495.*

husk faces a secret **Iroquois** religious or **healing** society made up of members who represent mythical farmers and who are admitted to membership following a prophetic dream or miraculous cure. With fringed hair and plaited cornhusk masks, for the eight days of the midwinter ceremony, members of the husk faces made puffing sounds, guarded the doors of the **longhouse**, and prophesied the outcome of crops and the number of babies to be born in the **tribe**. [See also **false face, healing, longhouse**.] *Unlike members of the false faces, husk faces said few words.*

husky an Arctic sled dog used for pulling heavy loads over snow and ice; a Siberian, spitz, or malamute. **Inuit** owners shaped pelts or hides into pad covers to protect the tender inner flesh of the dog's paws from ice cuts or stone bruises. In addition to pulling loads, the husky used its sense of smell to locate seals and walrus, which were its major sources of food. In summer, huskies were allowed to roam free. [See also **qamutit**.] *The Siberian husky weighs no more than 60 pounds, yet is able to haul heavy loads across frozen tundra.*

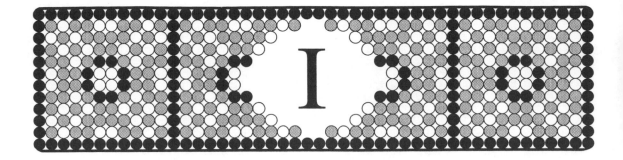

ice chisel a common **Eskimo** tool made from a pointed piece of bone or antler that was attached to a wooden grip by a **sinew thong**. Eskimo builders used ice chisels to cut large blocks of ice from a river. They removed the blocks to make fishing holes or to build **igloos**. [See also **buckhorn, igloo, snowknife**.] *The Toronto Museum features a drawing of an Inuit man using an ice chisel on a segment of ice floe.*

igloo or **iglu** a temporary domed shelter common to Canadian **Eskimos** that could be constructed on a stone foundation in a few hours by one or two people using an **ice chisel** or **snowknife**. The house was formed from a spiral of freshly cut blocks of ice or snow 1-2 feet long and 4-6 inches thick. The builder often built the house over the spot where the blocks were removed. The structure was glazed with snow to caulk the chinks. As the spiral was built up, the blocks were cut smaller. They tended to lean toward the center and hold up the structure. The last block was the key block, which had to be trimmed to fit the last hole.

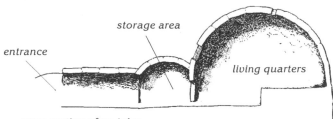

cross section of an igloo

entrance

storage area

living quarters

One block was pierced with the snowknife to allow smoke to escape. Then the igloo was covered with sod, turf, or skins or banked with loose snow to keep out the wind. An adjacent room served as a pantry or dog kennel; a porch or foyer of snow was built outside the door on a downhill slope to trap warm air. In front of the porch was a curved windbreak to protect the family from cold drafts. For protection from blizzards, the igloo might be sheltered on one side by a wall of ice blocks. A piece of gut or skin or a frozen block of fresh water might be added to a hole cut as a window. Inside, the igloo was fitted with sleeping platforms to keep the occupants away from the cold floor; **willow** twigs, grass, moss, and heather formed the mattresses, with skins serving as blankets.

The **Dorset** on Baffin Island were the first to use this form of residence, which was heated by blubber or **seal oil lamps**. For more permanent arrangements, Eskimos pegged canvas or skins loosely to the dome, creating an air space between the cloth and the wall as an added measure of insulation. Igloos made useful temporary dwellings, sometimes serving a family for more than a month, until a need for new hunting grounds forced it to move on. In winter, igloos were firm enough for an adult to stand on or children to slide down. In spring, when the roof began to melt, residents sliced off the top and replaced it with a piece of canvas. [See also **barabara, Dorset, Eskimo, ice chisel, innie, lean-to, nallaqtaq, qalgi, qarmat, qasgiq, snow-probe, Thule**.] *The term* igloo *can refer to many variations of Eskimo residences, including the nallaqtaq or tarp-topped ice house.*

Illinois a populous group of plains **tribes** that farmed and hunted buffalo and elk in the north-central United States. The Illinois shrank dramatically in number after fierce and protracted wars with the **Iroquois League** during the seventeenth and eighteenth centuries, followed by epidemics and displacement by European settlers. The Illinois, who currently live in Miami, Oklahoma, take their name from the French spelling of the **Shawnee** word for man. [See also **plains Indians, Pontiac**.] *After the death of Chief Pontiac in 1769, the Illinois lacked unity.*

Inca [ihn' kuh] an empire surrounded by colonies spread over 2,000 miles covering the coastal region of Ecuador, Peru, and Chile, and ranging inland to Bolivia and Argentina. In Cuzco, the capital city, the chief established his residence, headed the military, and was worshipped as a god. Named for the native word for prince, the Inca empire was famous for its 14,000-mile network of paved roads, as well as its courier service, stone temples, skilled surgeons and dentists, ventilated storehouses, gold ornaments, and terraced gardens.

map of the Inca empire

The Inca, who were clean shaven and dressed in tunics, cloaks, and **leggings**, used the **llama** as a work animal and source of transportation. They traveled from valley to valley over rope bridges woven of straw, vines, and spun rope. Their chief gods were the sun and moon and Viracocha, whom they revered as their creator. The Inca were virtually wiped out in 1533 by Francisco Pizarro's expedition. Although the tribe welcomed the Spanish as saviors predicted by sacred oracle, Pizarro's troops murdered the king and enslaved the survivors. [See also **huaca, Kon-Tiki, quipu**.] *Inca history dates to the semilegendary figure Manco Capac.*

Indian a Native American, member of a number of racial groups who migrated across a land bridge from Siberia to North America over a period from 20,000 to 40,000 years ago. Within 8,000 years, they spread north to Greenland, east to the Caribbean islands and south to Tierra del Fuego on the southern tip of South America. Although population figures are mostly guesswork, scientists believe that the rigors of Indian life kept the native population north of Mexico stable at 850,000 to 1 million; some estimates place the figure as high as 2 million. The native population decreased 90 percent after the arrival of Europeans. Today's U.S. census shows the Indian population at nearly 2 million in North America alone.

Over time, Native American **tribes** spoke more than 1,500 languages and adopted a variety of lifestyles, from **Inuit** snowhouse dwellers of the far north to nomadic **tepee** makers of the plains, **adobe pueblo** builders of the Arizona desert, and canal and temple **mound** builders of the Ohio Valley, Mexico, and Central America. Their arts and crafts ranged from the carved cedar **totems** of the Pacific Coast to the woven **yucca** huaraches of the **Pima**, **Yuma**, and **Zuñi**, from the **birch bark canoes** of the eastern woods Indians to the feathered garments of the **Maya** and **Aztec**. Their contributions to American life include foods, especially the potato, avocado, cashews, chewing gum, chocolate, beans, **corn**, **maple syrup**, blueberries, and **squash**; drugs, such as **quinine**, digitalis, and cocaine; and creative cuisine that mixed vegetables and meat in **succotash**, popped and soaked corn into popcorn and **hominy**, and roasted meat in a fire pit to produce **barbecue**. [See also **ahuacatl, Amerindian, Beringia, cacao, chicle, coca, healing, igloo, plains Indians**.] *On his arrival in the Western Hemisphere, Christopher Columbus thought he was in India and misnamed Native American people Indians.*

Indian flute a slim wind instrument made from a hollow limb or reed pierced with holes and ending with a carved bird head with open beak. **Plains Indians** used the flute in courting. By playing lyric, coaxing melodies, they expressed their longing for the girls of their choice. [See also **panpipes**.] *Swift Eagle was too shy to speak to Sunshine, so he courted her by flashing his mirror and playing original melodies on his Indian flute.*

Indian hemp a perennial plant yielding narrow seed pods that contain silky fluffs, which could be twisted into string. Indians used the toxic root and juice of the hemp plant to purge impurities from the body and to strengthen the heart. *While Cloud Dancer gathered roots, she kept her pony from nibbling the leaves of the powerful Indian hemp plant.*

Indian Removal Act an 1830 law that provided for the compulsory resettlement of Native Americans on designated land west of the Mississippi River in Kansas, Nebraska, Oklahoma, North Dakota, and South Dakota. Herded by soldiers along a difficult trail, often called the **Trail of Tears**, many Indians died from hunger, disease, exposure, and despair. Only 100,000 survived the brutal uprooting. Native Americans received $500,000 in repayment for the lands they lost as a result of the Indian Removal Act. [See also **Dawes Act, Indian Territory, Trail of Tears**.] *Of the Five Civilized Tribes—Cherokee, Chickasaw, Choctaw, Creek, and Seminole—who were forced to leave their homes, the Seminole were the most successful in avoiding the forced exile caused by the Indian Removal Act.*

Indian hemp

Indian Reorganization Act also called the Wheeler-Howard Act, this 1934 law restated the **Dawes Act** of 1887 (which was amended in 1891, 1906, and 1910) by establishing councils to help tribes cope with **reservation** life. Under the leadership of Commissioner of Indian Affairs John Collier, Congress provided more land for sale to individual Native Americans and encouraged conservation, tribal self-government, higher education, and investment in Native American businesses. This liberating legislation encouraged Indians to study and speak native languages, practice ancient religions, and return to traditional arts, such as pottery, **basketry**, weaving, leathercraft, and jewelry making. After two years of discussion and debate, 195 of 258 tribes chose to accept the government's proposal. [See also **Dawes Act**.] *Under the Indian Reorganization Act, Native Americans, including Alaskan Eskimos, have a greater role in the management of their own affairs.*

Indian Territory   midwestern acreage in Kansas, Oklahoma, Nebraska, North Dakota, and South Dakota where large populations of Indians were forced to settle. These areas were known as Indian Territory before they became states. [See also **Dawes Act, Indian Removal Act, Trail of Tears**.] *The largest expanse of Indian Territory lies in Oklahoma, where Wilson Rawls, son of a Cherokee mother, captured his boyhood memories of the region in his two young adult novels,* Where the Red Fern Grows *(New York: Bantam, 1961) and* Summer of the Monkeys *(New York: Dell, 1976).*

inipi   See **sweat lodge**.

iniskim [ihn' ihs • kihm] or **buffalo stone**   a rare stone or fossil; a sacred object used during buffalo ceremonies to summon herds of buffalo. **Blackfoot** tribe members kept iniskim or buffalo stones as personal good luck charms. The iniskim is believed to sing or speak, often offering encouragement during periods of disease, drought, or hunger. [See also **medicine, medicine bundle, medicine pendant**.] *Bold Runner valued his iniskim above all other tokens in his medicine bag.*

innie [ihn' nee]   a permanent or semipermanent sod or stone Eskimo residence; a variation of the short-term snow or ice **igloo**. [See also **barabara, igloo**.] *Enoch and his friends stacked their snowshoes against the side of the innie.*

i'noGo tied [ihn' uh • goh tyd']   a protective charm, literally house of the spirits, made from **blubber** and seal fur attached to a cord and fastened to the wrist, neck, or waist. The i'noGo tied guards Alaskan Indian children from harm. [See also **aungaak, medicine pendant**.] *The wise woman fastened the i'noGo tied on her granddaughter's belt.*

Inshtatheamba   See **Bright Eyes**.

inua [ihn' oo • ah]   the Alaskan **Eskimo** concept of spirit, which exists in people and animals as well as rivers, lakes, mountains, and wind. Inuas, like **tricksters**, are so powerful that they can change shape at will. To pacify the inuas, handicrafters painted faces of animals on masks, **kayaks**, **harpoons**, and tools. Ceremonial inuas often combined human heads on animal torsos. [See also **trickster**.] *Sgt. Lubbock of the Mounties located the lost kayak and identified its owner by the inua images painted on the hull.*

Inuit [ihn' uh • wiht] or **Inuk** [ih' nook] or **Nunavut** [noon' uh • voot] a native tribe of the Arctic. The word translates as the people, the **Eskimo** word for themselves. These nomadic hunters and fishers kept dogs to pull their sleds and moved from Siberia across Alaska, northern Canada, Thule, and other parts of Greenland. The Inuit trapped for hides and traded for tea, flour, coffee, and ammunition. Ipiutak, a site in Point Hope, Alaska, in 1939 yielded ivory carvings, masks, and primitive tools and weapons, relics of an early **Inupiak** tribe.

In modern time, the Inuit sometimes make their living as hunting guides and sellers of **soapstone** carvings. During the winter, Inuit business may be conducted by bush plane, which is the only way out of ice-choked waters and barren **tundra**. In 1992, Inuit tribes of Canada, led by Malachi Arreak, proposed an eastern territory called Nunavut or "Land of the People," which by 1999 would give autonomy to the 17,500 natives and title to 18 percent of the resource-rich 136,000-square-mile area, one-fifth of Canada. This valuable land, once known as the Northwest Territories, extends from Hudson Bay to Greenland and comprises thousands of islands and waterways. [See also **Déné, Eskimo, Inupiaq, Yupik**.] *An Inuit myth about Sedna, the woman in Adlivun, the land under the sea, includes a song about a land of the birds where residents have plenty to eat and sleep on soft bear skins.*

Inuk See **Inuit**. *An Inuk or Canadian Eskimo differs from the Alaskan Eskimo in customs, language, and traditions.*

inukshuk [ih' nook • shook'] a stone trail marker or cairn of the Canadian **Eskimo**. *Along the trails of the Auyuittuq National Park, inukshuks mark the best paths.*

Inupiaq [ih • noo' pee • ak] or **Inupiat** the **Eskimos** of northern Alaska as well as those speaking the Inupik language. [See also **Eskimo, Inuit, Yupik**.] *During the*

ih = sit; oh = soak; oo = soup; ow = sound; uh = such; y = side   **111**

nineteenth-century, missionaries studied the Inupiaq and made crude dictionaries of their language.

Inupik [ih • noo' pihk] or **Inupic** or **Inupiq** the language of **Eskimos** living in Greenland, Canada, and northern Alaska. [See also **Yupik**.] *The two major languages of the Eskimo are Inupik and Yupik.*

Iowa a peace-loving tribe of hunters and farmers that migrated from Mississippi to Iowa. Their Platte River village was visited by the **Lewis and Clark expedition** in 1804. Following severe losses from smallpox epidemics, many Iowas voluntarily gave up their lands and agreed to move to **reservations** in Oklahoma. Encouraged by ambassadors of King Louis-Philippe of France, a troupe of Iowan performers danced before the royal court at the Tuileries Palace, an event that was recorded in an 1846 painting. *The Iowa, who descended from the Winnebago, were originally named Ayuhwa, or the sleepy people.*

Iowa medicine man drawn by George Catlin

ipecac [ihp' ih • kak'] a viny plant that produces stems and roots valued by Indian healers of Central and South America. Indians used the dried roots of ipecac for religious purification rites, which cleansed the body of harmful or evil substances. [See also **black drink, healing**.] *Today, syrup of ipecac forms the basis of cough medicine; it is given to victims of poisoning because it causes vomiting, thus removing harmful substances from the stomach before they can enter the bloodstream.*

Iroquois [ihr' uh kwoi] an advanced, influential, but small farming tribe that settled portions of New York and traded with Canadian, French, and Dutch trappers. The Iroquois, whose name means real snakes, also called themselves Haudenausaunee, or people of the **longhouse**. They governed themselves through a matriarchal hierarchy of Clan Mothers, who directed political and domestic aspects of tribal life, including the selection of male leaders. Therefore, mothers, grandmothers, sisters, and aunts were highly honored tribal members. Another significant Iroquois figure was the Hageota, or storyteller, who entertained and educated with stories of the **trickster**.

The Iroquois were the first Native Americans to carry guns, and they earned a reputation for **blood feuds** with

a = sack; ah = sob; aw = sauce; ay = safe; ee = seek; eh = set

the **Mohawk** and **Algonquin**. In 1534, Jacques Cartier, who employed Iroquois guides, kidnapped Chief Donnacona's sons and took them to France to show to royalty. By 1670, Christianized Iroquois had begun Kahnawake, a native village across the St. Lawrence River from Montreal. In 1701, following a decisive defeat by a coalition of the Algonquin with Samuel de Champlain, the Iroquois signed the Montreal Treaty and pledged to fight the French. One renowned Iroquois **sachem**, Sa Ga Yeath Qua Pieth Tow, visited Queen Anne in her London palace in 1710.

In 1799, **Handsome Lake** encouraged the Iroquois to abandon witchcraft and accept The Good Word, which was revealed to him in visions. Four other leaders, **Joseph Brant**, Grangula, Dekanisora, and **Cornplanter**, achieved merit for military strategy and firmness, which white settlers respected and feared. One white adoptee, Mary Jemison, who joined the Iroquois in 1758, lived until the 1830s as a revered clan grandmother of the Buffalo Creek Reservation. Modern Iroquois live on reservations in Allegheny, Cattaraugus, Onondaga, St. Regis, Tonawanda, and Tuscarora, New York. [See also **blood feud, Joseph Brant, Cayuga, clan, Handsome Lake, Iroquois League, longhouse**.] *In 1917, the Iroquois, eager to display their Americanization, formally declared war on Germany by sending a runner to Washington, D.C.*

Iroquois League or **Hodesaunee** [hoh' duh • saw' nee] or **Five Nations** a confederacy or union, envisioned by **Deganawida**, an Iroquois **shaman**, and incorporated by the prophet **Hiawatha**. The league, composed of **Mohawk, Oneida, Cayuga, Onandaga**, and **Seneca**, fought Samuel de Champlain, founder of Quebec, who in 1609 joined with the **Algonquin** and Montagnais to assure French control of prime land in New France. The resulting ill will led to a century of wars. Joined by the **Tuscarora** in 1722, the Iroquois League aimed at settling internal differences and establishing territorial control. It remained strong until its collapse around 1790. The representative government of the league is thought by some historians to have been a model for the U.S. government's representative democracy. In 1880, Seth Newhouse, a Seneca scribe, recorded the constitution of the Iroquois League, which had been in effect for three centuries. The league's governing body, headed by lords, was composed of 50 chiefs, 9 Mohawk, 9 Oneida, 10

some Iroquois League clan symbols

Cayuga, 14 Onandaga, and 8 Seneca. The Mohawk were chosen by the **Great Spirit** to head the league because of their self-control and compassion. The Onandaga were appointed Firekeepers, or protocol officials, delegated to settle squabbles, thank the Great Spirit, open council sessions, and report on proceedings.

According to league rules, the Five Nations were intended to keep the peace and protect life, freedom, and property. Female relatives were expected to force chiefs to keep their word. A formal expulsion ceremony punished league members who did not take their duties seriously or who committed sins. The ritual symbol of a bundle of five arrows symbolized the league's goals: union, power, honor, and dominion. [See also **Algonquin, Cayuga, Deganawida, Hiawatha, Iroquois, league, Mohawk, Onandaga, Oneida, Seneca, Tuscarora**.] *The Iroquois League, led by Uthawah, met in the longhouse to debate civil matters, such as internal strife and relations with other tribes.*

Ishi [ee' shee] or **Tehna-Ishi** [tay' nuh • ee' shee] (1861-March 1916) the last survivor of the **Yahi**, a branch of the Yana nation, which lived near Sacramento, California, until miners and white settlers destroyed tribal remnants. Ishi witnessed violence between Indians and whites in early childhood. Following the deaths of the remaining three Yahi, he wandered alone for three years, keeping out of the way of white miners and railroad workers.

Ishi gave himself up near a corral outside Oroville in August 1911 and accepted protective custody in the local jail. Later, under the sponsorship of Dr. Alfred Kroeber, Ishi made his home at the Museum of Anthropology of the University of California, in San Francisco where he worked as the institution's caretaker and taught traditional crafts, cooking, healing, and lore. Named Ishi, or man, in the Yahi dialect, because he chose to keep his identity secret, he died of tuberculosis without revealing his true name. His friends at the museum conducted his funeral according to Yahi traditions. [See also **tobacco**.] *Two books immortalize Ishi: Alfred Kroeber's* Handbook of the Indians of California *(Wilmington, Del.: Scholarly, 1925) and Theodora Kroeber's* Ishi in Two Worlds: A Biography of the Last Wild Indian in North America *(Berkeley: University of California Press, 1961.)*

*a = s**a**ck; ah = s**o**b; aw = s**au**ce; ay = s**a**fe; ee = s**ee**k; eh = s**e**t*

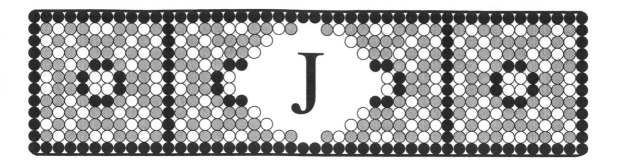

jack-lighting a method of hunting deer by lashing a lighted **pine knot** to the bow of a canoe and backing it with a birch-bark shield to reflect its glow. The reflection drew deer and other game, which were curious about the light. As the rower steered close to animal watering spots, hunters shot the deer with **bows** and **arrows** or darts from a **blowgun**. [See also **fire-lighting**.] *Moose Heart aimed his arrow at a doe, which was attracted by jack-lighting.*

jerky or **charqui** [chahr' kee *or* shar' kee] flank meat or fish that is cut into thin strips, soaked in salted water, then dried in the sun for three days or smoked over a slow **hickory**-wood fire. Indians made jerky on windy days to keep insects from dirtying the meat. Like pemmican, it is a handy and nourishing food for travel because it does not need cooking or other preparation and requires no special packaging or storage. [See also **llama, pemmican, smoking, squaw candy**.] *Jerky reputedly got its name from the jerking bite of mountaineers, who depended on dried meat during winter months.*

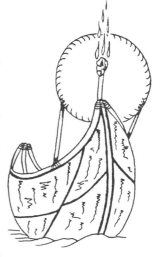

D. Timmons

canoe set up for jack-lighting

Jerusalem artichoke the potatolike tuber of a native wild sunflower. A staple year-round root crop, the tuber is eaten fresh like a radish; roasted and boiled, like turnips; or it is fed to livestock. *Because it furnishes insulin, the Jerusalem artichoke is sometimes eaten by diabetics.*

Joseph, Chief See **Chief Joseph**.

juneberry See **serviceberry**.

juniper a low-branching, shag-barked evergreen tree or shrub common to southwestern America and used by desert Indians as a source of fragrant wood and oil. The juniper has tangy gray-green or blue berries, which are

---

used as a condiment or spice or are pounded into meal. The berries are also strung on necklaces. Juniper wood makes a strong, lightweight **bow**, and good firewood, and roofing material. In early times, its bark was shaped into baby diapers. [See also **healing**.] *Juniper oil is used by Pueblo Indians as a strong spring tonic, postnatal restorative, and fragrant shampoo.*

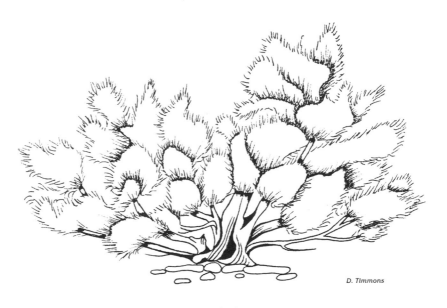

D. Timmons

juniper

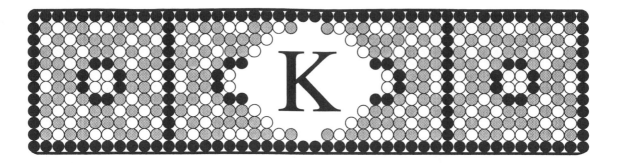

kacale See **koshare**.

kachina [kuh • chee' nuh] or **katchina** or **katcina** a member of a group of more than 250 benevolent ancestral spirits of the **Pueblo** and **Hopi**. The spirits lived six months underground and six months on Earth. During worship ceremonies, as a means of bringing rain and fertility, curing illness, or marking the passing of the seasons, dancers dressed in bright costumes and wooden masks of varying heights carved from cottonwood or cactus root. Although they sometimes chastised local misbehavers, kachinas were humorous, good-natured figures who brought gifts to children and laughter to the whole village. [See also **booger, healing, Hopi, koshare, mudhead, Pueblo**.] *According to the Hopi religion, when kachinas visit Earth, they always take a living spirit back with them.*

kado [kah' doh] the **Kiowa** name for the **Sun Dance**. [See also **Sun Dance**.] *To white observers, the fervent kado is an emotional experience.*

kammik [kam' mihk] thick sealskin boot that laces at the knee, worn by Canadian **Eskimo** hunters. For extra warmth, wearers line their kammiks with moss, bird skin, woven grass, or feathers. [See also **moccasin, mukluk**.] *Before settling in for the night, Naigo dried his parka, pants, and kammiks in front of the stove.*

kasghi See **qasgiq**.

katela [kuh • tee' luh] a secret society of **Sioux** women who acted out scenes from the lives of great warriors as a means of religious instruction for their tribe. *The katela dressed in masculine war regalia and weapons and even painted imitation wounds on their bodies.*

D. Timmons

kachina

---

ih = sit; oh = soak; oo = soup; ow = sound; uh = such; y = side

Kateri See **Catherine Tekakwitha**.

kayak [ky' ak] or **qayaq** a remarkably maneuverable one- or two-person hunting **canoe** that is 25 feet long, less than 2 feet wide, and only 1 foot deep. The kayak, which was invented by the **Dorset** of Baffin Island, in 800 B.C., had a willow-and-whalebone or driftwood frame covered in six or seven sealskins or **caribou** hide. Across the bow were fastenings to hold tools and weapons. Today, the standard one-person kayak, which weighs about 50 pounds, seats the paddler in a small oval opening, which is laced against the paddler's body with gut skin to keep out water and cold air.

Keokuk as painted by George Catlin

The occupant, who is virtually one with the boat, propels the craft silently across the water with a double-bladed paddle. The early kayaker dressed in a wetsuit fashioned out of seal or walrus intestine. If the kayak rolled over, the paddler could quickly right it with skillful moves of the paddle. The Nunivak Island kayak varies from the more common version by seating two paddlers back to back. [See also **bullboat, canoe, Dorset**.] *In a kayak, the lower portion of the paddler's body is concealed.*

keetaan See **prayer stick**.

Keokuk [kee' uh • kuhk] (1783-April 1848) a clever speaker, negotiator, and leader of the united **Fox** and **Sauk** after the capture of **Black Hawk**. Keokuk, who was born near Rock Island, Illinois, competed with **Black Hawk** for power during the War of 1812 and helped government forces hunt him down. Assigned to a Kansas **reservation**, Keokuk lived the remainder of his life under a cloud of suspicion and ill repute after he increased his wealth by selling Iowa lands to whites. [See also **Black**

*a = s**a**ck; ah = s**o**b; aw = s**au**ce; ay = s**a**fe; ee = s**ee**k; eh = s**e**t*

Hawk, Fox.] *Keokuk foolishly signed over huge areas of Indian land to the United States government.*

ki See **roundhouse**.

Kickapoo [kihk' uh • poo]   a fiercely independent tribe of horse breeders and raiders that originated in Michigan and settled southern Illinois and Indiana. Much of Kickapoo history is laced with intertribal rivalry with the **Osage**, **Ojibwa**, **Ottawa**, **Seminole**, and **Potawatomi**. In the early nineteenth century, two distinguished Kickapoo leaders, Mecina and Kennekuk, led in opposite directions. Mecina wanted to fight the uprooting of Indians from native lands; Kennekuk, both leader and prophet, counseled the Kickapoo to migrate farther from European settlers. The Kickapoo, who split over the sale of native territories, resettled in Mexico and Texas and, later, in Kansas and Oklahoma. *In defense of his tribe, Kennekuk, a Kickapoo spokesman, remarked that children do not eat breakfast until they have prayed to the Great Spirit.*

Kindle, Ben   an Oglala **Sioux** who memorized the oral chronicle of Sioux history from 1759 to 1925. Relying on mnemonic devices, Kindle studied the list of historic events narrated by his grandfather, Afraid-of-Soldier. Among the great events of the Sioux history, entitled *Winter Count* (Minneapolis, Minn.: Thueson, 1966), Kindle cites these:

1759 The Sioux tribes are scattered.
1763 Sioux implement makers obtain shells from the Platte and Missouri rivers and invent a shell knife.
1767 Sioux maintain peaceful coexistence with **Pawnee** and **Crow**.
1768 A civil war breaks out among **Cheyenne**, Standing Rock Indians, Oglala, and Rosebud.
1782 Sioux suffer a measles epidemic.
1791 Sioux tribes are introduced to the American flag.
1802 A white minister visits.
1833 A burst of shooting stars seems like an omen.
1861 Children suffer an outbreak of whooping cough.

1904   Reservation land is allotted.
1913   The Titanic sinks.
1917   President Woodrow Wilson drafts men for World War I.
1919   Sioux become citizens.

[See also **Sioux**.] *Ben Kindle believed the Sioux proverb, "A people without a history is like wind on the grass."*

King Philip (1638-August 12, 1676) or **Metacomet** [meh' tuh • cah' meht] the English name adopted by Metacomet, a **Wampanoag sachem**, son of Chief **Massasoit**, and brother and successor of Wamsutta. King Philip was taunted by European settlers for his dapper dress and proud posture. In 1675, following years of increasing European settlement, King Philip organized a coalition of Wampanoags with the **Narragansett**, **Pequot**, Nipmuck, Pocasset, Sakonnet, and others, then launched a two-year war against the 30,000 English settlers in New England. The war is known as King Philip's War.

Some tribes remained neutral during the war, while others sided with the English. King Philip's group attacked 52 of the 90 colonial villages and destroyed a dozen of them. Indian resistance ended when a combined force of militia and Indians cornered Philip in a swamp east of the Tounton River in Connecticut and killed him. To mark his humiliation, English settlers put his head on public display and sold his wife and son into slavery. The war was the first extensive military conflict in American history and was a tragic experience for the people of New England—both whites and Indians. [See also **Algonquin, Massasoit, Wampanoag**.] *A description of King Philip through the eyes of a white female taken prisoner in Lancaster on February 10, 1675, is found in* A Narrative of the Captivity and Restoration of Mrs. Mary Rowlandson *(Irvine, Calif.: Reprint Service, 1991).*

kinnikinnick [kin' ee • kuh • nik'] or **kinnikkinnik** the Algonquin name for a mixture of red willow or dogwood inner bark, **tobacco**, bearberry, and dry sumac leaves. Kinnikinnick was smoked in clay pipes for ceremonial purposes, such as the blessing of an infant, welcoming state visitors, or concluding a funeral rite. A ritual mix, it was used as a symbol of serious intent rather than for

*a = s**a**ck; ah = s**o**b; aw = s**au**ce; ay = s**a**fe; ee = s**ee**k; eh = s**e**t*

recreational purposes. [See also **tobacco**.] *When tobacco was scarce, settlers learned from Indians how to mix their own kinnikinnick.*

Kiowa [ky' uh • wuh]   a nomadic **tribe** of hunters native to the plains of the central and southwestern United States. Living primarily in southwest Oklahoma, the Kiowa's name means principal people. Driven out of the Black Hills of South Dakota by the **Sioux** in 1800, they encountered the **Lewis and Clark expedition** five years later. Kiowa history notes that the meteor shower on December 13, 1833, began a series of events that weakened their former strengths. A devout and noble people, they made peace with the **Arapaho**, **Comanche**, and **Cheyenne** and accepted residence on an Oklahoma **reservation** in 1868. A few decades later, according to Jim Whitewolf, Jesuit missionaries and nuns enticed Kiowa converts by giving them rosary beads.

N. Scott Momaday, professor of English at the University of Arizona and a noted Kiowa author, wrote *The Way to Rainy Mountain* (Albuquerque: University of New Mexico Press, 1976) and *House Made of Dawn* (New York: HarperCollins, 1989), for which he won the 1969 Pulitzer Prize for fiction. A significant part of his writing details the end of the Kiowa **Sun Dance**, which was last held in 1887 near Rainy Mountain Creek in southeastern Oklahoma. This break with their religious heritage, coupled with the death of the buffalo herds, crippled the Kiowa sense of oneness with nature. [See also **plains Indians, Satanta, Sun Dance**.] *In his retelling of native creation myths, N. Scott Momaday in* The Way to Rainy Mountain *declares, "You know, everything had to begin, and this is how it was: the Kiowas came one by one into the world through a hollow log."*

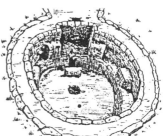

interior of an Anasazi kiva (without roof) showing the fire pit and sipapu

kit fox   See **dog soldier**.

kittiwake [kiht' tee • wayk] or **nauyak** or **nauyaq** [naw' yak] or **nauyaaluk** [naw' yuh • luk]   a white-and-gray seagull, the eggs of which the **Eskimo** prize as a delicacy. [See also **duck not yet**.] *Nuka climbed the sheer rock face and felt in its crevices for kittiwake nests.*

kiva [kee' vuh]   a circular or rectangular underground room dating to the ancient **Anasazi** and used by the

Pueblo as a men's club, weaving room, and worship area to petition their gods for good weather, healing, successful hunts and harvests, village unity, and the tribe's future. There was probably one kiva per **clan**. Entry was made by a ladder through a circular hole in the wooden roof to the stone floor below.

The **sipapu**, a small hole in the floor of the kiva, symbolized the birth of humanity from the underworld. A larger hole in the center of the floor contained a fire; a shaft in the wall served as ventilation for the smoke. The walls of the kiva were painted with sacred drawings of the gods; niches provided storage for ritual implements, such as **prayer sticks** and turquoise or shell beads, and for ceremonial offerings. Before the **Snake Dance**, snakes were housed, washed, and purified with prayers in the kiva. [See also **Anasazi, cabin court, Hopi, hot house, pit house, Pueblo, sipapu.**] *For the first time, Hopi initiates made their way down the ladder into the murky darkness of the kiva.*

komatik See **qamutit**.

Kon-Tiki [kahn • tee' kee] the Inca name for the creator of life. [See also **balsa, Inca.**] *Adventurer Thor Heyerdahl named his ocean-going reed craft the Kon-Tiki, which was also the name of his book and a movie based on his adventure.*

koodlik See **qulliq**.

Kooweskoowe See **John Ross**.

koshare [koh • shah' ray] or **koyala** [koi • yah' luh] or **kacale** [kuh • kah' lee] a member of a clown society who was painted with horizontal black and white stripes to represent a skeleton. The koshare lightened the mood of celebrants in **Pueblo** rituals by climbing a pole to retrieve a prize of food, dressing in women's clothes, playing practical jokes, gobbling gifts of food, or satirizing serious rituals with comic overreactions. [See also **heyoka, kachina, mudhead, Pueblo.**] *The koshare, the holy buffoons of Taos, New Mexico, tumbled, mimicked priests, begged, and performed comedy routines to entertain visitors to the annual festival.*

a = sack; ah = sob; aw = sauce; ay = safe; ee = seek; eh = set

kouse [kows] a root native to the North American plains that was beaten, then baked on rocks and eaten as bread. *Sacagawea taught hungry white explorers how to harvest and roast kouse roots.*

koyala See **koshare**.

kudlik See **qulliq**.

kuspuck [koos' puhk] or **kuspuk** a loose cotton shift or summer dress worn by **Aleut** women. [See also **Aleut**.] *The Inuit kuspuck was often worn over skin parka trousers.*

Kutenai [koot' ehn • ay] or **Kootenay** a **tribe** of gatherers, bison hunters, fishers, and traders native to Alberta and British Columbia. As a result of frequent wars and expanded trade, the Kutenai, relatives of the Piegan, became skilled in **sign language**, **beading**, **canoe** making, and **basketry**. By 1808, they established trade relations with Europeans. Scattered by resettlement on **reservations** in Idaho and Canada and by intermarriage with the **Chinook**, the modern Kutenai often work as guides, ranchers, and woodsmen. *Because of the tribe's extensive assimilation with English-speaking people, the Kutenai language has fallen into disuse.*

Kwakiutl [kwa' kee • yoo' t'l] a vigorous **tribe** of fishers and hunters native to the Pacific Coast of the Canadian northwest. The tribe was first visited by British traders in 1786. The early Kwakiutl prized pointed heads and bound children's skulls to flatten them. The tribe is known for its **potlatches**, or giveaway parties, and for native crafts, particularly red cedar **canoes**, flexible character masks, puppets, head and neck rings, button blankets, and **totems**. Anthropologist Franz

Kwakiutl family of the late eighteenth century wearing clothes of woven cedar bark with fur trim

Boas and linguist George Hunt helped to introduce white Americans to the Kwakiutl. [See also **giveaway, potlatch**.]
Dressed in ceremonial robe, headdress, apron, and train, Chief Willie Seaweed demonstrated the Kwakiutl passion for lavish details.

L

labret [lay' breht]   a weighty oval disc or plug of bone, stone, shell, or wood that **Tlingit** and **Haida** women wear on a **thong** that pierces the underlip and hangs to the chin. The purpose of the labret is to furl the lip downward and expose the inner tissue. Other types of labrets, such as those worn by **Eskimos**, are shaped like a spool and fit into a slit in the lip, which is pierced in childhood and is gradually widened by the insertion of larger labrets. Among the **Aleut**, the tuutok, or labret, a mark of manhood, is worn only by men. The Bering Sea Eskimo, on the other hand, differentiate between men's and women's labrets, which are worn to the side of the mouth: Men's styles are plug-shaped, and women's versions are hook-shaped, with dangling beaded ornaments. *Indians of the Gulf of Mexico wore the labret as a mark of nobility.*

labrets

lacrosse [luh • kraws']   a rough ball game similar to hockey or soccer played with a wooden or **buckskin** ball and a stick that ends in a loop covered with a woven **thong** net. In one form, a team consisted of 60 players; in another, 700 players took part. In ancient times, each player carried two sticks with which to maneuver the ball through goalposts, which were guarded by **medicine men**. Players often coated their bodies with either red or white pigment to signify the team that they played for. Because lacrosse served as a kind of military basic training, competition was keen, resulting in barks and yelps of victory and cries from the wounded. [See also **stickball**.] *In 1636, lacrosse was named by a French missionary who thought the playing stick resembled a bishop's cross.*

lanyard [lan' yuhrd]   a short cord made of rawhide or **babiche** and hung from the neck or waist to secure a pouch, such as a medicine bag or receptacle for **tobacco**, **jerky**, or fire-making materials. [See also **babiche, cording**.]

Passamaquoddy lacrosse racket and ball

Rhetta cuts long strips of cowhide and loops them around a post before braiding them into a lanyard.

lariat [lar' ee • uht]   a bridle, tie or picket rope, or lasso made from softened rawhide or braided horsehair; a **riata**. [See also **quirt, riata**.] *Mexican stock breeders taught desert Indians how to strengthen rope by braiding it and forming a lariat.*

latigo [lat' i • go']   a strap or cinch that fastens a saddle in place. *The lead rider halted the Thanksgiving Parade long enough to tighten a latigo.*

Arapaho girl's leggings

league   an interrelated group of **tribes**; a union or confederacy. Native groups formed leagues to give small tribes the strength and diplomatic authority enjoyed by large tribes. Another purpose of leagues was to promote trade, for example, the exchange of horses, medicinal herbs, and dyes from plains or forest tribes for cowrie or quahog shells, dried fish, or salt from coastal tribes. [See also **Five Civilized Tribes, Iroquois League, Sweet Medicine chief, Wabanaki Confederacy**.] *The Iroquois League maintained strong political ties to its Canadian neighbors.*

lean-to   a crude shed or shelter, often used to store tools, dried meats, vegetables, fruits, or fodder for livestock. A lean-to, like a loft or attic, was a common addition to a **hogan, longhouse, lodge**, or **igloo**; it allowed a family to enjoy uncluttered living space. [See also **hogan, igloo, lodge, longhouse**.] *The Bransons stored firewood and buffalo chips in a lean-to adjacent to their hogan.*

leather britches   bean pods strung on laces or cords and left near the fire to dry to preserve them from insects and mildew. Later, the beans are presoaked, parboiled, then simmered slowly with fat and salt. They are served with staples, such as wild onions, corn bread, and **sallet**. *Mountain settlers copied the Indian method of drying leather britches for hearty winter eating.*

leggings or **leggins**   flat leg coverings made of mountain-goat skin or deerskin. Unlike **chaps**, which cover only the front of the leg, leggings cover the entire leg. They are tightly tied or laced with leather string or **babiche**. Leggings

a = sack; ah = sob; aw = sauce; ay = safe; ee = seek; eh = set

protect the wearer from cold and are especially useful for walking or riding horseback through underbrush and cactus. Leggings or chaps can be fastened to **moccasins**, and the sides are often decorated with fringe, flaps, **quilling**, **beading**, paint, or locks from enemy scalps. [See also **babiche, chaps**.] *Without his leggings, Lanny might have been scratched by the burs on his long ride from Tucson to Tombstone, Arizona.*

leister [lee' stuhr]   a three-pronged fishing gig used by **Eskimo**, **Nootka**, and other northwest-coastal tribes; a **harpoon** featuring a central point of bear bone plus two protective prongs made of musk-ox horn and armed with bear bones. These three points kept fish from wiggling free. [See also **harpoon**.] *Much like modern fish hooks, the barbs on the leister turn inward to secure the catch.*

Leni-Lenape [leh' nee leh • nah' pay]   See **Delaware**.

Lewis and Clark expedition   an exploratory mission initiated by President Thomas Jefferson following the Louisiana Purchase of 1803. Ostensibly, the explorers were to search for a route to the Pacific Ocean and open possible trade contacts with Indians. Led by William Clark and Meriwether Lewis, the surveying party followed the Missouri River to the Rocky Mountains, then moved west to the Columbia River. After leaving St. Louis, Missouri, May 14, 1804, the explorers journeyed to a Mandan village in South Dakota, where they engaged **Sacagawea** as

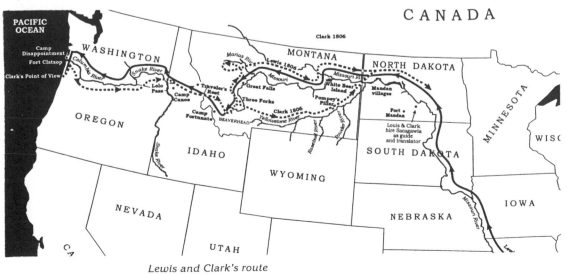

Lewis and Clark's route

translator and guide. The party journeyed by water and **portage**, and overland to the Pacific coast at the mouth of the Columbia River on the Oregon-Washington border, which they sighted on November 7, 1805. There they established Fort Clatsop. Following a different route, they arrived at their starting point on September 23, 1806. Although the Lewis and Clark expedition did not discover a water link between the Mississippi River and the Pacific Ocean, the group's report contained valuable information about plants, animals, and Indian tribes in the northwest United States, particularly the Flathead, **Nez Percé**, Clatsop, **Shoshone**, and **Mandan**. [See also **Mandan, portage, Sacagawea, York**.] *In his discussion with explorer Meriwether Lewis, President Thomas Jefferson assigned him to "explore the Missouri River, and such principal stream of it as . . . may offer the most direct and practicable water communication across this continent."* (Snyder, Gerald S. *In the Footsteps of Lewis and Clark*. Washington, D.C.: National Geographic Society, 1970, 11.)

Little Bear   See **Maconaqua**.

Little Turtle

Little Turtle or **Michikinikwa** [mih' shih • kin' ee • kwah] (?-1812) Miami war **chief** and ambassador who masterminded an alliance with the **Ojibwa**, **Delaware**, **Shawnee**, **Ottawa**, and **Potawatomi**. In September 1790, Little Turtle and his braves pretended to flee their burning villages to trap the forces led by General Josiah Harmar. Little Turtle taught his white attackers much about the effectiveness of guerrilla tactics, especially ambush, hit and run, and delay. He changed his tactics after he realized that white forces would not stop attacking Miami villages. Replaced by the more militant Turkey Foot, Little Turtle survived against General Anthony Wayne's forces at the Battle of Fallen Timbers on August 20, 1794, and was among the 1,000 Kickapoo, Miami, Ottawa, Piankishaw, Potawatomi, and Miami signers of a treaty completed on August 3, 1795, at Fort Greenville, Ohio. *After signing the Treaty of Greenville, Little Turtle remarked, "I am the last to sign it, and I will be the last to break it."* (*Encyclopedia Americana*. Danbury, Conn.: Grolier, 1987, Vol. 17, 603.)

llama [yah' muh *or* lah' muh]   a small pack animal, a member of the camel family, that was central to **Inca** work and worship. Llama meat was dried to make charqui, the Inca form of **jerky**. Incan ceremonies called for the decoration of a sacrificial white llama, which was offered to the Earth Mother. [See also **Inca, jerky**.] *Paco switched the herd of llamas into the arroyo and away from danger of coyotes.*

lodge   a large round or rectangular residence made of massive timbers formed into a frame above an underground foundation and covered with sod, dirt, or grass. The roof served as a second-story veranda for lounging, napping, playing games, and watching village ceremonies; it also provided storage space for **bullboats** and a work area for messy chores, such as trimming **pumpkins** and stringing **leather britches**. Outside the door was a vestibule or entryway, which supplied ventilation.

    Cheyenne lodges, which could seat 100 people and shelter horses and dogs, were often covered with buffalo hides. The Caddo built similar dwellings, shaped like curving cones or beehives, from poles and thatched grass. The **Nez Percé** provided a separate bachelor lodge for unmarried men and boys and a women's lodge to serve as a birthing chamber. **Mandan** women owned their lodges, to which husbands came to live. Also, the family who lived in the residence was called a lodge. [See also **lean-to, longhouse**.] *According to John Wesley Powell's diary of 1869, The Bishop, a Ute wise woman, explained that a lodge and all its furnishings must be burned after the death of its owner.*

lodge pole   a tree trunk that serves as the central support of a tent or **tepee**. [See also **tepee**.] *Sioux women hung their children's cradleboards on the lodge pole.*

longhouse   an extended residence or apartment house about 150 feet long and up to 25 feet wide. Lined with partitioned berths or lofts and a high, arching roof, the longhouse was made of stout elm timbers lashed together with basswood strips and covered by elm or cedar bark or woven mats. Longhouses sometimes featured covered porches on each end and painted **clan** crests above the door; several holes in the roof let in light and provided ventilation.

Another style of longhouse called for the regular placement of flexible saplings in two parallel rows. The saplings were bent and lashed together to form a barrel-shaped building. Tools, weapons, **cradleboards**, dried herbs, strings of dried apples and **squash**, braided ears of **corn**, **tobacco** hanks, drying pelts, medicinal roots, haunches of meat, and baskets of sunflower seeds were suspended from the ceiling. The early **Iroquois** and **Huron** lived in longhouses that sheltered an extended family, each family unit having its own fire and partitioned sleeping platform. [See also **hot house, husk faces, Iroquois, lean-to, lodge**.] *In the Yakima longhouse, a storyteller named Lucas Magpie told tales of Old Coyote, the trickster.*

longhouse

long knives a slang term for white soldiers brandishing rifles armed with bayonets. [See also **big knives**.] *Ute scouts spotted a party of long knives in the arroyo below.*

Long Walk a brutal forced march of **Navaho** from Arizona to Bosque Redondo, near Fort Sumner in eastern New Mexico. In 1863, troops led by Colonel Christopher "Kit" Carson slaughtered livestock and destroyed fruit trees and vegetable gardens to force the Navaho to move or starve. The 300-mile march began in March 1864. The U.S. government campaign to move the Navaho onto **reservations** concluded with four years' imprisonment of 8,491 people. A contingent under Manuelito, a rebel **chief** who refused to yield to Carson's troops, led 4,000 Navaho to western strongholds, but by September 1, 1866, they too surrendered. Two years later, Manuelito and Barboncito, his fellow chief, journeyed to Washington, D.C., to petition for Navaho rights. Upon the signing of a new treaty in the fall of 1868, the Navaho were allowed to return to Arizona and migrate on foot across the Chuska Mountains on the Arizona-New Mexico border to their sacred homeland, Canyon de Chelly. [See also **Anasazi, Navaho**.] *According to Chester Arthur, a Navaho chronicler and relative of Chief Henry Chee Dodge, the prophet Nahtahlith*

site of the Long Walk

saw in a vision that white soldiers would force his people to make the Long Walk.

Lost Colony a colony of English settlers who mysteriously disappeared from Roanoke Island, North Carolina, between 1587 and 1591. Three ships brought 81 men, 17 women, 9 children, and two Indians, who had come with them from England to the site of an abandoned 1586 settlement on Roanoke Island in July 1587. The newcomers repaired the houses and raised a palisade. When Governor White left for England in August, it was assumed that they would move 50 miles inland. War with Spain delayed the governor's return until August 1591. When he arrived, he found the settlement destroyed and the settlers, including his daughter and granddaughter, gone. Their destination and fate were unknown. Two clues, "CRO" and "CROATOAN" carved on a tree, led White to believe that they may have moved to the Indian village of that name, where one of the Indians who came with the settlers had relatives. Although Sir Walter Raleigh sent five successive research expeditions, the colonists' fate remains a mystery. A second clue turned up in 1623, when Chief **Powhatan** confessed that he had witnessed their slaughter. [See also **Pocahontas, Powhatan.**] *Some historians believe that the Lost Colony was assimilated into the Hatteras tribe, which was led by Chief Manteo.*

lovelock a braid at the side of the head, often woven with otter skin and decorated with a feather, charm, or beads for good luck. [See also **medicine bundle, roach, scalplock.**] *When he agreed to scout for the cavalry, Manitay had to give up his lovelocks.*

machete [muh • sheht' ee]   a thick-bladed battle knife or utility or harvest tool common to Central American sugarcane workers. The machete has a stout wooden grip and a wide, curved blade 12-30 inches long. It is usually swung in a sweeping, downward chopping motion to clear overhanging vines or to cut away the lower leaves of **tobacco**, sorghum, or **corn**. *Many Guatemalan natives carry machetes as a normal part of their apparel, much as farmers and hunters carry a pocketknife.*

mackinaw [mak' ih • naw] or **mackinac**   a thickly napped woolen blanket or short coat, often distinguished by a bold plaid. The term, which derives from the **Ojibwa** word for turtle, also applies to a flatboat with a pointed prow and squared stern, which was common to Great Lakes traders. *The campers hunched into their mackinaws and spread their hands to the fire.*

Maconaqua [ma • koh' nuh • kwah] or **Little Bear** or **Frances Slocum** (1778-1847)   a captive of the Miami who chose to remain with her adopted family rather than return home. Born in Wilkes-Barre, Pennsylvania, in 1778, Frances Slocum was abducted by **Delaware** Indians and later swapped to a Miami **tribe**. Named Maconaqua, or Little Bear, she became a prominent tribe member by marrying a **chief**, bearing two sons, and raising the standard of living by helping her village establish a herd of 100 cattle. In 1837, white trackers located Slocum and led her family to the village. Maconaqua, who no longer spoke English, refused to be enticed away from her Miami home, where she lived for the remaining 10 years of her life. *Maconaqua, who was adopted by the Miami, believed that her future as an Indian matriarch was much brighter than as a reclaimed squaw among white blood relatives.*

Madoc [may' dahk] or **Madog** [may' dahg] (fl. 1170s) Welsh explorer and Prince of Gwynedd who is reputed to have sailed to Mobile Bay in 1170 and to have returned in 1171 with a group of Welsh colonists. According to the legend, Madoc and his followers left behind the Welsh language and numerous children by Indian mothers. *As with most tall tales, the legend of Madoc seems much bigger than the man.*

Magnus Colorado   See **Mangas Coloradas**.

maguey   See **agave**.

Mahican [muh • hee' kuhn] or **Mohican** [moh • hee' kuhn]   a native **tribe** of forest hunters in the Hudson Valley region of New York State who were related to the **Delaware**, Housatonic, Manhattans, and Mohegans. In 1630, after smallpox, measles, alcohol, war with the **Mohawk**, and white settlers reduced their number, the Mahicans moved to Massachusetts. They later settled in Wisconsin, adopted the name Stockbridge Indians, attended religious schools, and learned European ways. After 1645, the line of hereditary chiefs ended with King Ben. Romantic novelist James Fenimore Cooper immortalized the Mahicans in *The Last of the Mohicans* (New York: Bantam, 1981), the most popular of his Leatherstocking Tales. Tschoop, a Mahican brave who is buried in Bethlehem, Pennsylvania, was the model for the fictional Uncas, Cooper's Mahican tracker. [See also **Narragansett**.] *In Cooper's* The Last of the Mohicans, *Chingachgook sadly reminisces to his white friend Hawkeye,*

> *we were one people and we were happy. The salt lake gave us its fish, the wood its deer, and the air its birds. We took wives who bore us children; we worshiped the Great Spirit. . . . My tribe is the grandfather of nations, but I am an unmixed man. The blood of chiefs is in my veins, where it must stay forever.*

(Cooper, James Fenimore. *The Last of the Mohicans.* New York: Bantam, 1981, 25.)

Mahpiua Luta   See **Red Cloud**.

maize [mayz] or **corn**   the **Taino** word for Indian corn, a staple grain for Native Americans and a major contribution to the world's diet. According to anthropologists, maize is the world's oldest food grain; it has been found in pottery and baskets dating to the first human settlements in the Western Hemisphere. Early varieties of maize grew only a few inches in length and produced from two to five kernels on each cob, ranging in color from white and light yellow to golden orange, red, and purple. Later varieties included dent, a starchy corn; flint, or ornamental corn; flour, or soft corn; popcorn, marked by small, pointed kernels; and sweet corn, the variety that contains the most sugar. Smut, a fungal disease that causes the kernels to grow grotesquely large, discolored, and misshapen, was eaten by the **Aztec** as a great delicacy.

To protect against wind and flood damage and to promote substantial roots, **Pueblo** Indians planted maize about 12 inches deep in mounds 5-6 feet apart. Woodlands Indians, particularly the **Wampanoag**, fertilized maize with fish heads and surrounded hills with climbing vegetables, such as beans, **gourds**, **pumpkins**, or **squash**, for maximum use of each plot. At harvest time, to ward off insect infestation, **Acoma** women dried ears of corn on the roof of their homes. Woodlands Indians dried corn in the sun and cooked it in winter with **maple syrup**.

Ground maize was used for medicinal purposes (for example, to make a dressing for an infant's navel or an oozing wound or as a treatment for intestinal parasites) as well as in religious ceremonies (for instance, to bless a newborn infant or to symbolize fertility at a wedding). Priests tapped children with ceremonial ears of corn to bless them. Cornsilk and cornhusks served several purposes, particularly as stuffing for mattresses, materials for making dolls and balls, cases for pudding or dumplings, **moccasins**, anklets, salt pouches, and ceremonial items. Corncobs were used as washcloths, stoppers, scrub brushes, and fuel.

Maize still plays a key role in Native American life. The **Navaho** anoint newborn children with holy maize pollen. In Bernalillo, New Mexico, the Santa Ana Indians obtained a grant to revitalize the cultivation of blue corn, which is used in ceremonies honoring infants and in the manufacture of natural cosmetics. Piki, a lacy blue corn chip, has become a popular delicacy. [See also **Green Corn Dance, hominy, milpa, piki, samp, Snake Dance,**

sixteenth-century drawing of maize

*a = s**a**ck; ah = s**o**b; aw = s**au**ce; ay = s**a**fe; ee = s**ee**k; eh = s**e**t*

squash.] *Hoecake, tortillas, hominy, grits, popcorn balls, samp, roasting ears, succotash, and other recipes featuring maize are native to the American kitchen.*

Makataimeshekiakiak See **Black Hawk**.

making medicine looking into the future; telling fortunes or interpreting dreams to help the dreamer make serious decisions, such as whether to seek a job or go to school or how to make a dangerous quest, hunt, or journey. One way of making medicine was through a ritual sweat bath, another by the eating of **peyote** or **mescal**. [See also **medicine, mescal, Native American Church, peyote, sand painting, sweat lodge**.] *Making medicine was the central purpose of the Cheyenne shaman's office.*

Maklak See **Modoc**.

maktak [mak' tak] or **muktuk** [muhk' tuhk] the delicate, sweet **blubber**, or fat, that lies near the skin of a baleen or beluga whale. To increase its flavor, the blubber is fermented, dipped in seal oil, and eaten either frozen or thawed. [See also **agvik**.] *The whaling team, safely returned from their voyage, parceled out maktak to each worker.*

Mandan [man' dan] a settled **tribe** of fishers and farmers native to the Missouri Valley who belonged to the **Sioux** language group. The Mandan lived in huge round multifamily dwellings made of earth and thatch, slept in four-poster beds hung with skins for warmth and privacy, and left circular earth **mounds**. Frequently in contact with European settlers, the tribe was studied by the **Lewis and Clark expedition** and painted and described by **George Catlin** and **Karl Bodmer**. The tribe was reduced to 13 percent of its original size following an 1837 smallpox epidemic started by a single wagon train. The survivors were absorbed by Arikara and **Hidatsa** tribes. One victim, Running Face, infected at the age of five in the epidemic of 1856, was photographed years later to show the pockmarks scarring his cheeks. [See also **George Catlin, Lewis and Clark expedition, mound, Okipa**.] *Shortly before he died from smallpox, Mato-Tope, or Four Bears, the last great Mandan chief, was painted in a ceremonial pose* *with a feathered lance in his left hand, buffalo horns on his head, and a war bonnet trailing the length of his body.*

mandrake See **mayapple**.

Mangas Coloradas [man' guhs cah • loh • rah' dahs] or **Magnus Colorado** [mag' nuhs cah • loh • rah' doh] or **Red Sleeves** (1781-January 18, 1863)   a tall, bold leader of the Mimbrano **Apache**, Mangas Coloradas was famous for his deadly aim with **bow** or rifle. He joined **Geronimo**, Victorio Mangas, his son, and **Cochise**, his son-in-law, in harassing Spanish and white settlers, miners, and soldiers by robbing stagecoaches and mine trains. Fluent in Spanish, Mangas Coloradas negotiated with local Spaniards. After Mangas Coloradas received a chest wound, Cochise saved his life by transporting him from Arizona to a physician in Mexico and threatening to kill the entire town if his father-in-law died. Mangas Coloradas, tricked by a false flag of truce in 1863, was captured by the U.S. Cavalry. At Fort McLean, Arizona, he was tortured with heated bayonets, then shot, mutilated, and dismembered. His skull was sold to a quack scientist. His followers were so incensed that they doubled their efforts to drive out white settlers. [See also **Apache, Cochise, Geronimo**.] *The savage treatment of Mangas Coloradas proves that the cruelties of the Apaches were no worse than treatment at cavalry prisons.*

manioc [man' ee • ahk] or **cassava** [cas • sah' vuh] or **tapioca plant** or **yuca** [yoo' kuh]   a tropical shrub cultivated for its starchy, tuberous roots and for its palm-shaped leaves, which are chopped as fodder for livestock. One of the earliest plants domesticated in the Western Hemisphere, manioc cultivation spread to Africa and Europe. The roots are boiled like yams or dried and beaten into a powder, which is used to thicken stew or pudding and can be fermented to make a beverage. Just as the **Pomo** prepare **acorn** meal, Central and South American bakers grate and rinse manioc roots to remove bitter, poisonous

Caribbean worker grinding manioc

*a = s**a**ck; ah = s**o**b; aw = s**au**ce; ay = s**a**fe; ee = s**ee**k; eh = s**e**t*

acids. They form the starch into loaves of bread or cook it as a hot cereal. As a cash crop, manioc also is sold to makers of glue, starch, and explosives; it is also used by weavers. [See also **tapioca, yuca**.] *The harvesting of maniac roots is a common practice dating to ancient times.*

Manitou [man' uh • too] or **Manito** [man' uh • toh] or **Manitoo** or **Manitu** the **Algonquin** name for an all-powerful animal or nature god, with whom individuals communicated through visions or dreams; the **Great Spirit**. *In* The Last of the Mohicans, *James Fenimore Cooper renders Uncas's prayer to Manitou:*

> *Manitou! Manitou! Manitou!*
> *Thou art great, thou art good, thou art wise:*
> *Manitou! Manitou!*
> *Thou art just.*
>
> *In the heavens, in the clouds, O, I see*
> *Many spots—many dark, many red:*
> *In the heavens, O, I see*
> *Many clouds. . . .*
>
> *Manitou! Manitou! Manitou!*
> *Thou art weak—thou art strong: I am slow:*
> *Manitou! Manitou!*
> *Give me aid.*

wood carving of Manitou from a Delaware house

(Cooper, James Fenimore. *The Last of the Mohicans.* New York: Bantam, 1981, 339.)

The **Sioux** equivalent of Manitou was Wakenda; the **Iroquois** used the name **Orenda**; in **Anishinabe**, the Great Spirit was Gitchee Manitou. [See also **All-Father, All-Mother, Great Spirit,** *Huron Carol,* **medicine dance, Ojibwa, Orenda**.] *Leaders of the Huron ceremony raised prayers to Manitou for bringing a profitable hunting season.*

Mankiller, Wilma P. (November 18, 1945-) social worker and principal **chief** of the **Cherokee** nation. A native of Tahlequah, Oklahoma, and ancestor of tribal leaders who walked the **Trail of Tears**, Mankiller, one of 11 children of Charlie and Irene Mankiller, became the first female chosen to serve as chief of a major American Indian tribe. Mankiller's family suffered financial losses in the 1950s and vacated the Oklahoma farm that was deeded to her grandfather by a U.S. government settlement. Under a federal project mainstreaming Indians, the Mankillers settled in San Francisco. Because of the high rate of unemployment and poor education and health of her fellow Cherokee, she dedicated herself to revitalizing the tribe.

At age 25, Mankiller joined an Indian rights occupation of the island of Alcatraz, a political act intended to draw public attention to the plight of Native Americans. Infused with the spirit of activisim, she studied sociology, receiving her B.A. degree and completing graduate work at the University of Arkansas. She returned to Oklahoma to help poor tribe members, founded the Community Development Department of the Cherokee nation, and served as the agency's director. In 1985, she succeeded Ross Swimmer as head of the Cherokee nation, which at that time, with 92,000 members, was second in population to the Navaho.

Chief Mankiller was reelected in 1987. Backed by her husband, Charlie Soap, she continues to emphasize tribal weaning from government help, improved health care, a higher employment rate, and a return to strong female voices in tribal government. She has received numerous leadership awards and in 1987 was named *Ms.* magazine's Woman of the Year. [See also **Cherokee, chief, Trail of Tears.**] *In her 1993 autobiography,* Mankiller: A Chief and Her People, *Chief Mankiller states, "Women can help turn the world right side up. We bring a more collaborative approach to government. And if we do not participate, then decisions will be made without us"* (Mankiller, Wilma P. *Mankiller: A Chief and Her People.* New York: St. Martin's Press, 1993, 242).

manly heart See **berdache**.

mano [mah' noh]   a stone roller or small millstone held in the hand and rubbed against grains, roots, berries, or nuts on a **metate**, or grinding board, to create flour or meal. For the **Aztec**, who ate tortillas at every meal, the family mano and metate were essential tools that were kept in a prominent spot near the hearth. [See also **metate, piki.**] *One of the first skills a bride was expected to demonstrate for her husband's family was competence with the mano and metate.*

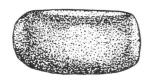

mano

a = sack; ah = sob; aw = sauce; ay = safe; ee = seek; eh = set

manta [man' tuh]   among desert tribes, a square piece of cloth used as a shawl or cloak or as part of a ritual costume. The manta could be pulled over the hair and held in place at the neck during windy or wet weather or as a ceremonial head covering, particularly for Indian women who converted to Catholicism. A diminutive form of the word, *mantilla*, is synonymous with wedding veil. *The Pueblo women embroidered their mantas with brightly colored geometric designs for ceremonial use.*

manzanita [man' zuh • nee' tuh] or **bearberry**   a low evergreen shrub of the heath family from which the Mono obtained a reddish brown berry to be made into fresh cider or dried for winter use in stew or hot cereal. Common to high elevations in the American Southwest, the red manzanita berry, named little apple in Spanish, has nutritional value and is used by native cooks in jelly, beverages, and snacks. [See also **healing**.] *Mono children beat the manzanita bush with sticks, then swept fallen berries into a basket.*

sugar maple

maple syrup   the syrup produced from the sweet sap of maple trees. Northern forest and Canadian Indians gathered the sap each spring and boiled it to make syrup or sugar. To tap the tree, sugaring-off parties made deep, Y-shaped slices through the bark, then at the bottom inserted a cedar spile, or spout, from which dangled a birch-bark bucket. Syrup was strained, then stirred with a wooden paddle in birch troughs for several days until the liquid evaporated, leaving behind crystals of maple sugar. Indian children prized maple sugar as candy, and cooks used it to flavor bread, stew, and porridge. It was also served over snow in a birchbark cone. The **Iroquois** fermented maple sap into beer, which they stored in hollow duck or quail eggs; the **Potawatomi** used the sap to make vinegar. *The maple tree, which provides sap for maple syrup, was so prized by the Iroquois that they thought of it as a special gift from Orenda, the Creator.*

Maquak   See **Mohawk**.

marrow   See **squash**.

Massasoit [mas' uh • soit'] or **Yellow Feather** (1580?-1662) a noble **Wampanoag chief** born at Pokanoket, a village near Bristol, Rhode Island. Massasoit ruled over a tribe in eastern Massachusetts, and in March 1621, welcomed English settlers to Plymouth. After meeting with Governor William Bradford's emissaries, Massasoit established a 24-year peace based on agreements about controlling violence, mutual protection, and suppression of weapons at meetings. Massasoit was succeeded first by his older son, Wamsutta, or Alexander, who died suddenly a few months later, and then by his younger son, Metacomet, better known as **King Philip**. [See also **King Philip, Samoset, Squanto, Wampanoag**.] *For helping the first English colony survive, Massasoit is immortalized in a stately statue in Plymouth, Massachusetts.*

mate [mah • tay'] a bitter, bracing South American tea made from the dried shoots and leaves of a holly native to Paraguay. The drink is sipped through a bombilla, or straw, to strain the dregs. Indian healers also use the drink as a stimulant, tonic, and treatment for upset stomach. Because of its high concentration of tannin and caffeine, mate tastes much like ordinary coffee or tea and is served with lemon and sugar or with milk. During long religious ceremonies, mate is drunk to heighten worshippers' awareness and to induce trances. *The gaucho ended his day by roasting a haunch of beef over a mesquite fire and brewing a calabash of mate.*

Matoaka See **Pocahontas**.

Matowaka See **Pocahontas**.

maxtli [mash' tlee] the wrapper or loincloth worn by **Aztec** men. Unlike the **breechclout** of **plains Indians**, the maxtli, much like the dhoti of India or the Hawaiian malo, was wrapped around the waist, between the thighs from back to front, and tied in a loose knot. [See also **breechclout, clout Indian**.] *Dressed in maxtli and yucca sandals, the Aztec worker was capable of hewing stone and moving it long distances on rollers.*

Maya [my' uh] an ancient nation that lived in Mexico and Central America from the first to the sixth century

A.D. and distinguished itself by such creative accomplishments as paper making; writing; counting by twenties; keeping calendars; studying astronomy; moving heavy blocks of stone; building with mortar; making highways, bridges, reservoirs, and aqueducts; and forming useful objects from rubber. Mayan chiefs, decked in resplendent feathered robes, headdresses, and gold ornaments, commanded great respect and reverence. Caracol, a Mayan center, reached its height after A.D. 562, when it defeated nearby Tikal, an ancient city in Guatemala. Military power extended Mayan control of 4,800 square miles of Peten and northern Belize. In the sixteenth century, Spanish conquerors enslaved Mayan workers and forced them to harvest sisal and cane crops. Stories of the Mayan cities of Chichén Itzá, Tikal, Uxmal, and Caracol, which thrived on the Yucatán Peninsula, filtered north and influenced mound builders in the Ohio Valley.

In 1986, fishermen discovered a clay figurine of a priest and a 4-ton basalt stele, a great oblong stone covered with Mayan writings. Although the writings have not been completely deciphered, they appear to record a 25-year period of planetary observations, including five eclipses dating from A.D. 128 to A.D. 153 and other heavenly events that Mayans would have connected with their gods. Recent archaeological studies of tombs and greater understanding of Mayan writings suggest that the Mayan culture may have come to a sudden cataclysmic end after a growing middle class revolted against the small, elite ruling class. [See also **mound, Olmec, pok-a-tok**.] *Today, some Mayan migrants from Guatemala live in cinderblock houses in Indiantown, outside Miami, Florida, where they work the citrus crop.*

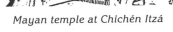

Mayan temple at Chichén Itzá

mayapple or **mandrake**   the yellow, oval fruit of a common plant that grows on single or forked stalks in rich bottom land and on hillsides. The mayapple plant produces an extremely powerful drug used by Indians to shrink growths and as a laxative. The toxic juice of the root treated deafness and served as an insecticide and crow repellant. [See also **healing**.] *In Conrad Richter's novel* The Light in the Forest *(New York: Bantam, 1953), True*

Son, a white captive adopted and reared by the Delaware, longs to end the misery of his return to his white family by eating the poisonous root of the mayapple.

maypop or **mollypop** or **passionflower** a small, viny plant covered with showy, fragrant, purple-and-white flowers, followed by egg-shaped fruit, which Indians ate like berries or made into a refreshing drink. Maypop was used as a cure for earache, boils, and swelling and to wean children. [See also **healing**.] *In Bermuda, perfume makers follow the traditional recipe of natives in making cologne, bath oil, and lotion out of maypop flowers.*

Arapaho medicine bundle

medicine a mysterious supernatural power or force over sickness, bad luck, weather, or enemies invoked by a **shaman** or **medicine man**. The eagle, a most prized bird among North American tribes, symbolized the power of nature and therefore carried strong medicine. Medicine headdresses and shields often were decorated with eagle wings and feathers or symbolic patterns painted or stitched into the fabric. Among Central American Indians, the mythical **thunderbird** paralleled the magic of the eagle. Desert tribes invoked magic or healing powers by painting with sand around a sick person or initiate, often using birds and other natural symbols. [See also **iniskim**, **making medicine, medicine man, prayer stick, sand painting, shaman, vision quest**.] *The Cheyenne invoked personal medicine by marking themselves and their horses with painted symbols, such as jagged lightning or sun signs, or binding the horses' tails and decorating them with eagle feathers.*

medicine bundle a collection of symbolic objects, such as whistles; bags of sacred soil; pipes; charms; herbs; roots, **mescal** or **peyote**; sweet grass bundles; quills; beads; or the tusks, beaks, talons, dried organs, or bones of an animal or bird, which represented the owner's dreams or other form of contact with the powers of nature. These tokens were kept in a treasured pouch, often made from the complete hide of a bird or small animal. When warriors prepared for battle, they wore these bundles around their necks, wrists, or ankles on **lanyards**, or they fastened them to **scalplocks** or **lovelocks** as protective charms.

In peacetime, the medicine bundle was hung from a tripod behind the **tepee** as protection for the family. The

a = sack; ah = sob; aw = sauce; ay = safe; ee = seek; eh = set

mother of the family watched over the bundle to protect it from contamination or theft. The owner took the bundle, a kind of portable altar, to a private place for worship and meditation. If a bundle did not ward off catastrophe, it could be discarded and replaced with a new collection of charms. At the death of the **bundle keeper**, the sacred duty passed to a son. [See also **bundle keeper, iniskim, lovelock, medicine man, scalplock, vision quest**.] *Little Cloud worked a complicated beaded design into the pouch that held her tribe's medicine bundle.*

medicine dance   a ceremonial act, entered in worship of **Manitou** or the **Great Spirit**, for the purpose of seeking a cure, assuring tribal harmony, or thanking the gods for good health. Before the medicine dance, participants were purified with ritual bathing and **tobacco** smoke, then entered a newly made lodge for hymns and chanting, an all-night sacred ritual, and more singing, which lasted for several days. The actual medicine dance followed, extending from sunrise to sunrise. Participants, who bribed their way into the dance with gifts to elders, were sworn to secrecy, especially about the ritual shooting and pretended death of the initiate, who then rises to life. Initiates who failed to take the medicine dance seriously were warned that they would soon die. [See also **Manitou**.] *In Paul Radin's* Autobiography of a Winnebago Indian *(New York: Dover, 1920), the speaker indicates that he is pleased and honored to assume his father's membership in the lodge so that he can take part in the medicine dance, yet he ends his narrative in disillusionment because the ritual seemed fake.*

medicine drum   a ceremonial drum tapped with the fingers or a padded mallet as an accompaniment to chanting or singing to summon the powers of the spirit world and to focus worshippers' concentration on the **Great Spirit**. The medicine drum was usually decorated with drawings from nature and symbols to heighten its value as a ritual object. When not in use, it was kept in a guarded place, much as the **medicine bundle** was protected and preserved. [See also **Native American Church, tom-tom**.] *Crowfoot tapped the medicine drum and chanted the ceremonial call to worship.*

medicine feast a ceremonial dinner at which prayers and choice pieces of game, such as the liver, heart, or other organs, are buried in the four corners of the room in honor of the **Great Mystery**. Devout members of medicine societies organized an annual medicine feast to thank the gods for an adequate supply of food or continued good health. [See also **Great Mystery**.] *After several seasons of hunger, the Arapaho organized a medicine feast to acknowledge their appreciation of a gift of buffalo meat.*

medicine man a valuable member of the **tribe** who could heal people, initiate young men, or consult the **Great Spirit** in times of distress or danger. The medicine man was often chosen because he was marked by disease; birth defect; or strange behavior, such as sleepwalking, epilepsy, mental instability, or depression. He served as herbalist, philosopher, political adviser, interpreter of dreams and omens, weather forecaster, finder of lost people or property, consoler, singer, or teacher of tribal morals and aims. His tools included a cane tube for blowing on herbal concoctions or sucking out tainted blood, and drums, bells, and **rattles** for summoning spirits. His medicines were often useful, such as wild-cherry-bark tea for coughs; caffeine to stimulate the nervous system; foxglove or digitalis to treat heart ailments; or **willow** bark, a pain medicine from which aspirin is derived.

Usually but not always male, a potential medicine man was selected as a child and for seven years studied the interpretation of cloud formations, herbs, and spiritual healing. He often dressed in a ragtag motley of animal skins, beaks, fish scales, feathers, hooves, fangs, and wings, which demonstrated his ties with nature. The medicine man could supervise apprentices, who helped him gather herbs, diagnose illness, and apply therapy. [See also **black drink, hatali, healing, heyoka, making medicine, medicine, medicine bundle, sand painting, sweat lodge, yuwipi**.] *Smoholla, a seer and medicine man of the Wanapum Indians, predicted that nature would punish the settlers for destroying the Earth.*

medicine pendant a ceremonial ornament, amulet, or charm made from bone, wood, feathers, shells, claws, teeth, fangs, or beads. Hung on a **lanyard** about the neck

Sioux medicine man drawn by George Catlin

a = sack; ah = sob; aw = sauce; ay = safe; ee = seek; eh = set

or attached on rawhide or **babiche** to ankle, wrist, or waist, the medicine pendant warded off accidents, predatory animals, or enemy warriors. A special medicine pendant was attached to the sunshade of the **cradleboard** to guard infants from harm or disease. [See also **aungaak, babiche, i'noGo tied, iniskim, prayer stick.**] *In Shoshone lore, the medicine pendant represented the power and protection of ancestral heroes.*

medicine pipe a powerful and symbolic ceremonial smoking pipe, the bowl of which was carved from **catlinite, steatite**, pipestone, limestone, shale, or slate and decorated with pendants, horsehair, or feathers. Stems, made of sumac or ash, were hollowed out with heated wires. A tamper or pipe tool was carved as a companion piece. The medicine pipe was used to establish peaceful intertribal settlements and to bless and protect the village. In many rituals, smoke was blown to the four winds as a means of pleasing the gods or calling down blessings. At the end of a ritual, the pipe was cleaned, the bowl removed from the stem, and the two pieces stored separately until their next use. [See also **calumet, catlinite, pipe bag, tobacco.**] *Red Wolf lifted the medicine pipe from the beaded bag, raised it prayerfully to the gods, and readied it for the ritual.*

medicine song a traditional ceremonial chant that is sung or spoken for a particular need, such as warding off disease or enemies or drawing strength from the rising sun or a shooting star. Some medicine songs go on all night, particularly those connected with the **peyote** cult. In N. Scott Momaday's *The Way to Rainy Mountain* (Albuquerque: University of New Mexico Press, 1969), a Kiowa family sings a three-part chant associated with the dedication of a new **lodge**, in which four societies gather leaves and branches for the ceremony. In a different mood, an **Eskimo** medicine song calls to the new moon as though it were a brother. [See also **mescal, Native American Church, peyote.**] *Wave Walker's medicine song requested help for his tribe, which suffered an epidemic of diphtheria.*

medicine wheel a ceremonial circle of stones 75-80 feet in diameter with a stone heap at the center and spokes radiating out to the rim. One example of more than 50 still in existence, the medicine wheel of Wyoming's

*ih = si*t; *oh = s*oa*k; oo = s*ou*p; ow = s*oun*d; uh = s*uc*h; y = s*ide

Bighorn Range contains six stone cairns evenly spaced along its rim. Anthropologists believe that such wheels, which exist across the plains from Alberta, Canada, to Wyoming, date to the 1300s and served a ritual purpose, possibly as a site of sun worship or as a calendar to predict the summer solstice, which Indians considered a magical time. *In Lawrence, Kansas, in 1981, folk artist Stan Herd created a modern medicine wheel—a 160-acre plowed earthwork or crop art featuring the face of the Kiowa chief Satanta.*

mesa

Menominee [meh • nahm' uh • nee] or **Menomini** or **Menominiwok** [meh • nahm' uh • nee' wahk]   a peace-loving **tribe** of hunter-gatherers and sturgeon fishers known for their skill in loomless finger weaving. Commonly called the wild rice people, they were related to the **Kickapoo**, **Potawatomi**, and **Fox**. Native to Michigan, the Menominee migrated along the Mississippi River and developed a system of gathering rice by beating it into their canoes with long poles and flailing it with bats to remove the husks. They preserved the grain by **smoking** or drying it in the sun, and they cooked it with **maple syrup** or added it to stew. According to Waioskasit, who described to Father Jean Nicolet the coming of the French around 1660, the Menominee abandoned their sedentary lifestyle and imitated European trappers, who earned large incomes from the sale of furs. *In modern times, Ada Deer, a Menominee writer and organizer, led protesters in a fight to restore government recognition of the tribe; another Menominee, Ralph Fredenberg, defended his tribe's rights to operate farms, logging industries, dairies, and lumber mills.*

mesa [may' suh]   a flat-topped hill composed of layers of rock and formed by rivers coursing through a plateau; a butte or tableland. **Pueblo** Indians often chose a location such as Bonita Mesa in Chaco Canyon, New Mexico, to establish their apartment-like stone or **adobe** living quarters in the walls. The gorge channeled the air so that it flowed past the cliff dwellings, cooling them. To help workers and families to carry heavy loads up the steep cliffs, builders cut steps in the mesa walls and between units. They also provided ladders, which residents pulled up to protect them from wild animals and hostile tribes. [See also **adobe, Anasazi, pueblo**.] *The winds about the mesa cooled the Hopi village, which had suffered the hottest summer in memory.*

*a = s**a**ck; ah = s**o**b; aw = s**au**ce; ay = s**a**fe; ee = s**ee**k; eh = s**e**t*

mescal [meh • skal'] a small, round bean taken from the **maguey** or **agave** plant, similar in use to the button obtained from the **peyote** cactus. Mescal is used as food, antispasmodic, intoxicant, and stimulant during an all-night prayer service. Laws in some states have forbidden the use of mescal, but members of the **Native American Church**, protected by constitutional rights to religious freedom, have pursued their form of worship by appealing to the courts. Where the courts have denied those rights, Indians have concealed their consumption of mescal in secret ceremonies. [See also **agave, making medicine, medicine song, Native American Church, peyote**.] *Mescaline, a non-habit-forming drug, is extracted from mescal and used to induce trances or visions.*

Mescalero [meh' skah • leh' roh] a group of the **Apache tribe**. [See also **Apache**.] *In his reflections on Apache relations with European settlers, autobiographer Percy Bigmouth, a Lipan Apache who later joined a Mescalero tribe, related his grandmother's tale of a Thanksgiving dinner shared with whites, whom the Indians taught to plant corn and pumpkins.*

D. Timmons

mesquite tree

Mesquakie See **Fox**.

mesquite [meh • skeet'] a spiny desert tree or shrub of the pea family. Desert Indians used its sugary pods and woody branches to entice bees and as forage for horses and cattle. From a mixture of mesquite flour, seeds, and berries, **Pueblo** Indians made *mesquitamal,* a favorite food. Other uses included flour for bread, mush, dumplings, pudding, stew, and beer. Mesquite gum was made into glue, hair dye, ointment, and mouthwash. *Yuma, Yaqui, Seri, and Mescalero cooks added mesquite beans to ground corn and cooked them in hot cereal.*

mestizo [mehs • tee' zoh] See **half-breed**.

Metacomet See **King Philip**.

metate [meh • tah' tay] a flat stone slab with a slight hollow in the center used by desert Indians as a base on which **corn**, seeds, chiles, and **acorns** were ground. By rolling a **mano** back and forth over grains on the metate,

metate

the cook reduced them into flour or meal for foods like **piki** or tortillas. **Hopi** cooks owned several grades of metates, each of which ground grain to a specific fineness. [See also **mano, piki**.] *With a mano or stone rolling pin, the Mescalero cook could quickly prepare enough grain for a family meal.*

métis [may • tee' *or* may • tees'] See **half-breed**.

Michikinikwa See **Little Turtle**.

Micmac [mihk' mak] or **MicMac** a peaceable **tribe** of hunters, gatherers, and seagoing fishers native to Nova Scotia, Gaspé, Cape Breton Island, Prince Edward Island, and New Brunswick. The name of the tribe means our allies. The Micmac, whom the Vikings encountered on their voyages to the Western Hemisphere in A.D. 1000, may have been the first Native Americans to see European explorers. The tribe also saw John Cabot's expedition reach landfall in 1497. The Micmac were successful at building **canoes** and establishing trade with French trappers. Unlike many of the northeast Canadian tribes, which died out from wars and European diseases, the Micmac remain on their ancestral lands. [See also **Abenaki, trickster**.] *According to Nova Scotian tradition, a Micmac brave named Silmoodawa was taken to France, where he demonstrated Indian hunting and cooking skills, then consumed portions of dried venison to prove that it was edible.*

mico See **miko**.

Midewiwin [mih' duh • wee' wihn] the Grand Medicine Society of the **Ojibwa**, a religious and social institution that combined religious ceremonies with **healing**. Membership in the Midewiwin offered male initiates a coveted place of prestige and honor as well as eternal life. Apprentices to the Midewiwin underwent long years of study with a medicine society elder to learn the magical incantations that cure disease. [See also **Ojibwa**.] *Silver Hair spent his winter evenings lecturing young apprentices on Midewiwin philosophy, particularly the concepts that applied to good health.*

Midwinter Festival a festival common to woodlands Indians, who welcomed the end of the old year by scattering ashes from a fire. The Midwinter Festival, which celebrated longer periods of sunlight and the coming of spring, ended with songs of thanksgiving, dancing, games, and clowns. Children, accompanied by an old woman, begged for gifts or **tobacco** in a Native American form of trick or treat. *Mud Woman's three grandchildren looked forward to gifts of maple sugar during the Midwinter Festival.*

miko [my' koh] or **mico** [mee' koh] a **Muskhogean** term for ruling or council **chief**. The attendants carried their miko on a ceremonial litter, which was draped with his ceremonial feather mantle. [See also **chief, mingo, sachem, sagamore**.] *The role of miko involved trying cases, settling squabbles, interpreting laws, and establishing ownership.*

milkweed a common plant that produces pairs of pods from which Indians extracted down or floss, a silky fiber that was spun into string. Another use of the fluff was as stuffing for **moccasins** and **cradleboards**. The shoots and pods of one variety of milkweed were boiled as a vegetable. [See also **cording, healing**.] *The Mono twisted milkweed fiber into fine, strong cording, which they wove into decorative and useful nets.*

milkweed

Milly See **Francis, Milly Hayo**.

milpa [mihl' puh] a cornfield hacked out of the wild, burned off, cultivated for a few years, then left fallow for 10 years until it was once again suitable for planting; a swidden. The purpose of burning a milpa was to eliminate briars, undergrowth, and weed seeds. Sterilization of soil with fire also reduced problems of nematodes and viruses. [See also **maize, slash and burn**.] *The Toltecs and Mayas cultivated their milpas with simple digging sticks or dibbles.*

mingo [mihn' goh] the **Chickasaw** word for **chief**. Also, as a proper noun, another name for the **Delaware**. In 1451, the Chickasaw mingo led an assault on de Soto's expedition at Mobilla in retaliation for the Spanish practice of capturing village chiefs and destroying Indian homes. [See also **cacique, chief, Delaware, miko**.] *Recorded in Thomas Jefferson's* Notes on the State of Virginia *(New York: Norton, 1972), dated 1774, is a statement by Logan, a Mingo brave, who boasted that he acted charitably toward the hungry and homeless and remained in his cabin while others went to war.*

Mission Indians a general term for Pacific Coast **tribes** of hunter-gatherers and fishers. The Mission Indians' lives centered on the **acorn**, which was the chief component of their diet. Individual tribes include the Cahuilla; Chumash; Diegueño; Gabrieleno; Luiseño, the largest of the group; and Serrano, which were named by Spanish missionaries. These well-meaning churchmen coerced natives into the Catholic faith during the height of mission construction, from 1769 to 1821, and eroded Indian dialects, customs, and native religions. One tribesman, Janitin, reported in 1878 that during the 1820s, zealous California priests had lashed and starved him, then baptized him under the name Jésus. A Luiseño convert, Tac, complied with mission rules and even visited Rome, but he died of disease at the age of 20. A few remote tribes, particularly the Hupa and **Pomo**, escaped contact with these European religious persecutions and

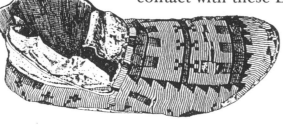

diseases and remained strong. [See also **Ishi, toloache**.] *In 1881, Helen Hunt Jackson, famed Massachusetts writer of* A Century of Dishonor: A Sketch of the United States Government's Dealing with Some of the Indian Tribes *(Irvine, Calif.: Reprint Service, 1988), championed the cause of 300 bands of Mission Indians, the poorest and most helpless of which received the most cruel treatment.*

Arapaho beaded moccasin

moccasin a soft rawhide slipper, either cuffed or lowcut, which could be stuffed with moss, deer hair, down, or **cattail** or **milkweed** fluff for extra warmth. Most moccasins, except for those worn by **plains Indians**, were relatively waterproof because they had no separate sole. For added warmth, moccasins could be attached to **leggings**. [See also **kammik, mukluk**.] *Ray's mother stitched up the split seam in the heel of his moccasin.*

moccasin game   an indoor winter game played by adults in which a small object, such as a bone, tooth, bead, bullet, stone, or fruit pit, is hidden in a moccasin for the designated player to find. *Teams of moccasin-game players kept score with small wooden sticks.*

Moctezuma   See **Montezuma II**.

mocuck [moh' kuhk]   a square-bottomed container with rounded sides that was formed from a single strip of **birch bark**; sewn with basswood strips, **willow** branches, sweet grass, cedar root, or wood splints; and sealed with pitch. The mocuck, which often had its own lid, was used as a storage box and was either placed in a loft or suspended from the **lodge pole** of a **tepee** by rawhide **thongs**. When transported over long distances, such as from village to maple grove, rice winnowing spot, herb bed, salt pit, or **jerky-** or salmon-drying frame, the mocuck could be attached to the carrier's head by a **tumpline**. [See also **stone boiling, tumpline**.] *Lena's mother filled the mocuck with pemmican, then carried it down to the stream so that she could stuff deer intestines with food for Late Moon's journey to the salt pits.*

Modoc [moh' dahk] or **Maklak**   a California **tribe** of **Chinook**-speaking hunter-gatherers and **obsidian** traders who yielded their tribal lands to U.S. government agents in 1864. They joined their relatives, the Klamath, on an Oregon **reservation** and maintained trading ties with the Yurok and Karok. In 1870, led by Chief Kintpuash, or Captain Jack, the Modoc forced their way back into former territories on Lost River near Tule Lake in Siskiyou County, California. They maintained a frail hold on local lava lakes for four years before being imprisoned in Quapaw, Oklahoma, then dispersed into **Indian Territory**. By 1980, their number had dwindled to 150. *Captain Jack, a Modoc chief, testified that Hooker Jim accused him of being an old squaw because he chose to run from skirmishes with the U.S. Cavalry rather than to make a stand and fight.*

Mohave dwelling

Mohave [moh • hah' vay] or **Mojave**   a **tribe** of farmers, fishers, and gatherers of the **Yuma** nation, the name of which means three mountains. The Mohave, who are related to the ancient **Anasazi** and their offshoots, the

---

Pueblo, are native to the area around the Colorado River, where in 1775 Father Francisco Tomas Garcés counted about 3,000 members. The tribe lives in loose **clans** with little internal control. The Mohave currently reside near Needles, California, in the desert that bears their name; in addition, some Mohave live in Arizona and Nevada. They subsist on wheat, corn, beans, and melons and eke out a living by selling pottery and beadwork. *The Mohave honored their dead by burning the body along with the owner's brush hut, stockpile of food, and personal possessions.*

Mohawk [moh' hawk] or **Maquak** or **Ganeagaono** a **tribe** of eastern woodlands Indians who joined with four other tribes in the original **Iroquois League**, which was envisioned by **Deganawida** in the fifteenth century, then formally charted about 1570 by his disciple, **Hiawatha**. The Mohawks' name in **Algonquin** means man-eaters. Most settled in Vermont, New Hampshire, and other parts of New England; others migrated to Canada. One outstanding Mohawk, Ely S. Parker, served as Mohawk representative to the Iroquois League and later as Ulysses S. Grant's personal secretary. Modern Mohawks are famous for accepting challenging construction jobs atop high buildings. [See also **Joseph Brant, Molly Brant, Deganawida, Hiawatha, Iroquois League, Catherine Tekakwitha.**] *Mohawks took pride in the leadership of Hiawatha, whom they revered as a god.*

Mohican See **Mahican**.

moiety [moy' uh • tee] a division of a **clan** into competitive halves; a subdivision or half-**tribe**. A moiety provides tribal stability by regulating intermarriage and offering additional advisers during times of stress. Members of a pair of **Seneca** moieties remained close by marriage, mutual hunting and gathering parties, and competition in **lacrosse** and other games. *The Oneida moiety system improves performance by establishing a natural challenge between rival halves.*

Mojave See **Mohave**.

mollypop See **maypop**.

a = sack; ah = sob; aw = sauce; ay = safe; ee = seek; eh = set

Montezuma II [mahn' tuh • zoo' muh] or **Moctezuma** [mahk' tuh • zoo' muh] or **Motecuhzoma** [mah' tay • kuh • zoo' muh] (?-1520)   a noble **Aztec** high priest who, after the death of his uncle, rose to the position of ruler of 5 million Mexicas of Central and South America. A native of Tenochtitlán, Mexico, Montezuma II was the grandson of Montezuma I. Fearing that Spanish explorer Hernán Cortés was the god Quetzalcoatl, Montezuma greeted him with gifts, only to have his people suppressed. Their customs and religion were outlawed by the Spanish. The Aztec rose up against Montezuma and stoned him. He died of his wounds or was murdered by the Spanish. [See also **Aztec, Quetzalcoatl**.] *Doña Marina, Montezuma's interpreter, assisted the Aztec leader in welcoming Cortés and his party to the city of Tenochtitlán.*

morache [moh • rahsh']   a Central American musical instrument composed of a notched rod resting on a hollow **gourd** and played with a stick; a guayos. *Tia leaned forward in her seat to watch the hands of the morache player.*

Motavato   See **Black Kettle**.

Motecuhzoma   See **Montezuma II**.

Montezuma

mound   early platforms, temple supports, ancestral monuments, or burial sites that mark Indian settlements. Ceremonial mounds that honored the dead were formed out of stone, earth, logs, or debris and walled with protective palisades and were shaped like birds, reptiles, or other animals. Members of the Adena and Hopewell tribes, influenced by stories about Mayan temples, built lengthy earthworks in the Ohio Valley from 1000 B.C. to A.D. 1700 and filled their chambers with woven goods, pottery, carvings, jewelry, stone tablets, copper tools, and the bones or ashes of their worthiest dead. One of North America's most impressive effigy mounds is the 1,300-foot Great Serpent Mound of southern Ohio, an uninhabited looped earthwork 4 feet high and 15-20 feet wide which resembles similar earth structures in Great Britain; other examples include these:

- the sloping bird mound at Poverty Point, a pre-Christian city in northeastern Louisiana;

- Angel Mounds, an earthen platform with sunken plaza, and Great Circle Mound, a circular ditch and geoglyph northeast of Indianapolis, Indiana;

- a step-pyramid at Monk's Mound in Cahokia, Illinois;

- Madira Bickel Mound of the ancient Timucuans on the west coast of Florida;

- Spiro Mound in southeastern Oklahoma, which was abandoned in the fourteenth century and reclaimed by **Choctaw** tribes in 1800;

- Old Stone Fort on the Big Duck and Little Duck rivers and Saul's Mound in western Tennessee;

- Lizard Mounds, Wisconsin, built by an unknown people and abandoned in the fourteenth century;

- Etowah, a flat-topped pyramid later used by the **Cherokee** as a fort, near Cartersville, Georgia;

- Giant Octagon, called the "navel of the world," in Newark, Ohio;

- Fort Ancient, a sacred mound enclosing a sacred grove on the Little Miami River, Ohio;

- Towosaghy, an abandoned mound city in southern Missouri dating to A.D. 1000.

[See also **Hohokam, Mandan, Maya**.] *Mound builders flourished for a thousand years, then mysteriously vanished after the mid-sixteenth century.*

Moving Robe   See **Tashenamani**.

muckamuck [muhk' uh • muhk] or **high muckety-muck Chinook** jargon for a person who eats too much. The English slang term has come to refer to a self-important or arrogant person; a strutter. *In Hal Borland's* When the Legends Die *(New York: Bantam, 1963), Charlie Huckleberry tries to be the muckamuck by giving all the orders.*

*a = s*a*ck; ah = s*o*b; aw = s*au*ce; ay = s*a*fe; ee = s*ee*k; eh = s*e*t

mudhead a humorous ceremonial figure in **Pueblo** and **Zuñi** rituals who portrayed the first people to emerge from the underworld. Wearing a black kilt and bandana, the mudhead sported a clownish mask made of a painted sack with lumps at the top and sides. To provoke laughter from the audience, mudheads sometimes ate dirt and mimicked priests. [See also **false fase, kachina, kiva, koshare, sipapu.**] *Chita's family photographed the mudhead, who posed beside the entrance to the kiva.*

mugwump [muhg' wuhmp] or **mugquomp** [muhk' wahmp] the **Algonquin** term for a chieftain or leader; an independent captain or kingpin. In 1884, the word mugwump was applied to freethinkers who broke away from James G. Blaine, candidate of the Republican party, to vote for Grover Cleveland, a Democrat. [See also **chief.**] *In English slang, the term* mugwump *refers to anyone who deserts a party to support its opposition.*

mukluk [muhk' luhk] or **muklok** [muhk' lahk] a stitched, one-piece **Eskimo** or **Aleut** boot, named for the gray seal. The mukluk, like the **moccasin**, has a tanned sole made of deerskin, moose or **caribou** hide, or sealskin and is lined with moss, caribou hair, or felt for extra warmth. [See also **kammik, moccasin.**] *Running along the tundra, Janie felt the cold through her mukluks.*

muktuk See maktak.

mullein [muhl' uhn] a common spiky herb with a single upright stem covered by fuzzy leaves and bright yellow flowers. The tallest varieties of mullein grow to 6 feet. **Cherokee** cooks picked mullein leaves in early spring and cooked them with other tender greens, which they ate as a tonic or appetite stimulant. Rolled mullein leaves dipped in animal fat also served as a makeshift torch. [See also **healing.**] *Mullein is in the snapdragon family.*

Muskhogean [muhs • koh' gee • uhn] or **Muskogean** or **Muskogee** [muhs • koh' gee] a native language group that covered the Southeast. Muskhogeans were members of the **Five Civilized Tribes**. White traders encountered Muskhogean villages from the Georgia coast into central Alabama. When pushed into Florida, Muskhogeans formed a tribe called the **Seminole**. [See also **Creek, Natchez, Seminole**.] *Both the Creeks and the Seminoles belong to the Muskhogean language group.*

muskrat a ratlike, web-footed water animal named for the Natick term *musquash*. At one time, Native American trappers from Alaska, Canada, and the continental United States valued the muskrat for its silky pelt, from which they earned a sizable income. European marketers, envying the widespread habitat of the American muskrat, tried to raise the animal but found that it overbred and destroyed gardens. *The end of the muskrat fur trade brought hardship to Great Lakes tribes.*

D. Timmons

muskrat

*a = s*a*ck; ah = s*o*b; aw = s*au*ce; ay = s*a*fe; ee = s*ee*k; eh = s*e*t*

Nahuatl [nah' hwah • t'l]   the Uto-Aztec language spoken by the **Aztec**, **Toltec**, and, currently, more than 1 million Mexicans. In the sixteenth century, when the Aztec nation was conquered by Spanish gold seekers, native servants, transported to European cities, spread Nahuatl words. The most familiar are Mexico, chili, avocado, coyote, and tomato. [See also **ahuacatl, Aztec**.] *In 1985, Nahuatl was listed among the 169 languages the U.S. Department of Education considered most critical to the understanding of science, economics, or international relations.*

nallaqtaq [nal' lak • tak]   a spring **igloo** or ice house with an open top covered by a tarp or **caribou** skin. As the ice melted, **Eskimo** families deserted their nallaqtaqs and took up residence in summer sod huts or tents. [See also **igloo, qarmat**.] *Because the weather turned unseasonably cold, Pete's fishing party built a hasty nallaqtaq.*

Nampeyo [nam • pay' oh] or **Snake Woman** (1860?-1942)   master potter of **Hopi** designs who flourished at the beginning of the twentieth century. Of mixed Tewa and Hopi parentage, Nampeyo, born in Hano Pueblo, Arizona, learned her craft from her grandmother and copied ancient designs. She shared them with anthropologist J. Walter Fewkes, who introduced Hopi crafts to Europe. Accompanied by her husband, Lesou, Nampeyo demonstrated her expertise at a crafts show in Chicago in 1898; by 1920, she was too visually impaired to continue her art. The Smithsonian Institution honored her work by purchasing some of her bowls, water jars, and vases. [See also **Hopi**.] *To assure that Hopi crafts would not die out, Nampeyo taught her daughter Fannie how to inscribe jars and bowls with the delicate black and red designs; Fannie passed on the skill to her daughters, Leah and Annie.*

nanook   See **nanuq**.

---

nantan [nan' tan]   an **Apache chief** or spokesman. [See also **chief**.] *A message from the nantan settled all questions about the direction the hunting party should take.*

nanuq [nan' ook] or **nanook**   the **Eskimo** word for polar bear. *The cry of nanuq brings Eskimo hunters to their feet.*

Narragansett [nar • ruh • gan' seht]   a **tribe** of tall, handsome farmers and hunter-gatherers native to Rhode Island, whom explorer Giovanni da Verrazzano described in 1524 as the most hospitable people he had seen on his voyage to North America. The Narragansett cooperated with Roger Williams, the founder of the state, but suffered heavy losses in 1676 during King Philip's War. They were absorbed into the **Mahican** and **Abenaki** tribes and intermarried with free blacks.

   The Narragansett language provided English with the words squash and squaw; the latter originally meant lady or queen but later came to be an insulting, antifemale term. The term Narragansett also applies to a breed of horses developed by the tribe. In James Fenimore Cooper's *The Last of the Mohicans* (New York: Bantam, 1981), the unusual placement of the feet—both left followed by both right—distinguished the trail of the Narragansett horse. [See also **King Philip, squaw**.] *Magnus, a female Narragansett sunksquaw, or sachem, served her tribe on a council of six influential leaders.*

narwhal [nahr' wahl]   a brownish gray Arctic mammal of the whale family. The **Inuit** prized the narwhal for its twisted ivory tusk, which ranges in length to 9 feet, and for its skin, which they dried and ate. The **Thule** depended on the narwhal for oil, **blubber**, and leather. [See also **blubber**.] *Idlaut's carving depicts an Inuit with his harpoon raised for a throw at a narwhal.*

nasaump   See samp.

Natchez [natch' ehz]   a sun-worshipping and **mound**-building **tribe** of farmers, fishers, and hunters of the **Muskhogean** nation, who lived along the Mississippi River and were visited by La Salle's expedition. Following disastrous wars with the **Choctaw** and French in 1730, the Natchez were scattered, enslaved, and virtually destroyed within two years. Remnants were absorbed by the **Chicka-saw**, **Creek**, and **Cherokee**. [See also **Muskhogean**.] *Today, the Natchez are listed among extinct Native American tribes.*

Natchez Trace   a 500-mile road completed in 1808 by U.S. Army engineers to link Nashville, Tennessee, with newly opened territory near Natchez, Mississippi. Named for the **Natchez** tribe, the road also enabled military forces to move men and supplies rapidly so that the army could quell Indian uprisings. *The Natchez Trace provided Indians and frontiersmen an easy route paralleling the Mississippi River.*

Native American Church   a formal worship society or cult established in 1918 to prevent government efforts to halt the use of **peyote** in religious vision ceremonies. Services, conducted from sunset to sunrise around a sacred fire within a magic circle, involve healing ceremonies, celebration, hymn singing, drumming, and trances achieved through the consumption of peyote. [See also **healing, making medicine, medicine drum, medicine song, mescal, peyote**.] *According to a report on the words of Alfred Wilson, former Cheyenne head of the Native American Church, "The Indian . . . stresses the importance of 'I am.' By this [Wilson] meant that the individual is a manifestation of the breath of energy of God."* (Collier, John. *Indians of the Americas.* New York: New American Library, 1947.)

nauyaaluk   See **kittiwake**.

nauyak see **kittiwake**.

Navaho women weaving a blanket

Navaho [nahv' uh • ho] or **Navajo**   a tight-knit **tribe** of desert-dwelling hunters, herders, farmers, traders, and silversmiths native to the southwestern United States. Originating in Canada and Alaska, the ancestors of the Navaho, kin to the **Anasazi** and Fremont tribes, migrated to the desert about the time of Columbus's voyages. A highly adaptable people, they learned to weave wool and create silver and turquoise jewelry, which today provide their major sources of income. The Navaho are the largest American tribe, inhabiting much of Arizona and New Mexico.

The word Navaho also refers to the Navaho language, which encompasses more than 80,000 native speakers, more than any other Native American language. In 1860, Navaho Chief Manuelito and his allies Delgadito and Barboncito set an example of defiance against American mistreatment; in 1944, Thomas Claw set a different kind of example for his people as a Marine code talker battling for Okinawa. [See also **code talkers, Long Walk**.] *"Night Way," a memorable Navaho prayer, finds beauty in all parts of a human life.*

Nazca [nahz' kuh]   a Peruvian culture dating from 200 B.C. to A.D. 600. The Nazca produced delicate embroidery; ceramic figurines; gold masks; and clay **panpipes**, which are similar to a harmonica. The tribe is best known for the Nazca Lines, a group of animal forms and geometric drawings several miles long near the coast of Peru. The lines were etched on the plain by the removal of surface stone. *The Nazca Lines, which may have been a calendar or astronomical chart similar to Stonehenge, expose a lighter-colored soil on the layer below, creating a light-on-dark design.*

Nelson, Edward W. (May 8, 1855-May 19, 1934)   an American naturalist who in 1877 explored the coastline of the Bering Sea for the U.S. Army Signal Service. Much lore about frontier Alaska dates to his writings, photos, specimens, and collected artifacts. Edward Nelson's observations provide a one-of-a-kind overview of Alaskan history before the intrusion of gold prospectors and missionaries. [See also **Aleut, Athapascan**.] *Without the writings of Edward Nelson, anthropologists would know virtually nothing about the ancient Aleuts.*

Nezahualcoyotl [neht' suh • hwahl • koi • yoh' t'l]   (*fl.* 1430s)   a Mexican poet-hero, religious leader, philosopher, and engineer who was crowned king of the Mexicas in 1431. *Nezahualcoyotl refused to eat until the poor had been fed, and he ordered corn planted at the roadside for anyone to harvest.*

Nez Percé [nehz' puhrs']   a **tribe** of fishers, hunters, and gatherers native to the northwestern United States and credited with breeding the Appaloosa, a western saddle horse. The Nez Percé were incorrectly named the pierced-nose Indians by French traders, who saw some braves with pieces of bone and shell through their noses. The people preferred the name Choopinitpaloo, or people of the mountain. **Chief Joseph**, a key figure in American history, led the Nez Percé within 30 miles of the border of Canada before being halted by authorities; on the way, his associate, Chief Looking Glass, was killed. [See also **Chief Joseph**.] *Wearing a fur hat and fox tail, Man-ce-muckt, a Nez Percé chief, posed for a portrait.*

Noah See **Seattle**.

nokehick [noh' kay • hihk] or **nocake** dried cornmeal made from parched **corn** that is beaten to a powder and carried in a leather backpack for use by travelers in making small cakes fried in a skillet or formed on a flat rock on an open fire. [See also **ash cake**.] *Algonquins taught Pilgrims how to fashion johnnycake out of nokehick.*

nomad a wanderer, herder, or forager; a person who lives in temporary residences. Nomadic Native American groups include hunters, fishers, herders, and gatherers, who followed migrating herds and flocks, schools of fish, and pods of whales or searched for grassy meadows or fertile fields of **camas** or **kouse** root or berries. *Some tribes of the American plains, for instance, the Navaho and Sioux, who hunted buffalo, were at one time nomads.*

Nootka woman wearing basket hat

Nootka [noot' kuh] a tribe of woodworkers, whalers, and fishers native to Vancouver Island in northwest Canada. The people are related to the **Kwakiutl** and were known for their boat building and for their colorful Salmon Rite, which celebrated the central food in their diet. The Nootka lived in sunken houses, the roofs of which were held up by beautifully carved and painted support posts. They first met European explorers in 1774 with the visit of Spanish adventurer Juan Pérez. [See also **potlatch**.] *Captain James Cook visited Nootka settlements in 1778, during his last Pacific voyage.*

---

*ih = s**i**t; oh = s**oa**k; oo = s**ou**p; ow = s**ou**nd; uh = s**u**ch; y = s**i**de*

nuglutang [noog' luh • tang] an **Eskimo** eye-hand co-ordination game that requires players to force a sharp-ened stick into a hole in a disk, which is suspended from the ceiling by a **thong**. *The champion player mastered nuglu-tang by keeping her eye on the hole in the disk.*

Nunavut See **Inuit**.

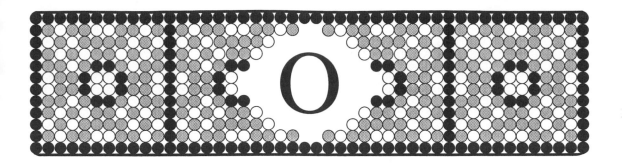

O'Bail, John   See **Cornplanter**.

obsidian [uhb • sih' dee • uhn]   a glassy, compact form of silica that was used to make hand-flaked blades; natural volcanic glass. Obsidian, which is usually greenish black, may vary from gray to red, brown, or even appear clear. From ancient times, Mexican Indians have quarried obsidian for mirrors, jewelry, choppers, and scrapers, as well as spear points, knife blades, and other weapons. California and Nevada Indians relied on obsidian as a valuable trade item. [See also **flaking**.] *The globules that are left after obsidian is formed into perlite are called Apache tears.*

Ohiyesa   See **Charles Alexander Eastman**.

Ojibwa [oh • jihb' wah] or **Ojibway** or **Chippewa** [chihp' puh • wah]   the largest **tribe** in the northern United States, the Ojibwa were nomadic woodland hunters and trappers native to Canada, who migrated to Wisconsin and the Great Lakes area. The white culture's name for the tribe was Chippewa, a mispronunciation of Ojibwa. It was one of the earliest Native American tribes to abandon primitive weapons for guns.

Residing in loosely defined **clans**, the Ojibwa ate potatoes, **squash**, beans, melons, and **corn** from their gardens, fish and fresh game from the woods, and herbs, wild rice, **maple sugar**, and berries gathered in the wild. They were famous for their skill with snares and the quality of their birch-bark **canoes** and lidded containers or **mocucks**. In his brief speech in 1761, orator Minavavana noted Ojibwa self-sufficiency, which he credited to gifts of the **Great Spirit**. Drawing on native lore, Henry Wadsworth Longfellow used Ojibwa myths in the writing of his epic poem, *The Song of Hiawatha* (New York: Dial Press, 1983). Because of their belief in the supernatural, the Ojibwa composed many stories and songs about the monster Windigo. A current Ojibwa writer and artist, Norval Morriseau, or Copper Thunderbird, painted a mural of native themes for the 1967 Exposition in Montreal. [See also **Anishinabe, Midewiwin**.] *In 1844, in the company of artist George Catlin, a visiting group of Ojibwa met with Queen Victoria and Prince Albert at Waterloo Gallery in London.*

Okipa [oh • kee' puh] a four-day summer ceremony among the **Mandan**, who celebrated creation and awaited visions from the spirit world. To hasten communication with the supernatural, young men danced themselves into a frenzy and were lifted on ropes that were attached to skewers through their chests or backs. [See also **Mandan**.] *Old Bear prepared himself to preside over the Okipa by dotting his flesh with clay, putting on a white wolfskin robe, and attaching foxtails to his feet.*

Old-Man a mythic character of **plains Indian** lore; a sage. Old-Man taught early tribes to revere nature, follow sacred law, and worship the **Great Spirit**. Old-Man symbolizes a Native American belief system that has evolved from ancient times. [See also **trickster**.] *Old-Man belongs to the literary heritage of Moses in the Bible, Merlin in Arthurian lore, Uncle Remus in African American lore, and Obi-Wan Kenobi, Luke Skywalker's adviser and mentor in* Star Wars.

olla [ahl' uh]   a wide-mouthed earthenware water jar or stew pot common to southwestern and Mexican tribes. The olla had large, looped handles on each side to aid in carrying and pouring. *Desert dwellers kept their water in a tall olla.*

Olmec [ohl' mehk]   an ancient Mesoamerican **tribe** of builders and traders that existed at Veracruz and Tabasco, Mexico, along the Gulf Coast as far south as Guatemala and El Salvador from 1500 B.C. to 400 B.C. The Olmec, the parent culture of the **Aztec** and **Maya**, worshipped **Quetzalcoatl**, the feathered serpent god. They were famous for their engineering projects—wide stone roads, pyramids, mozaics, plazas, **adobe** platforms, and canals. [See also **Aztec, Maya, Quetzalcoatl**.] *The Olmec* *developed a hieroglyphic system of writing and counting; they created delicate jade and basalt artworks, calendars, and soccer courts.*

Onandaga [oh' • nun • day' guh] or **Onondaga** another name for the **Iroquois**, also called the Onayatakono, or people of the standing stone. [See also **Iroquois League**.] *Audrey Shenandoah, an Onandaga storyteller and teacher, entertains children at the same time that she teaches them to respect the Earth and themselves.*

Oneida [oh • ny' duh] a **tribe** of the **Iroquois** language group that settled near Raquette Lake, New York. Members of the **Iroquois League**, the Oneida maintained close relationships with the **Onandaga** and **Mohawk**. Oneida women superintended large gardens of beans, **squash**, and **corn** and gathered other foods. The Oneida lived in bark **longhouses** or in multifamily compounds. After the arrival of the Rev. Samuel Kirkland, the Oneida supported colonists against England during the American Revolution. The nation was forced off its land and resettled in Wisconsin. A small tribe today, most remain in Wisconsin with smaller groups inhabiting Oneida, New York, and Ontario, Canada. [See also **Iroquois, Iroquois League**.] *Graham Greene, a full-blooded Canadian Oneida, gained fame in the early 1990s for his role as Kicking Bird in the film* Dances with Wolves.

One Who Travels See **Nancy Ward**.

One Who Yawns See **Geronimo**.

Onitositah See **Corn Tassel**.

oo-gruk See **ugruk**.

oolu See **ulu**.

Open Door See **Tenkswatawa**.

Orenda [oh • rehn' duh] the **Iroquois** concept of a divine spirit, which linked human beings and nature into a unified whole and could be summoned by ritual or magic. [See also **Great Spirit, Manitou, sweat lodge**.] *Orenda came to White Oak through powerful dreams, which he experienced in the sweat lodge.*

Osage [oh' sayj] a Siouan prairie **tribe** of farmers, horse breeders, trappers, traders, and bison hunters native to the Ohio Valley. The Osage, who call themselves the Wazhazhe, honor what is wakan or powerful. They were visited by Father Jacques Marquette, a French missionary, in 1673 and by the **Lewis and Clark expedition** in 1804. Pushed west by European settlers, they moved first to **reservations** in Kansas and then to Oklahoma in 1872, where oil and mineral rights brought them wealth. Famous Osage include Major General Clarence B. Tinker of the U.S. Air Force and prima ballerinas Marjorie Tallchief and Maria Tallchief. [See also **Kickapoo, Sioux**.] *In 1912, Playful-calf recalled how he learned from a secret Osage society*

> *of the light of the day by which the earth and all living things that dwell thereon are influenced; of the mysteries of the darkness of night that reveal to us all the great bodies of the upper world, each of which forever travels in a circle of its own unimpeded by the others.*

(Collier, John. *Indians of the Americas*. New York: New American Library, 1947, 108.)

Osceola [oh' see • oh' luh] or **Black Drink Singer** (1800-January 30, 1838) a **Muskhogean chief**, who was part Scottish and a native of Tallapoosa, Georgia. At the age of 17, Osceola fought during the First Seminole War. The uprising was caused by white settlers, who pushed his nation farther west into less habitable lands and forbade them to take along runaway black slaves, some of whom were married to Indians. Because Osceola's wife, Morning Dew, was the daughter of a slave mother and an Indian father, she was captured by slave catchers in 1835. Resistance to the U.S. government's authorized forced removal of Seminoles beyond the Mississippi led to the Second Seminole War. In April 1835, Osceola led 2,000 warriors, including 300 former slaves, against the U.S. Army. Nicknamed the Swamp Fox, he was captured by Andrew Jackson's troops in the Florida Everglades two years later and, clothed in war regalia, died of malaria in prison at Fort Moultrie, South Carolina. [See also **black**

Osceola

Indian, Seminole.] *In a famous speech, Osceola exhibited his religious faith by saying that the Great Spirit forbade him to follow the dictates of the whites; of his captors, he concluded dramatically, "They cannot hold me except in chains."* (Pastron, Allen. *Great Indian Chiefs.* Santa Barbara, Calif.: Bellerophon, 1993, 34.)

osier See **willow**.

otekoa [oh' tee • koh' uh] strings of white beads used as money. [See **dentalia, wampum**.] *Grayback tucked away his tribe's otekoa, which he planned to offer in exchange for kettles and cooking pots.*

Ottawa [aht' tuh • wah] an **Algonquin**-speaking **tribe** of traders native to the Great Lakes region that was pro-French during the French and Indian War. During the early seventeenth century, the Ottawa allied with the **Potawatomi, Ojibwa,** and **Huron**. They earned a comfortable living by trading with the French, who attempted to Christianize them. Suspicious of British intent, the Ottawa refused to negotiate and, in the mid-1700s, launched the Pontiac Wars. Eventually, they sided with the United States and gradually sold off their choicest northern acreage, which included prize timber. Today, the Ottawa live in Ontario, Manitoba, Michigan, Illinois, and Indiana, and on **reservations** in Oklahoma. [See also **Algonquin, Pontiac**.] *Chief Pontiac refused to halt aggression against European settlers, who he feared would take over Ottawa lands.*

Chief Ouray

Ouray [oo • ray'] or **Arrow** (1830-1880) a wily but honorable **half-breed** orator and **chief**. Born in Colorado of an **Apache** mother and **Ute** father, Ouray refused to be deceived or cheated by treaty makers and, by reporting the Indians' situation to the press, forced the U.S. government to give the Ute land at Los Pinos and White River. Despite Ouray's skill in diplomacy, he was too old and too ill from kidney disease to stop the resettlement of his people from the White River to less livable lands in Colorado and Utah. Still, in his last months, he undertook a journey to Washington, D.C., to plead for an amicable settlement. [See also **half-breed**.] *In 1881, Ouray's people were forced from Colorado onto lands rejected by the Mormons in Utah.*

owl woman   in the mythology of the **plains Indians**, the keeper of the bridge that leads across the dark river, one of the hurdles that the soul must pass on its way to the afterlife. To assure admission to the bridge, Indians are tattooed with symbolic markings on their faces or wrists. *The owl woman is said to hurl unidentified spirits into the river.*

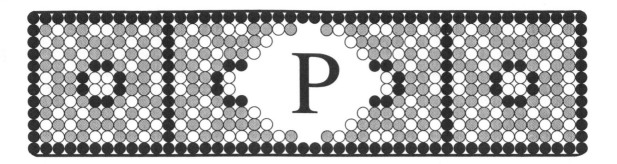

pad saddle   a soft skin bag stuffed with hair or moss and placed next to a horse's back beneath the saddle. *Each season, to protect his pinto from sores, Ray replaced the stuffing in his pad saddle.*

paho   See **baho**.

paint pot   a mineral rock containing iron oxide that can be ground into a colored powder for cosmetic or ritual use. [See also **dye**.] *The Hiwassee children scoured the rocky ledges for paint pots.*

Paiute [py • yoot'] or **Piute**   a nomadic **tribe** of hunters and fishers native to the southwestern United States that followed the ancient Fremont and **Anasazi** into the Great Basin between A.D. 1000 and A.D. 1500. The Paiute, also known as **Diggers**, were among the poorest Indians in the United States. They formed wide-spaced family groups, lived in **wickiups**, and kept on the move to locate food. European settlers seized Paiute lands, forcing them to scatter about the Southwest in search of roots, seeds, rabbits, and birds, which formed the bulk of their diet.

Paiute woman and baby

The Paiute were peace-loving people who were often enslaved by traders and transported to California. The Paiute are reported to have rescued wagon trains from disaster. The Truckee River was named in honor of a humanitarian Paiute chieftain. Two key spokesmen for the Paiute during the Bannock War of 1878 were war **chief** Egan and his prophet, Oyte. The Paiute prophet **Wovoka** preached a revival message of hope and won the **Sioux** chief Kicking Bear to his mystical religion. [See also **Ghost Dance, wickiup, Sarah Winnemucca, Wovoka**.] *Sarah Winnemucca set an example of courage for all members of the Paiute nation by serving as wagon driver and messenger through dangerous territory.*

palaver [puh • lav' uhr]   the frontier slang term meaning to chatter or talk freely; to confer or **caucus**. [See also **caucus**.] *Visitors and lacrosse players enjoyed a chance for a pleasant palaver.*

palisade around Florida Indian village

palisade [pal' ih • sayd]   a stockade or protective fence composed of tall wooden stakes sharpened at the top, placed close together, and interwoven with brush, cord, and sticks to keep out invaders and predatory animals. *The Iroquois often surrounded their villages with a palisade.*

pampas [pam' puhs]   the South American plains; a savanna or open grassland, which is ideal for stock raising. [See also **gaucho**.] *Argentine gauchos tend herds of stock on the pampas, where Araucanian Indians once roamed.*

pana [pa' nuh]   an **Eskimo** hunting knife attached to a shaft. The hunter steadies the pana in the snow, then entices a bear to lunge forward and impale itself on the point. The bear's weight forces its body down onto the pana. [See also **buckhorn, ice chisel, ulu**.] *Ugruk's skill with the pana earned him more bear pelts than any other resident of Baffin Bay.*

panpipes   a series of wooden tubes or reeds that are graduated in length and attached horizontally by lumps of wax or pitch or by a **sinew** or cord lashing. The musician blows into slots or holes in the top of the panpipes to create a musical scale. Panpipes are similar to a harmonica. [See also **Indian flute**.] *Taino and Inca Indians played native tunes on panpipes while keeping an eye on their flocks.*

Papago [pah' pah • goh]   a large, nomadic agricultural **tribe** that wandered southern Arizona in search of arable soil and plentiful water to cultivate **maize**, **squash**, and melons. The Papago, relatives of the **Pima**, earned a reputation for weaving striking baskets covered with geometric symbols. They also made a strong wine from saguaro cactus. Today, most of the Papago inhabit

reservation lands around Pima County, Arizona, or Sonora, Mexico, and keep their distance from white society. *Grandmother Noceo was the storyteller of the local Papago tribe.*

papaya [puh • py' yuh] or **pawpaw** or **papaw**   the large, globular yellow fruit of a tree, commonly called the custard apple. Prized by Indians for its pleasant flavor and ease of preparation, papaya tastes like sweet potatoes and can be baked whole or used to make nutbread. *Nola peeled papaya and mashed the pulp with honey to create a sweet dessert.*

papaya

papoose [pa • poos']   the **Narragansett** term for an infant or small child. [See also **cradleboard**.] *The Beothuk mother kept her papoose safely out of harm by tying her to a cradleboard.*

parfleche [pahr' flehsh]   a folded carrying case, skin envelope, or traveling bag used by **plains Indians**. The parfleche was made of a whole, unseamed rawhide and decorated with painted designs. Used to hold food, tools, medicine, paint, mirrors, or clothing, the parfleche was pierced and laced with ties so that the sides could be rolled up and secured in place on the back or behind a saddle. In the **tepee**, the parfleche was the equivalent of drawer space. [See also **babiche**.] *Several Lakota workers smoked the hide to soften it for use as a parfleche.*

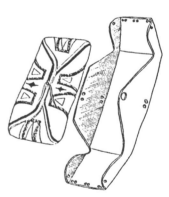

D. Timmons

parfleche

parka   an unlaced, one-piece hooded pullover jacket; an anorak. To protect themselves from the extremes of cold, **Eskimos** wore loose-fitting parkas and pants made of fish skin, strips of seal intestine, or **caribou** hide with the fur toward their bodies. These lightweight garments provided a layer of air, which kept the wearer warm and dry. The sleeves were loose so that wearers could pull their arms in and hug their chests for extra warmth.

In extreme cold, a sleeveless vest might help retain body warmth. To protect the face, Eskimos added wood or bone snow goggles, which fastened to the head with a **thong**. The woman's parka, or **amouti**, featured a U-shaped skirt and detailed embroidery, cormorant feathers, appliquéd skins, or red wool. The garment was loose enough to allow her to suspend an infant inside by a strap down the back. The parka required care to keep it soft.

If it became stiff, it was chewed or rubbed with oil to restore its texture. [See also **amouti, atigi.**] *Miyax asked for a parka lined in soft fleece and edged with wolverine fur.*

Parker, Quanah [kwah' nuh pahr' kuhr] or **Eagle** (1845-February 23, 1911) influential **Comanche** leader who fought the destruction of migrating buffalo herds and the Comanche way of life. The son of Chief Peta Nocona and his white wife, Cynthia Ann Parker, Quanah Parker led a Comanche band called Quahadas. To avoid moving his people to an Oklahoma **reservation**, for eight years he and his band evaded U.S. Army troops, who relentlessly pursued them. In 1875, Quanah Parker surrendered at Fort Sill, gave in to white ways, and became a successful businessman, diplomat, linguist, agricultural reformer, and judge. [See also **Comanche**.] *To prove his assimilation into white culture, Quanah Parker adopted his mother's surname and built a two-story ranch house, but he continued to live in a tepee.*

passionflower See **maypop**.

pa-tol [pah • towl'] or **patolli** [pah • towl' lee] a board game popular in the southwestern United States, played with dice and discs or markers in a circle of stones or on a cross divided into 52 squares, which represented a ritual time period. The rules of pa-tol are similar to those of backgammon. *Aztecs enjoyed regular pa-tol tournaments, which pitted several players in a championship match.*

patshall See **potlatch**.

pauluk [pow' look] or **poaluk** [poh' uh • look] a waterproof **Inuit** glove or mitten, which was made of skins lined or padded with soft down, moss, or felt for extra warmth. [See also **sphagnum**.] *The elder put on his anorak and boots, then stuffed moss into his pauluks before pulling them on.*

Pawnee [paw • nee'] a colorful **tribe** of hunters, farmers, and horse breeders native to the central plains states, particularly Nebraska. The Pawnee became famous for the quality of their **bows** and their skill as cavalry guides. Dating to A.D. 1200, they proudly referred to themselves as Chahiksicholhiks, or men of men, although their more familiar name means horn or hunter. The Pawnee and their relatives, the Wichita, moved north from Texas to Nebraska around 1300. First contact with white settlers, as described by Curly Chief, brought smallpox and cholera in 1849.

Photos from the mid-nineteenth century show the Pawnee males dressed in fringed **leggings**, **moccasins**, necklaces, earrings, and **toques**. By 1873, the tribe, like other **plains Indians**, was forcibly resettled in northern Oklahoma. One Pawnee leader, Sharitarish, visited President James Monroe and Secretary of War John C. Calhoun on February 4, 1882, and presented a **peace pipe**, robes, leggings, moccasins, and bear claws as a ceremonial gift. Modern-day Pawnee take pride in the artistry of painter Alvin Jake and the myths of Dolly Moore. *In advice to her son Lone Chief, the Pawnee mother advised him to stay true to his friends, even if he risked death.*

pawpaw See **papaya**.

peace pipe a holy object that Indians smoked to signify unity, welcome to strangers, and spirituality; a **calumet**. [See also **calumet, tobacco**.] *The smoke that curled from the bowl of the peace pipe suggested the mystic presence of the Great Spirit.*

pecan a Native American hardwood tree valued for its thin-shelled, sweet-flavored nuts. *The Catawbas gathered wild pecans and cracked them between flat stones.*

pemmican [pihm' ih • k'n] a nutritious, high-energy trail mix made from whatever ingredients were available, such as pounded bits of meat, fish, or **jerky** mixed with hot kidney fat, marrow, wild greens, nuts, or molasses. Acid berries, such as soapberries, **juniper** berries, elderberries, or buffaloberries, preserved the mixture. Pemmican was pressed into cakes and wrapped in animal skins or sewn up in animal intestines. Pemmican was served as quick-energy food for a journey or during food shortages. It resisted mold, needed no cooking or other preparation, and could be stored for up to five years. In the Pacific Northwest, pemmican was made from pounded fish bits mixed with berries and sturgeon oil or from

pecan

venison, suet, and seal oil. [See also **buffalo jump, jerky**.] *After white settlers began to eat pemmican, it became a valuable trade item.*

Penobscot [puh • nahb' skaht] See **Abenaki**.

Pequot [pee' kwaht] a New England **tribe** of the **Algonquin** nation and relatives of the Mohegan. The Pequot fought Dutch and English settlers in Connecticut in the Pequot War. Led by Sassacus, in 1636 the Pequot tried to end European settlement at the Massachusetts Bay Colony by killing livestock and burning houses. On May 25, 1637, Captain John Mason, allied with **Narragansett**, Mohegan, and Niantic warriors, overran the Pequot fort on the Mystic River in Connecticut. He defeated the Pequot; survivors were sold as slaves in the West Indies. *The Pequot, whose name means destroyer, are virtually extinct.*

persimmon [puhr • sim' uhn] the oval orange or yellow fruit of a common hardwood tree. Indian cooks usually make persimmon pudding or bread in the fall, after the fruit has lost its bitterness. *Native Americans dried persimmon pulp for winter use and saved the flat, black seeds for children to use in games.*

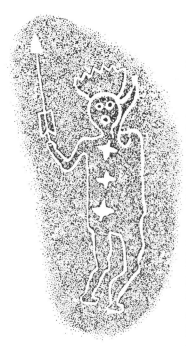

petroglyph [peht' ruh • glihf] a figure etched or engraved in stone. Petroglyphs of woodlands Indians often recorded successful hunts or made predictions, such as the outcome of an alliance. Some of the oldest rock carvings in the Western Hemisphere are found near Layou, St. Vincent, in the West Indies, where the **Carib** worshipped in the seventh century. European traders passing through the Great Basin of the southwest puzzled over **Hopi** petroglyphs and ruins of ancient houses. [See also **Carib, Hopi, pictograph**.] *A petroglyph at Canyon del Muerto, Arizona, depicts a column of mounted Europeans, who arrived around 1804; another elaborate historical carving in California's Santa Monica Mountains shows the Chumash encountering whites for the first time.*

two examples of petroglyphs

peyote [pay • oh' tee] a native cactus from which worshippers pick a sacred button or immature shoot. During the peyote ritual, worshippers sit around the fire, purify themselves with cedar smoke, chant, listen to the high priest, and eat peyote buttons or drink peyote tea, which causes them to see colorful, whirling visions or fall into a trance. The ritual use of peyote, which dates from prehistory, became increasingly popular around 1870, when **plains Indians** came under the control of European settlers. By turning to its magic, worshippers hoped to restore their ancient power. [See also **making medicine, medicine song, mescal, Native American Church**.] *Moon Singer encouraged other young Comanche men to chew peyote buttons, sing songs, and meditate.*

Philip, King   See **King Philip**.

Pickett, Bill (1870?-1932)   a feisty black **Cherokee** cowboy and rodeo star and silent-movie actor from Oklahoma who originated the sport of steer wrestling, or bulldogging, a means of forcing a steer to the ground by wrenching its neck and horns and biting its nose or upper lip. Pickett, who at the age of 10 decided to work cattle for a living, was employed on the range from South America to Texas. Along with associates Tom Mix and Will Rogers, he toured with his rodeo show in Europe, Canada, and Mexico. In 1914 his company performed in the arena for King George V and Queen Mary. Advertised as the "Dusky Demon," Pickett starred in *The Bull-Dogger,* a silent movie filmed in Jacksonville, Florida. [See also **black Indian**.] *Shortly after retirement, Bill Pickett was killed by the kick of a horse.*

Picotte, Suzette La Flesche   See **Bright Eyes**.

pictograph on a Sioux tepee drawn by George Catlin

pictograph [pihk' tuh • graf]   a picture, frieze, or design, often detailing, in simple drawings, historical events in chronological order. Drawn in 1898, 22 years after the event, Kicking Bear's pictograph of the **Battle of Little Big Horn** reveals General Custer's corpse lying near the battle leaders, **Sitting Bull, Crazy Horse, Rain-in-the-Face**, and Kicking Bear himself. During this same era, Yellow Nose, a **Ute** artist, drew on **buckskin** a pictograph of the **Ghost Dance**. [See also **Battle of Little Big Horn, Crazy Horse, petroglyph, Sitting Bull**.] *Pictographic style is usually two-dimensional and primitive, often depicting animals and human beings as stick figures.*

pigeon oil   the oil of the passenger pigeon, which was prized as cooking fat and a form of butter for cornbread. *Lone Doe opened a gourd of pigeon oil and offered it to her honored guests.*

pigweed   See **quinoa**.

piki [pee' kee]   a delicate, tasty, paper-thin cornbread. A staple in southwestern Indian society, piki is a thin, crackly black tortilla made from an ashy blue **corn** batter patted by hand onto a flat greased soapstone (**steatite**) slab or **duma** over an open fire. Twentieth-century merchants have rediscovered piki and begun to market blue corn chips and tortillas as a Native American delicacy. [See also **ash cake, duma, maize, mano, metate, pone, Pueblo**.] *In early times, Indians of the Southwest depended on piki for quick, easy nourishment.*

Pima village

Pima [pee' muh]   a settled **tribe** of small-framed farmers and canal-builders who lived in the southwestern United States. The Pima, whose name means no, were ancestors of the **Hohokam**. The Pima irrigated their fields and grew grain and forage to feed their livestock. They believed that war was so debilitating an occupation that they required returning braves to undergo healing therapy to help them adjust to normal life.

Pima villagers often sheltered white wagon trains from **Apache** raiders. After taking in the Maricopa, the Pimas intermarried and lost most of their cultural individuality. Their culture was further undermined in 1887 after white settlers drew off the waters of the Gila, Santa Cruz, and Salt rivers for farm irrigation, thereby reducing the Pima to destructive drought conditions. Consequently, their agricultural and gathering lifestyle altered dramatically by the turn of the century; in particular, they lost disease-preventing and healing plants. Ira Hayes, a distinguished Pima who was one of the flag raisers at Iwo Jima during World War II, fell victim to racism and rootlessness and died in poverty and misery. [See also **Hohokam**.] *A Pima ceremonial hymn concludes with rejoicing, dancing, and singing as headdresses wave.*

Pinaquana   See **Washakie**.

pine knot the base of a pine limb, which Native Americans used as an emergency light. *Lifting their lighted pine knots over the crevice, the braves looked down at the tracks of three lost sheep.*

pinole [pih • noh' lee] flour ground from parched **maize** or cactus seeds. Also, a bland drink made from ground corn and water, which was favored by women and children. *Chole quickly mixed pinole and water, formed the batter into balls, then patted out cakes to bake in the oven.*

piñon [pihn' yuhn] or **pinyon** a rough-barked pine tree native to the higher elevations of the American West; also, the nut from the piñon tree, sometimes called a pine nut. Because it is high in protein and fat as well as flavorful, it was used to make baby food. Piñon nuts were easily stored. Indian cooks relied on them, either raw or boiled, for flavoring stews and bread; they also added the nuts to salads or toasted the nuts on **willow** trays for snacks. They pounded green piñon nuts into a paste, which they molded into small cakes and fried or added to soups. The **Navaho** gathered pine nuts in the fall and winter as trade items. The nuts were valued as raw material for shoe polish, waterproofing, chewing gum, and a healing balm. *My Gosiute grandmother always tucks a few piñon nuts into my backpack.*

piñon pine

pinto [pihn' toh] a small, sturdy horse with a white coat blotched with dark, irregular patches. The breed takes its name from the Spanish word for painted. Also called a piebald, skewbald, or calico, the pinto, because of its dependable performance and steady gallop, was a favorite of buffalo hunters, both Indian and white, as well as riders for the Pony Express. *Mehaska rode bareback to Laramie on his pinto.*

pipe bag a pouch containing pipe, **tobacco**, tamping stick, and flint for striking a spark. [See also **calumet, kinnikinnick, medicine pipe, tobacco**.] *Day Watcher mixed walnut-shell dye with ash to create a dark shade of brown to color the pipe bag.*

---

pipe tomahawk an ingenious combination pipe and hatchet that could be used for smoking, chopping wood, or warding off an enemy. [See also **hatchet, tomahawk**.] *Standing Elk treasured his pipe tomahawk, which his grandfather had made.*

cross section of a pithouse showing pit, log frame, and notched ladder

pirogue [pee' rohg] a heavy **dugout canoe** formed from a single log and used as a fishing vessel for fresh water or salt. Caribbean raftsmen carved then burned the shell to make a pirogue from a great cypress log. [See also **canoe, dugout, poling, portage**.] *Fernando, Christopher Columbus's brother, reported seeing a pirogue seating 25 Mayan Indians covered by a canopy of palm leaves.*

pit house a permanent, semi-subterranean residence common to the **Anasazi**. Consisting of an antechamber and adjacent storage chamber, the pit house, dug several feet in the ground and topped by a roof supported by four timbers, contained a central fire pit and sleeping quarters. [See also **Anasazi, kiva**.] *The pit house was thought to be the forerunner of the ceremonial kiva.*

Pitiful Last See **Charles Alexander Eastman**.

Piute See **Paiute**.

Pizi See **Gall**.

plains Indians the 60 nomadic tribes of the American Midwest that began migrating south around 10,000 B.C. Tribes of the eastern plains, such as the **Mandan**, farmed **maize** and other crops and lived in villages of earth **lodges** during the growing season and hunted buffalo at other times. The western plains tribes lived the distinctive grasslands-nomadic lifestyle, notably hunting buffalo, riding horses, and living in portable **tepees**, which they moved on dog- or horse-pulled **travois**. Of all Native American cultures, the plains Indians are the only segment for which there exists a thorough written history. Their movement to the plains, hastened by drought to the south and European settlement to the east, forced Indians from Canada, the eastern woodlands, and the Rocky Mountains to abandon farming and adopt buffalo hunting. The most successful plains Indians remained mobile, avoiding

*a = s**a**ck; ah = s**o**b; aw = s**au**ce; ay = s**a**fe; ee = s**ee**k; eh = s**e**t*

contact with European settlers, who brought devastating diseases and stole their land. [See also **Arapaho, berdache, Blackfoot, Cheyenne, Comanche, contrary, Crow, dog soldier, heyoka, horse, Illinois, Indian, Kiowa, Mandan, Pawnee, Shoshone, tepee, travois, wickiup.**] *For more than a century, the plains Indians, who eventually comprised more than half the Native American population, were staunch defenders of the Native American way of life.*

plankhouse   the rectangular residence of Pacific Coast Indians, made of a wood frame covered by spruce or cedar planks. The walls of a **Kwakiutl** or **Haida** plankhouse are traditionally covered with brightly colored carvings of animals and birds. The supports, with their intricate re-creation of **clan** symbols, resemble **totem** poles. [See also **totem.**] *From the bay, the Nootka chief caught a glimpse of a fire on the hearth of his plankhouse.*

plankhouse

poaluk   See **pauluk**.

Pocahontas [po' kuh • hahn' tuhs] or **Pokahantes** or **Matoaka** or **Matowaka** [ma' toh • wah' kuh] (1595-March 21, 1617)   the beautiful, intelligent daughter of **Powhatan**, who served as an intermediary between her **tribe** and English settlers after saving Captain John Smith from decapitation at Werowocomoco, the Powhatan village outside Jamestown, Virginia, in 1608. Captured by the

plains Indian village drawn by George Catlin

English in 1613 and held hostage to keep her father from breaking the peace, she was taken to Henrico and converted to Christianity before being ransomed. As the wife of **tobacco** planter John Rolfe, she was named Lady Rebecca Rolfe and, in 1615, bore a son, Thomas Rolfe. Pocahontas traveled to London in 1616 and sat for an oil portrait. The next year, shortly before the return trip, she died suddenly, possibly of smallpox. She was buried near Gravesend. [See also **Algonquin, Milly Hayo Francis, Lost Colony, Powhatan.**] *According to John Smith's account of Pocahontas's courage, "She, under God, was the instrument to preserve this colony from death, famine, and utter confusion."* (Brandon, William. *The Last Americans.* New York: McGraw-Hill, 1974, 189.)

Pocahontas—from a painting done shortly before her death

pok-a-tok [pawk' uh • tawk]   a Mayan handball game played on a special court with stone goals at each end. Players wore padding on their hips, wrists, and elbows to enable them to hit a hard rubber ball without using their hands. [See also **Maya.**] *Mada's brother scored the most points by hitting the ball through the ring five times.*

pokeberry   the poisonous purple berry that grows in clusters on pokeweed, a common plant. Indian healers used the root of the plant as a purgative. Indian cooks boiled tender shoots of the pokeweed and ate them with wild onions and bland foods, such as cornpone or samp. [See also **healing.**] *In colonial times, colonists learned from Indians how to make ink from pokeberries.*

poling   pushing a **dugout**, **pirogue**, **mackinaw**, **chinampa**, or **bullboat** by means of forcing a long pole into a lake or streambed. The Mexica moved their produce to market by poling chinampas, or floating vegetable beds, down canals. [See also **bullboat, chinampa, dugout, pirogue.**] *Chingachgook knew that he could not risk giving away his position by poling the dugout to safer waters.*

Pomo [poh' moh]   a **tribe** of hunter-gatherers and fishers native to California and famous for weaving watertight baskets. The baskets held the **acorns** the Pomo collected and ground into meal and the grasshoppers they toasted for snacks. Pomo Indians were named red-earth people because they colored their food with dabs of red clay.

a = sack; ah = sob; aw = sauce; ay = safe; ee = seek; eh = set

They also marked their bodies with **tattoos** to indicate tribal stature and decorated their baskets with feathers, vines, and beads.

Much of Pomo life centered on rivers, where they anchored long, woven fish traps and fish baskets and collected giant clams. The shells they formed into beads and disks that served as money. Accomplished traders, the Pomo exchanged salt for goods from their Chumash and Hupa neighbors. Although they were peaceful people, according to Chief William Benson, the Pomo suffered near extermination during the mid-1800s by hostile white soldiers and gold prospectors. *Ona sang the Pomo song of the basket as she taught her two daughters the intricate weave.*

Ponca [pahn' kuh]   a small but prosperous plains **tribe** of farmers and horse traders native to the East, who migrated to Nebraska, Minnesota, and South Dakota. Already reduced to a few hundred from a smallpox epidemic, the Ponca met the **Lewis and Clark expedition** in 1804. The tribe negotiated with American officials in 1858; 10 years later, their lands were inadvertently given to the **Sioux**. In 1876, while escorting the body of his son to a burial site alongside the boy's sister on the Niobrara River, Chief Standing Bear was arrested. White attorneys appealed his case in a U.S. court so that Standing Bear would be able to complete his mission. The next year, the Ponca, along with tribes who fought at the **Battle of Little Big Horn**, were forcibly resettled in Nebraska and Oklahoma. The most noble of Ponca leaders during the last years of the tribe's greatness were Standing Bear, Big Elk, Big Snake, Hairy Bear, and White Eagle. [See also **Bright Eyes**.] *Incarcerated at Fort Omaha, Chief Standing Bear concluded that God intended the white race to overrun the country.*

pone   a flat bread, baked or fried, often made from two ingredients—cornmeal and water. [See also **ash cake, bean bread, duma, piki**.] *Hungry Choctaw travelers often baked pone on heated rocks, or dumas.*

Pontiac [pahn' tee • ak] (1720-April 20, 1769)   an influential **Ottawa chief**, Pontiac, born in Ohio of an Ottawa chief and an **Ojibwa** mother, joined with the French to defeat English settlers. Allied with the Ojibwa, **Seneca**,

---

ih = sit; oh = soak; oo = soup; ow = sound; uh = such; y = side

Delaware, Shawnee, Huron, and Kickapoo, on May 7, 1763, he set out to destroy nine of 10 British forts and trading camps. Pontiac's dream of a united Indian **league** was a noble but doomed experiment. After giving up his revolt against an overwhelming number of British, he was murdered in Cahokia, Illinois, by Black Dog, a Peoria assassin, who struck him on the head with a **tomahawk**. [See also **Algonquin, Illinois, Ottawa**.] *In a speech to his people, Pontiac said, "These lakes, these woods, these mountains were left us by our ancestors. They are our inheritance and we will part with none of them."* (Pastron, Allen. *Great Indian Chiefs*. Santa Barbara, Calif.: Bellerophon, 1993, 14.)

Popé [poh • pay] (1630?-1690) Tewa **shaman** imprisoned by the Spanish for witchcraft. On August 10, 1680, Popé led a rebellion against Hispanic settlers at San Juan, New Mexico, during which the Indians killed hundreds of Spanish missionaries, settlers, and soldiers. After the Spanish fled to El Paso, Popé washed baptized Indians in **yucca** soap to cleanse them of European corruption and herded cattle into churches to demonstrate his hatred for white people. As an elected leader, he helped restore traditions to his people, but alienated them by becoming tyrannical and arrogant. [See also **shaman**.] *Popé's destructive force burned all evidence of Spanish influence, including residences and churches.*

poquauhaug See **quahog**.

portage [por' tihj] the act of carrying a **canoe**, **pirogue**, or **dugout** from one body of water to another or over shallows or around falls and cataracts. From 1804-1805, the **Lewis and Clark expedition**, guided by interpreter **Sacagawea**, required frequent portages, which slowed the group's progress and exposed individuals to insect bites, quicksand, snakes, and other dangers. [See also **canoe, dugout, pirogue**.] *Assiniboin paddlers found portage necessary at narrow, rocky shoals or near steep falls.*

posketa See **busk**.

potato the starchy underground tuber of a common vegetable plant, native to the Andes Mountains, which is the world's fourth most useful food crop. Spanish explorers

a = sack; ah = sob; aw = sauce; ay = safe; ee = seek; eh = set

ate potatoes for the first time while visiting the **Inca** in Peru. The word is derived from *batata*, the **Taino** word for the tuber. The potato can be baked, boiled, roasted, fried, dried into flakes, ground into flour, or creamed in soup. It was once thought to cure impotence. *At one time, ground potato was used as a cleaning agent.*

Potawatomi [pah' tuh • wah' tuh • mee]   a peace-loving **tribe** of fur traders and horse breeders native to Michigan. The Potawatomi, relatives of the **Ottawa** and **Ojibwa**, migrated to Wisconsin, then to Idaho, and ultimately to an Oklahoma **reservation**. The word *Potawatomi* means people of the place of fire. In 1788, one of the most famous Potawatomi women, Catherine, married Paris-educated Jean Baptiste Pointe Du Sable, the French-Haitian founder of the city of Chicago. *In 1830, Potawatomi Chief Senachwine prophesied that the Indian would become extinct.*

potlatch or **patshall** [pat' shuhl]   a formal winter feast and dance at which a wealthy host increased personal prestige and attained honor by giving guests expensive gifts, such as copper jewelry, shells, or blankets. The potlatch is a tradition of the **Nootka**, **Haida**, Bella Coola, Puyallup, and **Kwakiutl** of the Pacific Northwest. The celebration features gift giving, singing, dancing, feasting, and oratory. It can be given for any social purpose: to celebrate a wedding, new house, or initiation, to invest a crown prince, christen an infant, mark an adoption or death, end a feud, make up for a serious fault, or honor a notable relative. In 1921, Canadian officials outlawed potlatch celebrations, but reinstated the custom 30 years later. In the interim, Kwakiutls pursued the tradition by disguising potlatches as Christmas celebrations, holding secret potlatches, or separating the dance from the gift giving, which was held on a separate date. [See also **Carrier, copper, giveaway, Haida, Kwakiutl, Nootka, Salish, Tlingit**.] *Runners carried invitations for the traditional Tsimshian potlatch.*

Poundmaker (1826-1886)   a **Cree** chief who surrendered to General Frederick Middleton in 1885. A native of southern Manitoba, Poundmaker led a party of French explorers across the prairie to Calgary. Allied with **métis**

---

ih = sit; oh = soak; oo = soup; ow = sound; uh = such; y = side

or **half-breed** French, led by Louis Riel in 1885, Poundmaker tried to stop European settlers from overrunning Indian lands and building railroads. He surrendered and was imprisoned, but gained his freedom a year later shortly before his death. [See also **Cree**.] *Poundmaker and Riel sparked the only major Indian war in Canada's history.*

Powhatan [pow' uh • tan] or **Wahunsonacook** [wah' hoon • sow' nuh • kook] (1550-1618) a **chief** of the Powhatan and leader of a confederacy of 30 **tribes** that lived between Maryland and Jamestown, Virginia. From a family of four boys and two girls, Powhatan understood that white settlers could improve Indian life by relieving it of misery and poverty. As reported by Captain John Smith in 1609, Powhatan was made king by European settlers, was adorned with a crown sent from England, and was robed in raccoon skins. He is remembered for trying to make an example of John Smith, who led white settlers into Indian territory. With Powhatan's blessing, his daughter, Princess **Pocahontas**, married John Rolfe, a European, thereby symbolizing a harmonious union of Indian and European races. [See also **Algonquin, Milly Hayo Francis, Lost Colony, Pocahontas**.] *In a speech to the Algonquin Confederacy in 1609 in Gloucester County, the aging Powhatan refused to mince words when he warned members to cease their jealousies and warring.*

Powhatan

powwow an **Algonquin** term meaning a meeting, tribal convention, caucus, or formal ceremony, often accompanied by feasting, craft displays, and dancing. Indian delegates painted their faces for powwows, a sign of seriousness and dedication. [See also **caucus**.] *The unified Algonquin nations held a powwow to discuss their plans.*

prayer stick or **keetaan** [kee' tahn] a ceremonial baton, dowel, reed, or wand the size of a pencil or slightly larger. Used by Indians as prayer beads or religious medals are used, the prayer stick serves as a reminder of the order and importance of ritual chants. The **Hopi** used a feather to similar purpose. The **Kickapoo** prayer stick was covered with scores of tiny slash marks and decorated with eagle feathers. **Navaho** priests stuffed hollow prayer sticks with feathers, down, pollen, or bits of colored stone. The **Pueblo** buried prayer sticks after they were used.

a = sack; ah = sob; aw = sauce; ay = safe; ee = seek; eh = set

[See also **baho, kiva, medicine, medicine pendant**.] *A Zuñi held his prayer stick and chanted to Mother Earth to bring winter by covering the Earth in snow.*

prickly pear or **tuna** a cactus common to the southwestern desert. **Navaho** cooks gather the plant's plump, sweet, red fruit for snack food. Prickly pear pads are dried, boiled in a syrup, roasted, or formed into a pulp; baked as small cakes; made into pickles; or cooked into jelly and preserves. Strips can be chewed like chewing gum. The seeds can be dried and ground into flour, which resembles **tapioca**. Prickly pear pads have also been used to bind wounds, to feed cattle, or to make mortar. *Handling the prickly pear requires care because of the sharp spines that cover the outer surface.*

prickly pear

Pueblo [pwehb' loh] a highly organized **tribe** of farmers native to the southwestern United States dating 8,000 years. The Pueblo were divided into five subgroups: **Zuñi**, Tiwa, Tewa, Keres, and **Hopi**. They were famous for their skill in weaving, **basketry**, and pottery, which they taught the **Navaho** and the **Apache**, who had been their enemies in early times. The Pueblo were a contented people. As James Paytiamo wrote in his 1932 memoir of the Acoma Pueblo, elderly pueblo dwellers delighted in sitting and sleeping in the sun and playing with the children.

Two famous twentieth-century Pueblo potters are Maria Martinez, of the San Ildefonso Pueblo in New Mexico, and Nampeo, of Hopi Pueblo Hano, Arizona, both of whom rely on artistic methods dating to the first century B.C. The Santa Ana Pueblo Indians have in recent times alleviated their poverty by creating markets for a rare, native strain of blue corn, which is sold as meal, parched corn or corn nuts, or is used as an ingredient in moisturizer, soap, and body oil. [See also **Hopi, kachina, kiva, koshare, piki, sipapu, Zuñi**.] *The early Pueblo Indians prayed before and after hunting deer as a means of honoring what fed them and glorifying Earth's unbroken cycle of birth and death.*

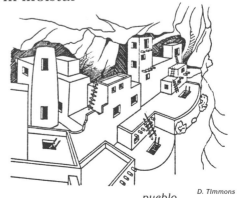

pueblo D. Timmons

pueblo [pwehb' loh] a flat-roofed, terraced multifamily dwelling; a village common to the southwestern desert. Similar to medieval castles, pueblos, such as Bonita

Mesa in Chaco Canyon, New Mexico, were first built of stone. They were later constructed from **adobe**. Interconnected in a step design, they were set against tall buttes or atop **mesas** or cliffs for maximum protection from attack and extremes of weather. Ladders provided access to the top floors. Windows and small storage rooms could be sealed with sandstone slabs to keep out rats, mice, and insects, which threatened the tribe's food supply. Adjacent reservoirs demonstrate the necessity for guarding the water supply. [See also **adobe, Anasazi, mesa, Zuñi.**] *Living in pueblos meant that Pima and Papago families became well acquainted.*

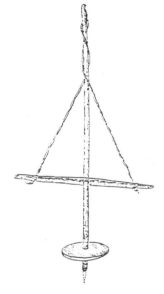

pump drill

puffball a dried fungus that **plains Indians** used as a disinfectant. *Many Coups's wife, Stag Woman, dried the infant's navel with the powder from a puffball.*

pulque [pool' kay] a fermented drink made from the juice of the maguey, a plant of the **agave** family. The **Aztec** revered pulque as a holy beverage, which was thought to have been invented by the god **Quetzalcoatl.** [See also **agave, Aztec, Quetzalcoatl.**] *The high priest poured pulque into a calabash and set it on the roadside altar.*

pump drill a fire-making device similar to a **bowdrill.** The pump drill consists of a wheel fastened over a vertical stick with thongs. By winding the **thong** around the stick, the user winds the wheel to the top, then presses down, causing the stick to twirl against a piece of wood below, creating sparks. [See also **bowdrill.**] *Indians of the southwestern desert ignited dry moss by manipulating a pump drill.*

pumpkin the orange, melon-sized fruit of a common annual vine related to the **squash** family. Indians dried rounds of pumpkin before a fire, then stored them for later use in cooked dishes or ate them on the trail like **jerky.** A special treat were dried pumpkin seeds, which were parched in hot ashes. Pumpkin seeds were thought to cleanse the body of parasites. [See also **healing, squash.**] *Pumpkins, like winter squash, are easily stored for winter use.*

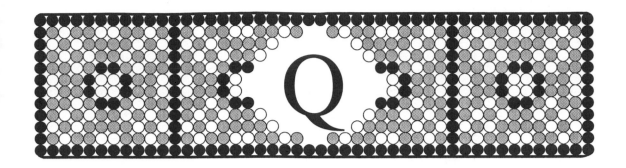

qalgi [kahl' gee] an **Eskimo** snow house or meeting house large enough to house an entire village for a whale feast. [See also **igloo, nallaqtaq, qarmat, qasgiq**.] *Uakuak helped his uncles build the qalgi for a week of games, feasting, dancing, and discussion of business and civic matters.*

qamutit [ka • muht' iht] or **komatik** [koh' muh • tihk] a wooden sled 20-30 feet long and 1 foot high that is pulled by dog teams. The body of the sled is made of crossbars covered by a tarp or skins. Bedrolls, food, gear, and weapons are packed on top, draped with a sled cover, then lashed down in a diamond pattern with **thongs**. The drivers can sit on top of the 4-foot load or run alongside to keep warm. Drivers must coat the runners with mud and glaze them with lukewarm water to keep the qamutit from settling into the ice. [See also **husky, toboggan**.] *Because he had no more fish or caribou scraps, Iksik loaded his qamutit with dog-food pellets.*

qarmat [kahr' mat] a temporary, rectangular two-family **Eskimo** dwelling constructed each fall on a rocky ledge or on the foundation of an abandoned rock house. Residents built up the sides with stone and dirt clods, placed wood or bone rafters across the top, then draped the crossbeams with sealskins. They insulated between the skins with layers of moss. [See also **igloo, nallaqtaq, qalgi, qasgiq**.] *The qarmat provided shelter until there was enough snow for building an igloo.*

qasgiq [kas' kik] or **kasghi** [kahs' gee] a rectangular men's sod house, a prominent social club and guest house common to the Bering Sea **Eskimo** and central to ceremonial life. While educating young men in ritual lore, spirit dances, mythology, and religious rites, male residents used the qasgiq as a place to make wood or ivory handicrafts, tools, and weapons; to smoke and plan

---

*ih = **s**it; oh = **s**oak; oo = **s**oup; ow = **s**ound; uh = **s**uch; y = **s**ide*

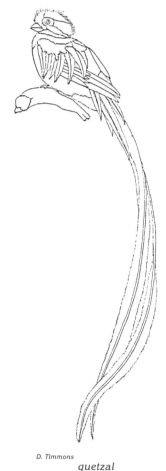

D. Timmons

quetzal

community events; and to take sweat baths. [See also **igloo, qarmat.**] *In his photos and notes, ethnologist Edward W. Nelson describes villages containing sod huts, qasgiqs, and storage sheds.*

qayaq   See **kayak.**

quahog [koh' hahg] or **poquauhaug** [poh • qwaw' hahg] a thick-shelled, heart-shaped clam, common to Long Island and New Jersey shores, which yields a purple lining valued for the making of beads for **wampum**; a cherry-stone clam. [See also **dentalia, wampum.**] *Munsi clamming parties dug baskets full of quahogs for roasting in deep pits.*

quamash   See **squamash.**

quetzal [keht • suhl']   a rare, long-tailed bird found in Central America with green and red iridescent plumes almost twice the length of its body. The plumes symbolize freedom. [See also **Quetzalcoatl.**] *Aztec nobles prized the tail feathers of the quetzal for ceremonial decorations.*

Quetzalcoatl [keht' sahl • koh • aht'l']   the feathered serpent that is the chief **Aztec** god and creator, who rescued humanity by shedding his blood. **Montezuma II** and his followers associated Quetzalcoatl with Hernán Cortés, a Spanish explorer who arrived on the god's birthday and whose white-sailed ships resembled the god. Quetzalcoatl, a peace deity dating to a legendary eleventh-century priest, represented the wind, life, arts and crafts, agriculture, and learning. [See also **Aztec, Montezuma II, Olmec, pulque, quetzal**.] *Carved statues of Quetzalcoatl show a vibrant bird-spirit with outspread wings and open beak.*

quilling [kwihl' ling]   a type of embroidery by which individual quills from porcupines or birds were softened, dyed, flattened between the teeth or with a bone tool, bent, then sewn with **sinew** or plant fibers onto a garment, pouch, quiver, **parfleche**, **moccasin**, or knife sheath in a decorative pattern, or lined up side by side to cover an entire area, such as a yoke or sleeve. Quillers also used beads and additional fibers, including nettle or thistle-down, buffalo wool, and moose hair. To make dyes for quilling, Indian women relied on walnut hulls for brown, butternut for black, bloodroot and sumac for red and orange, blueberries for gray and blue, and goldenrod and yellowroot for yellow. [See also **awl, beading, dye**.] *By the time she was a grandmother, Little Doe had worn down her teeth from quilling.*

quinine [kwy' nyn]   a drug derived from the bark of the cinchona tree, which native healers used to combat malaria. [See also **healing**.] *Native medicines, particularly ipecac, quinine, slippery elm, goldenseal, digitalis, willow bark, and coca, have been useful to modern pharmacologists.*

quinoa [keen • wah'] or **pigweed** or **quinua** [kee' noo • uh]   a common Peruvian plant from which Indians harvest a valuable cereal grain for making flour or eating whole in soup and hot porridge. Quinoa is also a valuable forage for livestock and can be mixed with water and fermented to make beer. *Modern scientists are investigating the nutritional properties of amaranth, quinoa, and other ancient grains.*

quipu [kee' poo]   a row of knotted strings attached to a cord. The quipu served as a numerical list or record. **Inca** chieftains recorded on quipus the size of a village, its harvests, the number of warriors, and local rainfall. [See also **Inca**.] *Xototl taught his apprentices how to record time on a quipu.*

quirt [kwuhrt]   a riding whip made of braided rawhide attached to a short grip made of wood, antler, turkey leg, or bone and ending with a wrist guard. [See also **lariat, riata**.] *Cheyo plaited the quirt from strips of rawhide.*

ceremonial quirt of the Arapaho

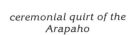

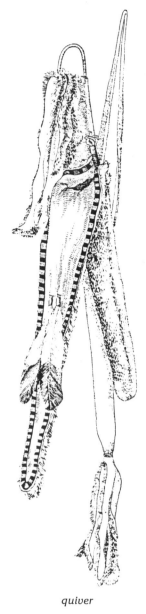

quiver

quiver a long, narrow case for carrying arrows. Quivers, which were made from **buckskin**, coyote pelts, bark, or fish skin, were slung over the shoulder or under the arm opposite the **bow** arm in such a way that a warrior could draw out an **arrow** and fit it into a **bowstring** with one smooth motion of the arm. [See also **arrow**.] *Yurok quivers were cut out of smooth sealskin.*

qulliq [kool' lihk] or **koodlik** or **kudlik** [kood' lihk] an oblong, saucer-shaped soapstone (**steatite**) lamp filled with burning seal or whale oil, used to heat and light an **igloo**. [See also **blubber, seal-oil lamp**.] *To keep the qulliq flame from burning too fast, Marina suspended dripping blubber overhead, which oozed oil slowly onto the moss wick.*

*a = s**a**ck; ah = s**o**b; aw = s**au**ce; ay = s**a**fe; ee = s**ee**k; eh = s**e**t*

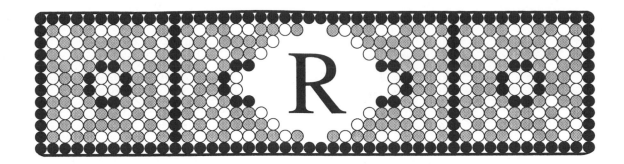

rabbit drive   a hunting method used by the **plains In-dians** by which they herded rabbits into a net 4 feet high and 100 feet long. Hunters clubbed the rabbits and ate the meat. Their pelts were made into clothing or cut into strips and woven into blankets. [See also **fire-surround**.] *The Paiute cut the soft pelts gained from the rabbit drive into strips, then wove the strips into coverlets for their infants.*

rabbit stick   See **throwing stick**.

Rain-in-the-Face (ca. 1835-September 14, 1905)   a doughty **Sioux** warrior from Standing Rock, North Da-kota, in the Black Hills, on the forks of the Cheyenne River. **Charles Eastman** interviewed Rain-in-the-Face at his log cabin and learned that the noted fighter was an ordinary brave, not of royal blood. Rain-in-the-Face was a strong friend of Hóhay, an **Assiniboin** leader, and of Wapáypay, who was hanged for raids on whites. Rain-in-the-Face also knew the great leaders of his day—**Red Cloud**, Spotted Tail, **Crazy Horse**, **Sitting Bull**, and Big Foot. In a sham fight with **Cheyenne** boys in about 1845, an adversary punched Rain-in-the-Face in the nose; the resulting shower of blood earned Rain-in-the-Face his name. He earned his reputation for toughness at a raid on Fort Totten, North Dakota, in 1866, but his most significant role lay in witnessing and reporting on the **Battle of Little Big Horn**. Rain-in-the-Face denied killing General Custer but claimed to have cut the heart from his brother Tom, who had put Rain-in-the-Face in prison. [See also **Battle of Little Big Horn, Tashenamani**.] *Before the Battle of Little Big Horn, Rain-in-the-Face declared, "I must be in the forefront of the charge. I must fight until I die."* (Pastron, Allen. *Great Indian Chiefs*. Santa Barbara, Calif.: Bellerophon, 1993, 44.)

ceremonial rattle

ramada [ruh • mah' duh]   a simple woven mat atop four corner poles, which Indian families used as a sunshade for cooking, weaving, eating, playing, and napping; a pavilion or arbor. The **Pima** construct ramadas of **mesquite** posts and cover them with cottonwood or willow crossbeams covered with arrowwood stems or **cattails** and finished with wheat straw and mud. [See also **chickee**.] *Maricopo workers liked to winnow grain and grind meal under their ramadas.*

rattle   a ceremonial shaker or clacker made from natural materials, such as pairs of hooves, a turtle shell, dew claws, or a **gourd** filled with stones or bone fragments, to imitate the sound of an animal. Rattles were an integral part of religious ceremonies and helped establish the common rhythm of the dance. *Pizi strapped rattles onto his ankles and danced the complex steps of the Buffalo Dance.*

Red Cloud or **Mahpiua Luta** [mah • pee' wah loot' tuh] (1822-December 10, 1909)   a vigorous chief of the Oglala **Sioux**. Born near North Platte, Nebraska, Red Cloud earned recognition in his youth for his bravery and military skills. He joined **Crazy Horse** in trying to keep white settlers from seizing Indian lands in Montana and Wyoming and from building the **Bozeman Trail**, an extension of the Oregon Trail that led to western goldfields. Following the **Sand Creek Massacre**, his stubborn offensive against U.S. forts ended in 1868 with a government retreat and abandonment of the Bozeman Trail project. Red Cloud is known as the only Indian to have won a war against the U.S. Army; he once visited President Ulysses S. Grant to petition for fair treatment. Because he gave up his leadership, he fell from power in 1881. He grew feeble and blind, and he died on the Pine Ridge **reservation**. [See also **Bozeman Trail, Sand Creek Massacre**.] *To a crowd in New York, Red Cloud declared, "The Great Spirit made us both."* (Pastron, Allen. *Great Indian Chiefs.* Santa Barbara, Calif.: Bellerophon, 1993, 46.)

Red Cloud

Red Jacket or **Sagoyewatha** [suh • goi' yuh • wah' thuh] (1758-January 20, 1830)   a **Seneca** leader from New York State. Red Jacket was famous for his charisma, tact, and political savvy. His grandson, General Eli Parker, served during the Civil War as secretary to General Ulysses S.

*a = s**a**ck; ah = s**o**b; aw = s**au**ce; ay = s**a**fe; ee = s**ee**k; eh = s**e**t*

Grant. Red Jacket, who earned his name while fighting in a British uniform, maintained his hold on European settlers by secretly selling them land. [See also **Handsome Lake, Seneca**.] *Near the end of his life, Red Jacket noted optimistically, "Think not I mourn for myself. I go to join the spirits of my fathers, where age cannot come."* (Pastron, Allen. *Great Indian Chiefs*. Santa Barbara, Calif.: Bellerophon, 1993, 22.)

red man the racial generalization of red man began in the early seventeenth century, when English and French settlers encountered the Beothuk of Newfoundland, who colored their skin with red ocher. [See also **Shawnawdithit**.] *Despite the designation as red men, Native Americans represent a variety of skin colors, body types, and features.*

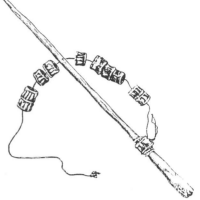

ring-and-pin game

Red Sleeves See **Mangas Coloradas**.

reservation a piece of land set aside for Indian use. [See also **Dawes Act, Trail of Tears**.] *The Oglala Sioux live on the second-largest reservation, called Pine Ridge Sioux Reservation.*

riata [ree • aht' uh] a rope with a loop in one end; a lasso. [See also **lariat, quirt**.] *For practice, cowboys like Bill Pickett flung their riatas at rapidly moving targets.*

ring-and-pin game a game calling for the skillful toss of a ring, which is caught on the end of a pin, bone, stick, or other long, pointed object. [See also **ajagak**.] *Indian children constructed their own ring-and-pin games.*

roach a tall ruff of hair that was brushed straight back from the forehead or into an upright row or ridge. Often, the wearer made the roach more dramatic by singeing or plucking the outer portions of the scalp and letting the **scalplock** grow long behind. Eastern Indians sometimes fashioned an artificial roach from the bristly hair of deer, porcupine, or moose; the roach was dyed a bright color and fastened in place by a V-shaped roach spreader, through which the wearer threaded the scalplock and fastened it in place with a carved pin. Among forest

D. Timmons

roach

Indians, only a brave was allowed to wear an artificial roach. [See also **lovelock, scalplock**.] *James Fenimore Cooper's fictional Uncas, the last of the Mohicans, wears his hair in a roach adorned with a single eagle plume dangling over his left shoulder.*

rock pit a type of underground oven created by lining a pit with rocks. Cooking in a rock pit required a hot fire, which was then extinguished and a clay dish containing food was nestled in the coals. Because the rocks stored heat, the food cooked slowly and evenly. *Lone Cloud lowered the dish of venison stew into the rock pit and covered the top to hold the heat until morning.*

Roman Nose or **Woquini** [woh • kee' nee] (?-September 17,1868) a notable and influential **Cheyenne** chief who was more than 6 feet tall and renowned for bravery. A member of the distinguished war chiefs who sought revenge for the **Sand Creek Massacre**, he was killed in battle against the U.S. Cavalry on the Arikaree River in Colorado. [See also **Black Kettle, Cheyenne, Sand Creek Massacre**.] *Roman Nose reported to General Winfield Scott Hancock that his soldiers resembled those who butchered the women and children at the Sand Creek Massacre.*

John Ross

Ross, John or **Coowescoowe** or **Kooweskoowe** [koo • wehs' koo • wee] (October 3, 1790-August 1, 1866) **Cherokee chief** who led one of General Andrew Jackson's regiments at the Battle of Horseshoe Bend. Born at Lookout Mountain, Tennessee, Ross was a council president at the age of 29 and a chief by age 38. When gold was discovered on Cherokee land, the state of Georgia ordered the Indians to move. Ross sought to have the order overturned based on a treaty signed by the United States and the Cherokee. He took his case to the U.S. Supreme Court but lost. In 1838, Ross led the Cherokee over the **Trail of Tears** to the Oklahoma territory. [See also **Cherokee, Five Civilized Tribes, Trail of Tears**.] *John Ross is remembered for a 47-year career as spokesman for his people.*

roundhouse or **ki** [kee] a **Pima** structure formed of thatch or wicker over cottonwood or **willow** supports, shaped into a mud-covered dome from 20-50 feet wide and 6 feet high. Shelving was supported by cactus thorns or saguaro ribs suspended from the ceiling. [See also **hogan, Pima**.] *The sturdy Pima roundhouse was large enough to accommodate a festival and strong enough to withstand strong gales.*

rubber   an elastic substance, made from the refined sap of a tree native to Central and South America, which is used to make balls, mallets, syringes, drums, bottles, bands, torches, and waterproofing for bark cloth. Christopher Columbus introduced rubber to Europe after seeing the **Taino** of Haiti playing with rubber balls. *The Mojo of Paraguay and the Omagua of Brazil made rubber balls by shaping the boiled sap over a clay center, then forming a hollow by crushing the clay and removing it through a slit.*

Sac See **Sauk**.

Sacagawea [sa' kuh • juh • wee' uh] or **Bird Girl** or **Sacajawea** (1786-April 9, 1884) a **Shoshone** interpreter and explorer who was born in the Rocky Mountains. In 1799 she was kidnapped by the **Hidatsa**, who took her to North Dakota. According to legend, Sacagawea became the slave of a Hidatsa chief, who staked her as the prize in a betting match. The chief lost, and Sacagawea became the property of Toussaint Charbonneau, a 40-year-old French trader who lived with the **Mandan**. In 1804, she was chosen to guide and interpret for the **Lewis and Clark expedition** from Fort Mandan, North Dakota, to the Pacific Ocean and back. Her pregnancy concluded with hard labor, which Captain Lewis relieved with a pinch of powdered snake rattle. Following the birth of her son, Pompey, or **Jean Baptiste Charbonneau**, on February 11, 1805, Sacagawea carried him in a **cradleboard** on her back as she translated native languages and helped trade for horses. According to expeditionary records, she reunited with her brother, Chief Cameahwait, in southwestern Montana on August 17 and arrived at the Pacific Ocean on November 7. Sacagawea's husband earned $500 for his part in the expedition; she received nothing. [See also **Jean Baptiste Charbonneau, Lewis and Clark expedition**.] *According to the journal kept by William Clark, the presence of Sacagawea on the expedition "confirmed . . . our friendly intentions, as no woman ever accompanies a war party. "* (Snyder, Gerald S. *In the Footsteps of Lewis and Clark.* Washington, D.C.: National Geographic Society, 1970, 162.)

sachem [satch' uhm] a **chief** or leader who served as spokesperson for an entire nation and negotiated serious questions at council meetings, such as the creation of alliances or the settlement of intertribal squabbles.

Generally, a sachem passed succession to his nephews, who had stronger claim to the sachem's position than did his sons. [See also **cacique, chief, miko, sagamore**.] *Without the sachem, no one could make a decision about where and how to move the tribe to winter grounds.*

Sacred Circle the symbolic unity, harmony, or wholeness found in nature, including the four seasons and the four directions. The shape of the **tepee**, the wheeling flight of the eagle, and many ceremonial decorations and hoops suggest the perfection of the Sacred Circle. Indian camps, based on the Sacred Circle, positioned each family dwelling in its allotted place with the door of the tepee facing the rising sun. [See also **tepee**.] *To protect him from harm, Little Bear inscribed the Sacred Circle on his buckskin vest.*

sagamore [sag' uh • mohr] a subordinate **chief**, who served the **Algonquin** as war captain and **sachem** or adviser. James Fenimore Cooper refers to his **Mahican** character Chingachgook as a wise and noble sagamore. [See also **chief, miko, sachem**.] *On the advice of his sagamores, Chief Spotted Elk divided the horses into small herds and hid them among the willows.*

sage a fragrant green herb used in cooking, religious rites, and healing. Indians used sage tea as a beverage and as a skin rub to combat fever. [See also **healing**.] *Before his vision quest, Lame Duck crushed dried sage leaves in the palm of his left hand and blew the dust toward the east.*

Sagoyewatha See **Red Jacket**.

Sak See **Sauk**.

salal [suh • lal'] a small, spiky shrub or heath plant, common to the north Pacific Coast, that produces many-seeded berries the size of grapes. The **Kwakiutl** use the deep purple salal berries in cooking. *Marta sprinkled fragrant salal berries over alder sprouts.*

Salish [say' lihsh] or **Shuswap** [shoo' swahp] a nation of tribes from the Pacific Northwest, including the Okanogan, Nisqually, Shuswap, Coeur d'Alene, Bella

Salish woman of the late nineteenth century wearing handwoven blanket clothing

Coola, and Tillamook. Salish Indians survive on hunting, fishing, and clam gathering and are noted for holding potlatches. [See also **potlatch**.] *A common name for Salish tribes is Flatheads.*

sallet [sal' liht]   the tender, green tips of young plants, such as pokeweed, amaranth, or **quinoa**, which are parboiled, drained, then cooked in fat. *In early spring, several Creeks took their baskets to the meadow and gathered enough sallet and wild onions for the whole tribe.*

Samoset [sam' oh • seht] (1590-1653)   a member of the Pemaquid Indians and a **Wabanaki Confederacy** leader from Bristol, Maine, who in 1621 introduced **Massasoit** to the Pilgrims of Plymouth Colony, led the settlers to the interpreter **Squanto**, and sold them 12,000 acres, the first parcel of land bought by European colonists. [See also **Massasoit, Squanto, Wabanaki Confederacy**.] *Samoset's command of English puzzles historians, who cannot account for the source of his knowledge.*

samp or **nasaump** [nah' sawmp]   a coarse **corn** mush, porridge, or hot cereal made from pounded grain that is boiled, whipped, and served with milk or butter and **maple syrup** or is made into samp cakes, which resemble flapjacks. [See also **maize, sofkee**.] *The Narragansett taught American colonists how to make samp.*

Sand Creek Massacre   a devastating betrayal of Chief Black Kettle's band of **Cheyenne** and **Arapaho** on November 29, 1864, on the Sand Creek River in Colorado. The massacre was a direct outgrowth of tensions resulting from the discovery of gold in Colorado. Although **Black Kettle**, White Hand, and Left Hand flew an American flag to indicate allegiance to the U.S. government, 500 cavalrymen led by Colonel John M. Chivington and Major Scott J. Anthony, slaughtered and mutilated about 150 of Black Kettle's people. A government inquiry stripped Chivington and his militia of their commendations for heroism. [See also **Battle of Little Big Horn, Cheyenne, Red Cloud, Roman Nose**.] *In a written report, George Bent, a Cheyenne eyewitness to the Sand Creek Massacre, declared bitterly, "I heard [Black Kettle] call to the people not to be afraid,* *that the soldiers would not hurt them; then the troops opened fire from two sides of the camp."* (Brown, Dee. *Bury My Heart at Wounded Knee.* New York: Henry Holt, 1970, 88.)

sand painting a **Navaho** and **Pueblo** craft that combines colorful sand, powdered minerals, rice, meal, petals, and pollen into pictures. Sand painting began as part of initiation ceremonies or healing rituals, which were conducted in a sacred **hogan**. The youth or patient often sat at the center of the painting while the masked **shaman** and his helpers made geometric or mythic figures on the ground, shook rattles, and chanted powerful incantations. Sometimes the painter placed grains of sand directly on a patient's body at the place where the disease caused pain or fever. Hosteen Klah, a Navaho, preserved traditional sand painting designs and colors in woven pieces. [See also **hatali, healing, making medicine, medicine, medicine man**.] *Crow Mocker, who limped too badly to be a warrior, gained fame for his sand painting.*

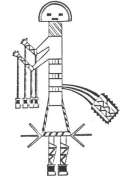

figure of a god from a Navaho sand painting

sarape See **zarape**.

sassafras [sas' uh • fras] a tall, aromatic laurel tree from which Indians obtained twigs, oil, roots, and bark to be boiled into tea, which was taken as a seasonal tonic or cough syrup. Pith and leaves were boiled as a thickener for stew. [See also **healing**.] *Maria preferred a bit of maple sap in her sassafras tea.*

Satanta [suh • tan' tuh] or **White Bear** (*ca.* 1820-October 11, 1878) a **Kiowa** chief during the 1870s, when the Kiowa were losing control of their lands. Satanta joined Kicking Bird, Lone Wolf, and other notable plains leaders in trying to negotiate one last time for their rights before settlers and soldiers took all their property and reduced them to beggars. After his arrest on February 25, 1875, Satanta was sent to a Texas prison, from which he leaped to his death. [See also **Kiowa**.] *In a speech concerning Native American rights, Satanta defiantly stated the Kiowa point of view: "I have heard that you intend to settle us on a reservation near the mountains. I don't want to settle. I love to roam over the prairies. There I feel free and happy, but when we settle down we grow pale and die. . . . "* (Brown, Dee. *Bury My Heart at Wounded Knee.* New York: Henry Holt, 1970, 88.)

Sauk [sawk] or **Sac** [sak] or **Sak**   an **Algonquin tribe** of hunters and farmers native to Michigan and kinsmen of the **Fox** and **Potawatomi**. The Sauk are famous for their wise and noble chief **Black Hawk** (1767-1838). Because of rivalry with the **Iroquois**, the Sauk settled in Wisconsin, then migrated to Iowa, Illinois, Kansas, and Oklahoma. *The Sauk originally referred to themselves as the people of the outlet.*

savanna [suh • van' uh] or **savannah**   a smooth meadow or grassland, sometimes caused by a **fire-surround**, an Indian hunting tactic by which the Indians burned several miles of land to drive animals to the center, where they were shot or clubbed. [See also **fire-surround**.] *Across the savanna, runners caught sight of a herd of buffalo.*

savvy [sav' ee]   a frontier slang term meaning to understand. Also, practical skill or know-how. *Wilma has the savvy to maintain and repair her own motorcycle.*

scalping   the removal of a portion of the skin and hair from the skull. Historians dispute the origin of scalping; some claim the practice was introduced to woodlands Indians by European bounty hunters. Scalping ranged in severity from the removal of a quarter-sized circle of skin to the removal of the entire scalp and ears. *In a speech to the British in Detroit in November 1781, Captain Pipe, a Delaware chief, reported that he had been supplied with hatchets by his white superiors and had scalped victims, even though the practice was repulsive to him.*

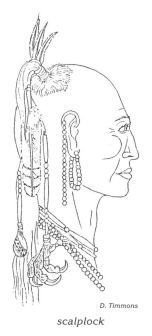

D. Timmons

scalplock

scalplock   a small circle of braided and decorated hair on the crown of the head. The feathers, down, shells, beads, and ceremonial ornaments on a scalplock represented the soul. When an enemy removed a scalplock, he subdued the spirit of his opponent but did not necessarily kill him. A brave who remained alive after being scalped was treated like the walking dead. [See also **lovelock, medicine bundle, roach**.] *To escape the bother of overhead tangles and burs, plains Indians usually shaved the sides of their heads, then plaited a small scalplock at the top.*

*a = s**a**ck; ah = s**o**b; aw = s**au**ce; ay = s**a**fe; ee = s**ee**k; eh = s**e**t*

Schoolcraft, Henry Rowe (March 28, 1793-December 10, 1864) an American adventurer-sociologist who observed Native American life. A native of Watervliet, New York, Schoolcraft served as geologist and topologist on an expedition to the Great Lakes in 1819. Following three years of scholarly work among tribes in Missouri and around the Great Lakes, he took the post of Indian agent to the **Ojibwa** at Mackinac, Michigan, in 1822. He married an Indian woman and negotiated treaties. He then produced a scholarly encyclopedia, *Historical and Statistical Information Respecting the Indian Tribes of the United States*, a project of the U.S. Congress illustrated by Seth Eastman. *The work of Henry Schoolcraft served as basis for Longfellow's* The Song of Hiawatha.

seal oil lamp a standard **Eskimo** lamp made with an oval soapstone (**steatite**) base varying from 12-40 inches long and fitted with wicks made of grass or moss, which could be adjusted to raise or lower the flame for lighting and cooking. The owners lit seal oil lamps by striking pyrite with flint or iron. To make the most of rising heat, they placed soapstone cooking vessels on a rectangular frame over the lamp; above that they hung a rack of drying clothes. [See also **blubber, qulliq**.] *Uakuak anchored the stewpot over the seal oil lamp, then tossed in enough blubber to feed several guests.*

Seattle or **Sealt** [sihlt] or **Sialth** [sihlth] or **Noah** (1780?-June 7, 1866) a handsome, curly-haired Suquamish **chief** and orator. Seattle was the son of Chief Schweabe. He witnessed the arrival of the British ship *Discovery* at Puget Sound in 1792. Seattle converted to Christianity and used his tribe's ample stock of fish and venison to help feed starving European settlers. By 1854, as leader of six Duwamish and Suquamish tribes, Seattle realized that European settlers were outnumbering natives. In 1855, following an eloquent speech to President Franklin Pierce's agent, Seattle agreed that area tribes would settle on Washington **reservations**. *Seattle influenced attitudes toward nature by declaring that the Earth was sacred to his people and that people and the Earth are interrelated.*

Seminole [sehm' uh • nohl]   a Florida **tribe** of swamp-dwelling hunters and gatherers native to Georgia, which joined with the Yuchi and Oconee to form a single tribe. The Seminole built burial **mounds** to honor their dead. Named for the root word for wild or runaway, Seminoles preferred to be called peninsula people. They were victimized by Spanish settlers, then by Andrew Jackson's troops, who forced them south following the First Seminole War of 1817. The Second Seminole War, which **Osceola** led beginning in 1835, lasted seven years and resulted in more resettlement. In 1841, Chief Coacooche was captured and imprisoned at Fort Brooke in Tampa, Florida. Most Seminoles then moved to Oklahoma **reservations**. The handful that remained in Florida settled around Lake Okeechobee, where today they excel in arts and crafts. [See also **Milly Hoya Francis, Green Corn Dance, Muskhogean, Osceola**.] *The Seminole nation takes pride in the accomplishments of numerous strong leaders: Wild Cat, Neamathla, Francis, Boleck, Halek, Coacooche, and Osceola.*

Seneca [sihn' uh • kuh]   a **tribe** of farmers, hunters, and traders native to New York State. In the **Algonquin** language they are called Osininka, meaning "people of the stone." Their rivals called them a "Nation of Snakes"; the term *snake oil* derived from the Senecas' use of natural oil from a Pennsylvania river for war paint and pitch to waterproof their canoes. They were also referred to as "people of the great hill" and, because of their position on the end at **Iroquois League** meetings, "keepers of the western door." Seneca chiefs, notably **Cornplanter**, **Red Jacket**, and **Handsome Lake**, were powerful forces among the Iroquois League. The ritual duty of the Seneca at league sessions was to keep out crawling creatures, which were bad omens, and to take charge of strangers who carried messages. Involved in warfare with European settlers, the Seneca suffered defeat in 1777 when Chief Cornstalk and his sons were captured and killed. On November 11, 1794, a treaty guaranteed the Seneca permanent land in the Allegheny Mountains. By the middle of the nineteenth century, the Seneca were forced to merge with the **Cherokee**. In 1873, Donehogawa, or Ely S. Parker, was named first native commissioner of Indian affairs. [See also **Cornplanter, Handsome Lake, Iroquois**

*a = s**a**ck; ah = s**o**b; aw = s**au**ce; ay = s**a**fe; ee = s**ee**k; eh = s**e**t*

League, Red Jacket.] *The words of George Heron in 1961 before a House Subcommittee on Indian Affairs express the modern Seneca's dual loyalties to country and tribe.*

Sequoyah [suh • kwoi' yuh] (1760-1843)   a lame **Cherokee** linguist and diplomat. Sequoyah, the son of a Cherokee woman and a white trader named George Guess, was born in Tuskegee on the Tennessee River. A silversmith and painter by trade, in 1821 he invented a syllabary, which was a simplified phonetic method of reading and writing the Cherokee language. Although early in his life he was suspected of witchcraft for inventing letters that talked, he gained prestige in midlife for fighting with Andrew Jackson's forces and in old age often served as official ambassador for his tribe. A statue in the U.S. Capitol in Washington, D.C., honors his memory. [See also **Cherokee**.] *Sequoyah, who was at first ridiculed, soon brought innovations to his people, including an intertribal mail system.*

Sequoyah

serviceberry or **juneberry** or **shadbush**   the sweet, juicy reddish purple fruit of a shrub common to the southern Appalachians and related to the rose. Indians used the serviceberry, dried or fresh, as a flavoring for various dishes such as **pemmican**. Its wood served as construction material. *New York colonists learned from their Mahican neighbors to value a good stand of serviceberries.*

shadbush   See **serviceberry**.

shaman [shah' muhn]   a Siberian term for magical healer. In some tribes, the shaman is a man of great power, influence, and wealth; in others, he earns his living like other tribe members. In the **Inuit** culture, a shaman must be a wise leader, a prophet endowed with magical powers to cure illness with herbs and incantations, conduct the dead to their final rest, or communicate with spirits. An Inuit shaman is expected to perform magic feats, such as flying to the moon, changing into a polar bear, battling evil spirits, or sawing off a limb, then replacing it. A shaman of the **plains Indians** falls into a trance, giving the impression of being seized by a spirit, which often rattles furniture or creates a breeze to demonstrate its presence. Much of the stock of the shaman's

Tlingit shaman with a fin symbolizing the killer whale

trade is obvious trickery, such as ventriloquism or sleight of hand. In some primitive tribes, a shaman who fails too frequently is put to death. [See also **berdache, Deganawida, hatali, healing, medicine, medicine man, Popé, yuwipi.**] *A Salinan shaman, confronted by skeptical Catholic priests at a San Antonio mission, made rain, then had to make it stop because the priests feared a flood.*

Shawnawdithit [shaw' naw • dee' tiht] or **Nancy April** or **Shawanahdit** [shah • wah' nuh • diht] or **Shananditti** [shah • nahn • diht' tee] (?-1829)   the last survivor of the Beothuk, a migratory **tribe** of hunters and whalers who were living in Newfoundland at the time of John Cabot's exploration in 1497. Shawnawdithit, a native of St. John's, Newfoundland, was the last source of information about Beothuk religion and culture, which included painting the skin red with ocher powder. [See also **red man.**] *Captured in 1823, Shawnawdithit was the last Native American to be positively identified as a Beothuk.*

Shawnee [shaw • nee'] or **Shawanee** or **Shawanos** [sha' wuh • nohs]   a nomadic **Algonquin tribe** of farmers and hunters native to the Ohio Valley and famous as guides, hunters, and woodsmen. From 1692 to 1694, Shawnee scouts led Dutchman Cornelissen Arnout Viuele over the Susquehanna, Ohio, and Wabash rivers. Forced by the **Iroquois** from their ancestral home in the seventeenth century, the Shawnee resettled in Kentucky and Tennesse, where they tended fields of corn, melons, and beans. They continued their migration to Pennsylvania, but met serious opposition in 1822 from General William Henry Harrison at the Battle of Tippecanoe. Pushed farther south and west, they drifted into Missouri, Kansas, Texas, and Oklahoma, where they allied with the **Cherokee**. The most famous Shawnee leaders were the twin brothers **Tenkswatawa** and **Tecumseh**, who encouraged all tribes to join in a single union. [See also **Cherokee, Tecumseh, Tenkswatawa.**] *A historic letter, sent from friendly Shawnee to President Thomas Jefferson in 1809 and signed by Old Snake, Wolf, Black Hoof, Young Snake, Beaver, and Chief Wahappi, thanks the U.S. government for sending Kirk, a useful Quaker who taught the natives European farming methods.*

*a = s**a**ck; ah = s**o**b; aw = s**au**ce; ay = s**a**fe; ee = s**ee**k; eh = s**e**t*

shield   a small piece of protective armor made from a circle or oval of rawhide from the neck of a buffalo, which was hardened over a slow flame or in a fire pit. The hardened hide was soaked with glue and attached to a **willow** frame. The shield was worn on a neck thong so that it could be carried in front of the left arm during battle or slung over the left shoulder when not in use. Blessed with medicine prayers, the shield was decorated with totemic figures, **quilling**, hair, or feathers. *Old Bear's shield was decorated to commemorate skirmishes with white miners and settlers.*

rawhide shield cover of the Arapaho. The symbol in the center represents the morning star, the circles represent the sun, and the black dots represent bullets the shield will stop.

shinny or **shinty** or **shinney**   a **plains Indians** game for men or women in which a small ball is lifted from a pit with curved sticks and kicked through a goal. *Shinny, which resembles ice or field hockey, is a game common to most American tribes.*

Shooting Star   See **Tecumseh**.

Shoshone [shuh • shohn' ee] or **Shoshoni**   a populous **tribe** of hunter-gatherers and horse breeders native to the western United States and also known as the Snake, Digger, Grass Lodge Indians, or valley people. They lived in cone-shaped **wickiups** and subsisted on meager foods, including wild plants, rabbits, and other small animals. Later, under the influence of the **Comanche**, they adopted **tepee** living and other **plains Indians** characteristics. The Shoshone, whose ancestors date to 8,000 B.C., supplied Lewis and Clark with horses during their westward expedition. During the mid-nineteenth century, when trading activity increased along the Old Spanish Trail through the Great Basin and on the banks of the Colorado River, the Shoshone were frequently enslaved and sold in California. [See also **Lewis and Clark expedition, Sacagawea, Washakie**.] *In the Shoshone legend, "Old Man Coyote and Buffalo Power," teller Arthur Big Turnip advises that you shouldn't begin what you can't finish.*

Shuswap   See **Salish**.

Sialth   See **Seattle**.

Siboney   See **Ciboney**.

---

ih = sit; oh = soak; oo = soup; ow = sound; uh = such; y = side   **205**

sign language a fluid set of two-handed signals or gestures known to most plains tribes. Sign language was used for trade and intertribal councils and later for communication with white traders, missionaries, and soldiers. To keep their presence a secret, Indians used hand signals as a means of silent communication. The signs, which were greatly refined during the eighteenth and nineteenth centuries, were limited to concepts of weather, objects, plants, animals, size, amount, speed, and human responses and actions, such as walk, sad, pleased, and sleep. *Sign language proved useful to Native Americans traveling far from home and to outsiders, including European priests, peddlers, ferry pilots, Pony Express riders, stage drivers, and military scouts.*

sinew [sin' yoo] the tendon taken from the back of a buffalo, horse, elk, or deer and used as cord or sewing thread for seaming garments, fastening arrowheads to shafts, strengthening **bows**, lashing on **leggings**, or tying loads to **travois** or pack horses. Seamstresses chewed the sinew to soften it, then rolled it to make rope. [See also **bow, spear**.] *Paiute leggings were often laced with lengths of sinew, which neither stretched nor stiffened from frequent wetting and drying.*

Sioux warrior drawn by George Catlin

Sioux [soo] a populous **tribe** of horse breeders and buffalo hunters native to the central United States. The western Sioux were divided into seven subgroups: the Oglala, Brulé, Miniconjou, Two Kettle, Hunkpapa, Sans Arc, and Blackfoot, who met annually at a grand council to settle problems and exchange news. Because of their tight confederation, the Sioux referred to themselves as Ocheti Shakowin or the seven council fires. As plains tribes weakened from the extinction of the buffalo, resulting hunger, and wars with white settlers, some Sioux turned to the hopeful message of **Wovoka**, the Paiute prophet. Crushed by the massacre at **Wounded Knee**, Sioux strength was further weakened by resettlement on **reservations** spread over the Canadian provinces, Minnesota, Nebraska, North Dakota, and South Dakota. Notable Sioux women include writer Ella Deloria and Evelyn Yellowrobe, a professor of English speech at Vassar College. [See also **Dakota, Charles Alexander Eastman, Ben Kindle, Osage, Paiute, Tashenamani**.] *According to Mari*

Sandoz's book These Were the Sioux *(Lincoln: University of Nebraska Press, 1985), a young girl was taught that the people's honor lies in its women.*

sipapu [sih • pah' poo] a hole filled with clean sand in the bottom of a **kiva**. Through the sipapu **kachinas**, or spirits, enter this world and souls return to the underworld. Care of the sipapu, which was a tribal honor given to male members, involved sifting and spreading fresh sand. The Arizona sinkhole on Beaver Creek is known as Montezuma's Well, which local people claim was the birthing center for native peoples. [See also **kachina, kiva, mudhead, Pueblo**.] *Initiates to the kiva regarded the sipapu with great reverence.*

Sitting Bull or **Tatanka Iyotake** [tuh • tan' kuh ee • yoh • tah' kay] (1831-1890) a distinguished **chief**, prophet, and **medicine man** of the Hunkpapa **Sioux** from Many Caches, South Dakota. A mystic, Sitting Bull is famous for walking barefoot in the dew to feel the heartbeat of Mother Earth. He earned military honors at the age of 14 and joined the Strong Hearts, an honorary warrior society. He was deeply moved by acts of courage and adopted an **Assiniboin** youth, Jumping Bull, who in 1857 tried to fight the Sioux with a child-sized bow. Sitting Bull called white men thieves and liars at a public ceremony honoring the transcontinental railroad.

Sitting Bull

Sitting Bull helped organize the offensive against General George Custer, escaped to Canada, then accepted an offer of amnesty in 1881. Following two years in prison, he maintained his dignity while performing in Buffalo Bill Cody's Wild West Show. As a member of the troupe, he toured Europe during the last two years of his life. He was shot to death on the Standing Rock **Reservation** in South Dakota by native police for his part in the **Ghost Dance** religion. His remains, which were revered by his followers, were taken to Fort Yates, North Dakota, then moved in 1953 to Mobridge, South Dakota. [See also **Battle of Little Big Horn, Chief Joseph, Gall, Wounded Knee**.] *Near the end of his life, Sitting Bull sang his famous dirge, "A warrior I have been. Now it is all over. A hard time I have."* (Brown, Dee. *Bury My Heart at Wounded Knee.* New York: Henry Holt, 1970, 313.)

---

siwash fruit cake [see' wash]   an Alaskan **Eskimo** delicacy made from a thick gel scraped from the inner core of the hemlock tree. The gel is dried in cakes, then mixed with water, oil, and berries, formed into a flat disk, and baked. *Mr. Uhl requested a special platter of siwash fruit cakes and baleen for the reception.*

Skidoo® [skih • doo']   the brand name of a snowmobile, which is also used as a generic term for all such vehicles. In some respects, the Skidoo has replaced Inuit dependence on sleds and huskies, but for pleasure jaunts, nothing beats a dog team, which is quieter and requires no gasoline or mechanical repairs. [See also **husky, toboggan**.] *The Inuits' use of Skidoos, house trailers, and motorboats has changed the perception outsiders have of the native lifestyle.*

skin-drag   a long trailer of hide that an Eskimo traveler attaches to the shoulders to carry personal belongings, food, and other necessities for a long trek over frozen country. The skin-drag leaves the hands free for carrying children or other burdens or allows the traveler to pull chilled hands inside the **parka** or **amouti** for warmth. *Naka used a bone needle to fasten shoulder straps to her skin-drag.*

slash and burn   a primitive agricultural method by which farmers burn trees, weeds, and brush, then plant crops in the ashy remains, which serve as fertilizer and soil sterilizer. When the land is sapped of nutrients after two or three years of cultivation, the farmers move on to new areas, leaving the old site to grow wild for five to seven years. [See also **milpa**.] *To increase cultivated lands and pastures, Amazon Indians destroy great stretches of the rain forest by the slash-and-burn method.*

Slocum, Frances   See **Maconaqua**.

smoke signals   a method of sending silent coded messages, which **plains Indians** used while stalking buffalo or communicating with distant war parties. Smoke was controlled by adding green sticks, grass, or buffalo chips to a slow wood fire. The flame was covered with a dampened hide or blanket, then released to send puffs of smoke into the air. [See also **buffalo chips**.] *Smoke signals enabled a circle of scouts or hunters to remain in wordless communication as they drew close to a herd of buffalo or searched for wild horses.*

smoking a method of preserving food, particularly fish or venison, by layering slabs over a wooden or cane rack and lighting a slow fire of fragrant hardwood sticks, herbs, and grasses underneath. Other methods of smoking included suspending chunks of meat, fish, or shellfish on sticks or stringing them on tough **bear grass** before hanging over the fire. This method also killed parasites in the meat and destroyed flying insects. [See also **jerky**.] *Elderly Oto villagers helped out each fall by smoking the herring and shad the children brought from the weir.*

Snake Dance a late August ceremony of the **Pueblo** in which dancers hold live snakes in their mouths and encircle the village four times as a means of bringing rain. Dressed in kilts and clutching snake-stick wands that are decorated with symbolic zigzags, participants flutter a snake whip or eagle feather duster; the action terrifies the snakes, which fear the eagle as a natural predator. At the conclusion of the dance, the snakes, which represent ancestral spirits, are dusted with cornmeal, then released at the four corners of the village so that they can carry the tribe's prayers to the rain gods. [See also **Hopi, maize**.] *Zuñi priests take charge of collecting snakes and housing them in the kiva until they can be used at the annual Snake Dance.*

Snake Woman See **Nampeyo**

snare a **lariat** or noose baited and attached to a sapling so that a bird or animal taking the bait will dislodge the sapling and become entangled in the loop. Use of snares in hunting requires few tools and no weapons or traps and makes less noise than guns. Women and children often set snares so that they could augment the village's supply of meat from bigger animals. *Listening attentively, Kit Fox learned how to conceal a snare in the edge of the brush.*

snare

snowknife a curved tool of ivory or horn the shape of a butcher knife with a foot-long blade and a handle long enough to be gripped by both hands. The **Eskimo** use the snowknife for chopping blocks of snow into a temporary shelter against a blizzard. [See also **ice chisel**.] *Akomalik says that it is better for a lost hunter to cut protective blocks of snow with a snowknife than to waste energy wandering about in dangerous weather.*

snow-probe an **Eskimo** tool of bone or ivory used to test the quality of snow to determine if it will make a strong snow house. [See also **igloo**.] *Inuit hunters determine the depth of layers of snow and ice by forcing their snow-probes through the crust.*

snowshoe a netted or woven rawhide platform attached inside a circle or oval of wood resembling a tennis racket. The snowshoe fastened to a **moccasin** to enable a tracker or traveler to move more easily on soft snow. The Maidu of northern California made a simple circular snowshoe from a wooden hoop strung with grapevines. The **Ojibwa** celebrated the coming of winter with a snowshoe dance. [See also **babiche**.] *Weasel Tail's wife loaned their guest a pair of snowshoes, which he wore during the buffalo hunt.*

Maidu snowshoe

snowsnake a game in which a flexible rod, stick, bone, or other vertical gaming piece 5-9 feet long and tipped with lead is slid across a level track or trough of ice or ground and over barriers. Players grasp the snowsnake by a thickened end piece, then hurl it lengthwise at a goal. The snake, which was seasoned with oil or beeswax, was turned up on end to mark where it stopped. *Games of snowsnake required a sharp eye and deft turn of the wrist.*

soapstone See **steatite**.

sobia [soh' bya] a quartz crystal kept in a pouch for use in magic. *The Mandan shaman considers a sobia essential to his healing ritual.*

sofkee [sahf' kee] or **sofkey** or **sofki** a staple dish of sour mush composed of coarsely pounded **corn**, which was soaked in ash water, drained, mixed with marrow and ground nuts, then simmered in an open kettle for daily meals and snacks. Each diner dipped into the community pot with a sofkee spoon, which was usually whittled from

*a = s**a**ck; ah = s**o**b; aw = s**au**ce; ay = s**a**fe; ee = s**ee**k; eh = s**e**t*

wood or antler. [See also **chemuck, coontie, samp**.] *Semi-nole and Creek families often served steaming bowls of sofkee and topped them with corn dumplings.*

spear a Native American hunting or military weapon, like a dart or **arrow**, which was fitted together from the materials at hand. The shaft was usually made of hard-wood or reed, which was straightened over fire and some-times carved, painted, and aged before it was fitted with a point. Sharpened bone, quartz, or flaked flint points, indented on the side, were laced into the end of the haft. Lacings were usually **babiche**, vine, or **sinew** or tendon. Often displayed as ceremonial staffs, as demonstrated by **Huron** tribes, spears were frequently decorated with a collar of soft down, underfeathers, or fur and pendant tail feathers, which bore symbolic meaning, such as the rank of the spear carrier. [See also **arrow, atlatl, babiche, flaking, sinew**.] *For desert and forest tribes, hunting with a spear was less cumbersome than carrying quiver, arrows, and bow.*

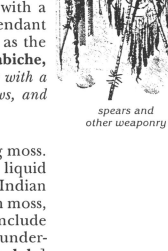

spears and other weaponry

sphagnum [sfag' nuhm] a common peat or bog moss. Indians used the spongy moss to pack or apply liquid medicines to wounds or to absorb body fluids. Indian mothers packed their cradleboards with sphagnum moss, a forerunner of the disposable diaper. Other uses include warm linings for mittens and **moccasins** and an under-layer for bedding or **ground cloths**. [See also **pauluk**.] *Lucy stripped open the mattress, then removed the old matted sphagnum, shook it out, and draped it over willow limbs in the sun.*

spirit dog See **horse**.

spirit water whiskey. The introduction of distilled al-coholic beverages from Europe contributed to Indian dependence on white society, making the Indians easier to exploit. Today, alcohol abuse is a major problem among Native Americans, who suffer twice the rate of alcoholism as other populations. [See also **hooch**.] *Indian agents tricked members of the Fox embassy by serving them spirit water before pressuring them to sign away their land rights.*

---

*ih = s**i**t; oh = s**oa**k; oo = s**ou**p; ow = s**ou**nd; uh = s**u**ch; y = s**i**de*

squamash [skwah' mash] or **quamash**   the sweet, edible bulb of the camas lily, which was roasted as a delicacy. It is sometimes referred to as the Indian potato. [See also **camas**.] *Sacagawea eased the explorers' hunger by locating squamash, which she roasted beneath hot coals.*

Squanto [skwahn' toh] or **Tisquantum** [tih • skwahn' tuhm] (1580-1622)   a Pemaquid translator, guide, and diplomat from Pawtuxet, Massachusetts, who was enslaved by Captain Thomas Hunt in 1614 and taken to Spain for three years. In 1620 Squanto welcomed English settlers to Plymouth, Massachusetts, and taught them to fish and to grow and preserve native foods, particularly **corn** and **squash**. He also helped negotiate a peace treaty with **Massasoit** and the **Wampanoag** tribe. Squanto died in Cheatham, Massachusetts, of a contagious disease, probably scarlet fever or smallpox, which he caught from members of Governor Bradford's expedition. [See also **Hobomak, Massasoit, Samoset**.] *Most school Thanksgiving pageants feature Squanto as a helper and friend to the Pilgrims.*

squash or **askootasquash** [as • koo' tuh • skwash] or **marrow**   the **Narragansett** word for a green or yellow vegetable that grows on a vine and is a staple in Indian cooking. Originating in Peru and Chile and spread through the Western Hemisphere, squash was usually planted among supportive hills of corn. There are a number of varieties of squash, including butternut, acorn, and summer squash. It can be dried, baked whole, stewed, boiled, fried, or pureed. The flowers can be cooked in soup, and the seeds toasted for snacks. [See also **maize**.] *A favorite Aztec recipe for squash uses the blossoms, which are stuffed with ground meat and spices then tied with a string and cooked over hot coals.*

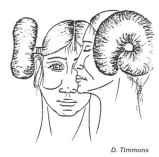

D. Timmons

squash blossom

squash blossom   an elaborate **Hopi** hairdo in which hair was parted in the middle, then shaped around a U-shaped wood frame to form a circular whorl over each ear. The creation of the squash blossom hairdo symbolized that a young woman was eligible for marriage. *Sadie sat still while her mother shaped the squash blossom, tucking the ends firmly into place.*

a = sack; ah = sob; aw = sauce; ay = safe; ee = seek; eh = set

squaw the **Narragansett** word for woman or wife. White settlers turned the word into an insulting reference to any Indian female and used the term *squaw man* to ridicule a white man married to an Indian. *Squaw and papoose are common words in Hollywood versions of Indian family structure.*

squaw candy an **Eskimo** or **Aleut** treat made from thin strips of salmon dried in the sun until chewy. [See also **jerky**.] *Mike, an Iliamna Eskimo, always packed jerky and squaw candy in his backpack.*

steatite [stee' uh • tyt] or **soapstone** or **talc** a soft, brown or gray mineral suitable for carving into **arrow straighteners**, utensils, pans, or pipe bowls and stems. Indians of Catalina Island quarried steatite to be carved into cooking and serving dishes because the material could withstand high temperatures. Because of its flexibility, steatite was also a valuable trade item. [See also **catlinite**.] *Steatite bowls found near Santa Barbara, California, are carved with diamond patterns.*

stele [stee' leh] an upright stone slab, shaft, or free-standing column carved with numbers, letters, dates, symbols, and hieroglyphs. Stelae (the plural form of stele) often pictured historical events, portraits, or gifts. *A Mayan stele was a common sight near temples and along causeways.*

stickball a traditional **Seminole** game played around a tall pole or tree, which participants hit with a small deerhide ball. Male players used a spoon-shaped wooden racket; women played with their hands. [See also **lacrosse**.] *Village games of stickball drew cheers from the crowd in the courtyard.*

stomp dance a ritual spring dance preceding the **Green Corn Dance** among **Creek** and **Seminole** tribes. A serious nighttime ritual, the stomp dance required people to purify themselves by bathing and drinking cleansing potions. The performance of the dance took place on the square ground, a central courtyard or **chungke** court. Processions, shakers and **rattles**, songs, and a central fire

---

were important aspects of the ceremonial dance. [See also **black drink, Green Corn Dance**.] *Lois Cabe's family dressed with care for the annual stomp dance.*

stone boiling a method of cooking by dropping heated stones into a **mocuck**, animal stomach, waterproof basket, or skin bag filled with liquid. Cooks used long-handled tongs to grasp the hot stones. Metal pots and pans were valuable trade goods because they greatly reduced the cook's work and broadened the variety of foods and styles of cooking. [See also **mocuck, tripe**.] *Buffalo Woman cooked the moose tongue by stone boiling, then peeled the meat and served it on carved wooden platters.*

D. Timmons

stone boiling

Strong Heart Society See **dog soldier**.

subarctic Indians nomadic natives of northwestern Canada who migrated across the Bering Strait around 10,000 B.C. These **tribes** of the **Athapascan** language group include the Dogrib, Ingalik, Koyukon, Kutchin, and Slave Indians, who developed into forest tribes dependant on the **caribou** for food and skins. Like their neighbors, the **Eskimo**, subarctic tribes built their sod houses partially underground. The subarctic culture declined from the influence of European settlers and the scarcity of game. [See also **Beringia**.] *Subarctic Indians often competed with the Eskimo and the Chipewyan for control of local game, the hides of which they sold to European traders.*

succotash [suhk' uh • tash] a native vegetable dish made with a bit of stewed beef, game birds, seafood, or pork fat and available vegetables, such as pumpkin, squash, potatoes, corn, or green beans, and thickened with sunflower seeds. *Like chocolate, hominy, avocado, squash, potato, and tomato, succotash is one of many common Native American food terms.*

sunburst a characteristic pattern or decoration made of concentric circles of spikes or points representing the sun's rays. The sunburst symbol suggests the generosity of the **Great Spirit**, who makes the Earth green by flooding it with sunlight. *Kino's jacket sported a traditional embroidered sunburst pattern across the yoke.*

a = s**a**ck; *ah* = s**o**b; *aw* = s**au**ce; *ay* = s**a**fe; *ee* = s**ee**k; *eh* = s**e**t

Sun Dance a significant summer ritual of **plains Indians** that in early times represented creation. The Sun Dance emerged from a need of nomadic tribes to establish a central religious experience. The annual gathering, which lasted for three or four days, took place in a circular court centered by a cottonwood pole, and distributed power to members of the tribe through the sacrifice of the buffalo, the animal symbol of the sun. Dancers, painted bright colors and dusted with crumbled **sage**, often blew whistles or tortured themselves by cutting slits in their flesh and inserting skewers fastened to ropes, which they tied to buffalo skulls or to a ceremonial cottonwood pole in the center of the camp. As they danced to the drumbeat, they might pull hunks of flesh from their bodies as sacrifices to the **Great Spirit**.

For a time, the government forbade the Sun Dance as a harmful ritual. After the ban was lifted, Indians resumed the practice. The **Cheyenne** version involves a complex arrangement of dance steps, offerings, songs, fasting, smoking of sacred **tobacco**, and incantations or prayers. The sacrifice of the sun dancers is considered beneficial to the entire tribe. [See also **kado, Kiowa, Tai-me**.] *According to Dick Washakie, a Shoshone chief, the Sun Dance is a traditional worship form during which participants pray for the sick.*

sweat lodge or **inipi** [ih • nee' pee] a place for prayer, chanting, and ritual purification to make tribe members more acceptable to the **Great Spirit**. The sweat lodge, dug into the side of a hill or built as a domed framework of branches covered with skins, featured a hole in the earth where heated stones were sprinkled with water to produce a cleansing steam. Following a period of fasting and visions, individuals first drank a therapeutic **black drink**, an emetic made from holly or yaupon, followed by soothing tea, then returned to the sweat lodge to reveal the messages they received from the gods. [See also **making medicine, medicine man, Orenda, vision quest**.] *The shaman offered bowls of smoldering sweet grass for worshippers to inhale while reclining in the sweat lodge.*

Sweet Medicine chief a general term applied to the head of the **Cheyenne** council. Named for a legendary **Cheyenne** prophet who established order among bickering tribes by setting up an annual Council of Forty-Four, the Sweet Medicine chief's code of honor, courtesy, self-restraint, and good grooming set the tone for behavior for other leaders. [See also **Cheyenne, league.**] *In his last prophecy, the Sweet Medicine chief predicted that the buffalo would die out and that white settlers would change the lifestyle of the Cheyenne.*

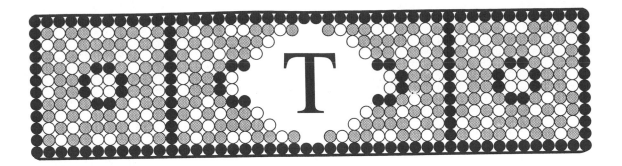

taboo or **tabu** the sociological term for a law or rule forbidding an act for moral or religious reasons, such as marriage to a person of a particular **clan** or **moiety**. Among the **Eskimo**, it was taboo for a newborn child to touch the snow platform of the **igloo** in which it was born. **Plains Indians** often segregated women in separate lodges during their menstrual cycles and denied their return until they had undergone ritual bathing. The Naskapi required girls to wear skin veils and gloves during their menstrual periods. In other tribes, certain foods were forbidden, particularly for pregnant women and **medicine men**, warriors before a battle, or adolescents not yet accepted into tribal adulthood. The **Cheyenne** forbade women, **half-breeds**, and whites from entering the **lodge** where the Sacred Arrows were kept. The Hupa reserved spoons for men; women ate with mussel shells. *Rainmaker obeyed the taboo that forbade him to allow his medicine bundle to touch the ground.*

Tai-me [ty • may'] a **Kiowa** god represented by the **Sun Dance** doll. The 2-foot image of Tai-me, a dark green stone decorated with white feathers, ermine, and blue beads, was central to the annual ceremony, during which it was displayed in the medicine **lodge** on a stick. The rest of the year, Tai-me resided in a rawhide box. *Satanta taught his people to respect the divinity of Tai-me.*

Taino [ty' noh] a gentle, hospitable Caribbean **tribe** of farmers of the **Arawak** nation. The Taino encountered Christopher Columbus on his first voyage to the Americas. They led him on an expedition from San Salvador to Cuba and Haiti, where he searched for China. Caguana Indian Ceremonial Park, a reserve near Utuado, Puerto Rico, preserves a twelfth-century Taino settlement, where natives played a form of soccer on 10 paved courts and drew **petroglyphs** to their gods among stone monoliths and ritual altars. [See also **Arawak**.] *Columbus's journal describes the gentle, peace-loving ways of the Taino.*

talc See **steatite**.

Tammany [tam' muh • nee] or **Tamanen** [tam' uh • nihn] or **Tamanend** [tam' uh • nihnd] or **Tamany** (1625-1701) a **Delaware chief** who in 1683 sold William Penn the territory of Pennsylvania in exchange for a chest of beads, mirrors, bells, combs, scissors, blankets, and pots and pans. [See also **Delaware**.] *Tammany waited for three years before receiving payment from white settlers for the land on which they built Philadelphia.*

tapioca a starchy grain made from the grated root of the cassava or **manioc** plant and used as a thickener for soup and broth, in milk pudding, or to make a fermented drink. [See also **manioc, yuca**.] *Tapioca, in addition to its culinary uses, is used to make fabric starch and sizing, glue, and explosives, and as forage for livestock.*

Mohave woman with tattoos on her face and arms

Tashenamani [ta • shay' nah • mah' nee] or **Moving Robe** (*fl.* 1870s) a **Sioux** woman who was present at the **Battle of Little Big Horn** as a mourner for her brother, who was killed in a skirmish with white soldiers. According to **Rain-in-the-Face**, with her war staff over her head as she rode her horse, she inspired male warriors to compete for valor. [See also **Battle of Little Big Horn, Rain-in-the-Face, Sioux**.] *Tashenamani's example helps to dispel the myth that Indian women were absent during military engagements or had no power or influence over tribal affairs.*

Tashunka Witko See **Crazy Horse**.

Tatanka Iyotake See **Sitting Bull**.

tattoo a form of skin beautification or ceremonial scarification or marking to indicate initiation or nobility. **Mohave** Indians tattooed their faces and bodies as a type of adornment by sketching on a charcoal design; pricking the flesh with stone or wood slivers, bone, or thorns; then rubbing more charcoal into the wounds. When the surface healed, the tattoo appeared dark or light blue. Hupa

*a = s**a**ck; ah = s**o**b; aw = s**au**ce; ay = s**a**fe; ee = s**ee**k; eh = s**e**t*

Indians used colored pigments to fill the wounds that formed tattoos. **Eskimo** women tattooed young girls by stitching their chins with a bone needle pulling threads blackened with soot. The **Tlingit** tattooed adolescent girls on the hand as a mark of initiation into womanhood. The **Osage**, however, reserved tattooing as marks of valor for warriors and for their wives and daughters. *The Tupi Indians, native to the Amazon jungle, wear no clothes and decorate their bodies with colored spirals made from vegetable dyes, which serve as a form of genealogical identification.*

Tecumseh [tuh • kuhm' suh] or **Tikamthi** [tuh • kahm' tee] or **Tecumtha** [tuh • kuhm' tah] or **Shooting Star** (1768-October 5, 1813) a humanistic **Shawnee chief** from Piqua, a village near Springfield, Ohio, and twin brother of **Tenkswatawa**, with whom Tecumseh attempted to ally all eastern tribes into a strong front against white settlers. A proud man, in 1810 he proclaimed to Governor William Henry Harrison his noble heritage and his pride in achievement, for which he thanked the **Great Spirit**. That same year, Tecumseh traveled from the Great Lakes south to the Gulf of Mexico on a goodwill tour.

Tecumseh gained a reputation for making persuasive speeches about the idealized community of Prophet's Town on the Tippecanoe River, which set the example of the perfect Native American settlement. He proclaimed, "No tribe has the right to sell [land], even to each other, much less to strangers. Sell a country? Why not sell the air, the great sea, as well as the earth?" (Pastron, Allen. *Great Indian Chiefs.* Santa Barbara, Calif.: Bellerophon, 1993, 26.)

Tecumseh

While fighting for the British, Tecumseh was killed by General Harrison's men during the War of 1812. Tecumseh died in native dress, which he put on because he foresaw that he would not survive the Battle of the Thames near Chatham, Ontario. To protect him from mutilation or undignified burial, his followers declined to identify the body. [See also **Algonquin, Black Hawk, Shawnee, Tenkswatawa.**] *In a nostalgic speech on the banks of the Wabash River in July 1811, Chief Tecumseh noted that many tribes "vanished as snow before a summer sun."* (Brown, Dee. *Bury My Heart at Wounded Knee.* New York: Henry Holt, 1970, 1.)

---

ih = sit; oh = soak; oo = soup; ow = sound; uh = such; y = side

Tehna-Ishi See **Ishi**.

Tekakwitha, Catherine [tek • uhk • wihth' uh] or **Kateri** [kuh • teh' ree] (1656-April 17, 1680) an **Algonquin** Catholic missionary known as the Indian saint. A **Mohawk** captive from Ossernenon, New York, Catherine survived smallpox at the age of four. At age 11, she accepted the teachings of three Jesuit missionaries who visited her family. She was baptized into the church in 1676, but was forced out of the parish by disapproving whites and Indians, whom she angered by refusing to work on Sunday or to take a husband. Tekakwitha fled to a retreat at Caughnawaga, Montreal, where she became the first Native American nun. *Introduced at the Vatican as the Lily of the Mohawk, Catherine Tekakwitha was nominated for sainthood in 1932.*

Tena [tay' nuh] See **Athapascan**.

Tenkswatawa [tihnk • swah' tuh • wah] or **Tensquataway** or **Tenkswataya** [tihnk • swah' tay • yuh] or **Open Door** (1768-1837) a **Shawnee** prophet and twin brother of **Tecumseh**. In 1805, Tenkswatawa, who was blind in his left eye, disclosed a far-reaching vision of a unified world of Indians who lived by the old ways, before corruption by European settlers. By correctly naming the time of a solar eclipse, Tenkswatawa increased his prestige. On November 7, 1811, he was defeated by General William Henry Harrison's troops at the Battle of Tippecanoe Creek, where Tecumseh had left Tenkswatawa with instructions to remain at peace. Retired from public life after the death of his twin, Tenkswatawa lived in Canada, then settled in Kansas, where he sat for a painting by **George Catlin**. [See also **George Catlin, Shawnee, Tecumseh**.] *In a speech delivered to the Indiana governor in August 1808, Tenkswatawa urged Indians to abstain from drinking whiskey and to follow the Great Spirit.*

*a = s**a**ck; ah = s**o**b; aw = s**au**ce; ay = s**a**fe; ee = s**ee**k; eh = s**e**t*

tepee [tee'pee] or **teepee** or **tipi** a cone-shaped shelter common to **plains Indians**. A tepee was 10-16 feet in diameter. It was formed of 20-30 buffalo hides stretched over 16-20 cedar or pine poles. An Indian woman could stitch a tepee in a day or two and erect it in a few minutes. Its three main poles were arranged in tripod formation. The floor of the tepee was made of hides and furs; the outer shell was a semicircle of hide lashed together with wooden or bone lacing pins and held to the ground with pegs. A flap on the east side was left open to serve as an entrance; it could be covered with hide and secured with pins in drafty weather. Near the tepee's entrance, some owners hung deer-hoof clackers, which served as a door knocker. The cluster of poles left enough space for smoke to escape through a pair of smoke wings or flaps at the top, which were maneuvered into place with long poles.

A **dew cloth** and inner lining kept out drafts and supplied interior decoration. In the summer, the entire lower edge of the tepee cover could be rolled up for ventilation. Tepee furniture included fluff-, moss-, or grass-lined **buckskin** couches which could be used for sleeping or sitting. **Willow** backrests made the couches more comfortable for sitting. Tripods held weapons, ceremonial dress, and **medicine bags**. When tepee covers were no longer serviceable, Indian women cut them up and recycled them to make children's clothes, bags, and **moccasin** soles. [See also **dew cloth, lodge pole, Sacred Circle**.] *In comparing white and Indian residences, Flying Hawk noted the tepee is better because it is easier to clean and transport and remains warm in winter and cool in summer.*

terrapin a small, edible turtle common to fresh water and tidal waters of the East Coast. The Indians prized the terrapin for both its meat and eggs, which were used in soup or stew, and its shell, which was made into cups, spoons, dishes, and ceremonial **rattles**, which were used in ceremonial dances and **healing** rituals. *Bright Path owned a spoon that his great uncle had carved from a terrapin shell.*

D. Timmons

terrapin

Thayendanegea See **Joseph Brant**.

thong a rawhide string, cord, lacing, or tie. Thongs were important parts of native costume. They tied **leggings** and **chaps** in place, supported **roaches**, bustles, quivers, and headdresses, and fastened **tobacco** and medicine bags at the waist. [See also **babiche**.] *Laughing Waters softened and rolled rawhide and cut it into lengths to be used for tent thongs.*

Thorpe, Jim See **Carlisle Indian School**.

throwing stick or **rabbit stick** a primitive, curved hunting weapon of the desert Indians. Throwing sticks resembled boomerangs and were used to stun wild turkeys or rabbits, a staple in the southwestern diet. *Jed One-Eye's throwing stick was marked with carvings of migrating geese.*

Thule [too' lee or thoo' lee] a prehistoric native Alaskan people of A.D. 900-1600 who migrated as far east as Greenland, then disappeared, probably because of climatic shifts. The Thule snared birds; fished; gathered mussels and shellfish; and hunted whales, seals, caribou, bears, walrus, oxen, and small mammals. Their partially sunken homes, supported by whale bones and covered with skins and sod strips, were erected on rock ledges along the shore. While traveling they depended on tents in the summer and temporary snow houses or **igloos** in the winter. The adaptability of the Thule influenced their descendents, the **Eskimo**. [See also **Dorset, Eskimo, igloo**.] *A few stone and ivory carvings and implements are the only remains of Thule culture.*

Hopi thunderbird design

thunderbird a protective spirit; the mythic bringer of spring, lightning, and thunder, which was thought to live on high rocky slopes and cliffs. Native Americans etched the thunderbird on **petroglyphs**, painted its likeness on clothing and horse flanks, embroidered it on **moccasins** and **tepees**, and created huge **mounds** in the shape of a stylized bird with outstretched wings. Worshippers often summoned the thunderbird by swinging the **bull-roarer**. [See also **bull-roarer, petroglyph**.] *The clan totem was topped with a thunderbird, a symbol of good weather.*

*a = s**a**ck; ah = s**o**b; aw = s**au**ce; ay = s**a**fe; ee = s**ee**k; eh = s**e**t*

Thunder-Rolling-in-the-Mountains   See **Chief Joseph**.

Tikamthi   See **Tecumseh**.

Timucua [tih • muh' koo • uh]   a **tribe** of tall farmers and fishers of central and southern Florida. Visited by Jacques le Moyne in 1564, the Timucua are immortalized in line drawings featuring elaborate wedding ceremonies, herb tea rituals, neat villages composed of beehive-shaped huts, and alligator hunts. Explorers were disarmed by the courtesy of warriors, who exchanged skin **breechclouts** with European visitors; the women's robes, which were fashioned from Spanish moss; and the intricate red and black **tattoos** of both men and women. *Outina and Saturiwa, chiefs of the Timucua, shot reed arrows tipped with flaming moss into enemy villages.*

tipi   See **tepee**.

Tisquantum   See **Squanto**.

tlachtli [tlahk' tlee]   a ritual game played by **Aztec** teams on an I-shaped court. The object was to use some part of the body other than the hands to bat a small rubber ball, symbolic of the sun, into the far end of the court or through a stone hoop. The best players used skillful movements of hips, knees, and elbows. [See also **Aztec**.] *Gambling at games of tlachtli drew Rain Flower's interest away from the boring chore of grinding maize with stone mano and metate.*

Tlingit [tlihng' giht *or* tlihnk' iht *or* klihnk' iht] a populous **tribe** of fishers, gatherers, and fur traders native to Alaska. Like the **Nootka**, **Kwakiutl**, **Chinook**, **Haida**, and **Athapascan**, the Tlingit depended on the sea for their livelihood. The Tlingit distinguished themselves by making double-pointed daggers, huge, oceangoing cedar **dugouts**, **plankhouses**, goat-wool and cedar-bark blankets, **totem** poles, spruce-root baskets, and wooden armor topped with stylized headpieces. They were known for holding elaborate **potlatches**. The outside world learned about the Tlingit after Russian fur traders encountered their villages in

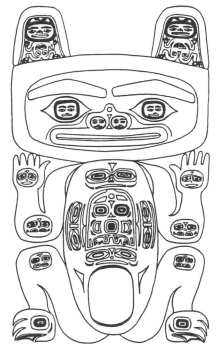

modern Tlingit design representing a bear. This design was carved on a house front; the hole in the abdomen is the entrance.

1741 and from the published journals of naturalist John Muir describing his travels to the Pacific Coast in 1917. [See also **potlatch**.] *The Tlingit myth about Raven tells how this mythical bird brought light into the world and separated forest Indians from coastal tribes.*

tobacco a plant or mixture of leaves sprinkled or smoked for community, medicinal, or ceremonial purposes or used as a trade item. Tobacco use dates back at least 2,000 years: the **Maya** were using tobacco in religious rituals in the first century B.C. The **Taino** welcomed Christopher Columbus and his crew by giving them tobacco leaves. Forest Indians left a gift of tobacco in place of a felled tree. When **Ishi**, the last of the Yahi, died, his white friend, Dr. Alfred Kroeber, sprinkled tobacco powder on the Pacific Ocean to mark Ishi's spirit's trail to the afterlife. **Plains Indians**, including the **Cheyenne**, **Arapaho**, and **Cree**, offer tobacco before they cross an expanse of water. Pipe and chewing tobacco, as well as snuff and crude cigars, were standard items in the pouches carried by the males of many tribes. The **Cherokee** used crushed tobacco leaves to cure asthma, boils, chill, flu, toothache, convulsions, muscle spasms, and the pain of childbirth. To welcome guests or to open negotiations at a council meeting, powdered tobacco was sprinkled or burned to combat evil spirits. English settlers, impressed that Indians could stave off hunger for several days by smoking tobacco, applied it to wounds, sores, congested chests, aching teeth, chapped skin, and arthritic joints as a trusted cure-all. When the plant became scarce, tribes resorted to making **kinnikinnick**, a makeshift tobacco. [See also **calumet, healing, Ishi, kinnikinnick, medicine pipe, peace pipe, pipe bag**.] *Because no wild tobacco grows in northeastern California, the Achomawi traded for seed with their neighbors, the Shasta Indians.*

toboggan [tuh • bog' ihn] a long, narrow sled with a curled front end and either a wooden platform or two runners or rails, often made of buffalo ribs or whale bone. Invented by the **Déné** around 3,000 B.C., the toboggan, which was crafted out of spruce plants, was tapered front and back, bolstered with crosspieces, and covered with skins. For shock absorbers, toboggan makers laced the frame with **babiche**. For long journeys, toboggans were coated with frozen moss and clay and glazed with warm

*a = s*a*ck; ah = s*o*b; a*w* = s*au*ce; a*y* = s*a*fe; ee = s*ee*k; eh = s*e*t*

water to lessen friction, then hitched to teams of dogs. [See also **qamutit, Skidoo**.] *Micmac children looked forward to winter days when they could ride the toboggan and throw their snowsnakes.*

Tocmetone See **Winnemucca, Sarah**.

toloache [toh • loh' ah • chay]   a ritual at which participants drank preparations made from boiled jimson roots or thornapple blossoms to cause prophetic dreams, visions, or trances. The **Mission Indians** of California valued toloache rituals, which forecast the future of their tribes and initiate young members into the tribes. [See also **healing, Mission Indians, vision quest**.] *Only tribe members may participate in a toloache ceremony.*

Toltec [tohl' tehk]   an extinct Mexican **tribe** of farmers, traders, and builders dating from A.D. 900 to A.D. 1200, forerunners of the **Aztec**. Led by Mixcoatl and his son Topiltzin, the Toltec established a network of independent states. Toltecs are known for their architectural skill, as demonstrated by the pyramids, ball courts, colonnades, and frescoes of Chichén Itzá. They also crafted gold and silver jewelry; wove fibers and feathers into bright ceremonial capes; and refined methods of cultivating and using **corn**, cotton, and **squash**. [See also **Aztec**.] *The Toltec capital, Tollen, now called Tula, in the state of Hidalgo, was destroyed in 1160.*

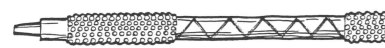
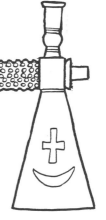

tomahawk   a useful tool, throwing weapon, belt ax, or ceremonial club made from a stone, **obsidian**, or metal head attached by vines, **babiche**, or rawhide binding to a wooden or bone grip or handle. The **Algonquin** tomahawk, with a leather-covered grip that rounded into a knob, contained a triangle of flaked stone, bone, or shell on the end. [See also **hatchet, pipe tomahawk, war club**.] *Soaring Bird's tomahawk blade was lashed to a piece of white oak, which was inlaid with quartz.*

tomahawk with pipe

---

tom-tom a small, single-head drum played with the fingertips. The tom-tom could be used for ceremonial purposes or to send messages. [See also **medicine drum**.] *From the valley came sounds of an Ottawa tom-tom.*

Tonalamatl [toh • nah' lah • mah • t'l'] a sacred book of behavior codes, which was read to **Aztec** students and which future priests learned to read and interpret. The Tonalamatl was made of single folds of paper and contained **pictographs** detailing history, manners, morals, prayers, and pious customs. [See also **Aztec**.] *Apprentices carried the Tonalamatl to its special place on a covered shelf by the altar of Quetzalcoatl.*

toque [tohk] a close-fitting mound of cloth worn as a brimless hat or ceremonial headdress, particularly among Indians of the Southeast. *Sequoyah is usually pictured wearing a toque and smoking his calumet.*

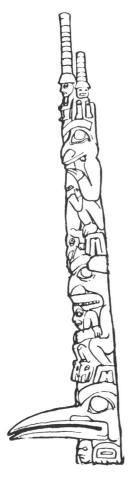

Haida "totem pole" on the front of a plankhouse

totem [toh' tuhm] a family or **clan** symbol in the shape of an animal or some stylized aspect of nature, such as a bear, fox, snipe, wolf, or eel, as demonstrated by the tortoise **tattoo** on the chest of Uncas, James Fenimore Cooper's title character in *The Last of the Mohicans* (New York: Bantam, 1981). The totem honored a common ancestor, noted land ownership, or commemorated clan events or accomplishments. Frequently, it was drawn on the outside of a tepee. Among the **Kwakiutl**, the totem was carved on a cylindrical post erected outside a chief's house as a sign of prestige, a memorial to an important ancestor, or a three-dimensional family tree. Some totem poles were hollowed out for burial chambers; others bore the remains of leaders at the top. The **Haida** positioned an elaborately carved totem in front of each plankhouse as a distinctive family crest. [See also **clan, plankhouse**.] *The Tsimshian totem, which rose two stories high, was painted with bright woodland faces and topped by the effigy of a grizzly bear.*

trailer a long extension on either side of a feathered war bonnet. Like military medals, each feather of the trailer represented a heroic feat. During the thick of battle, a determined warrior might spear the ends of his trailer firmly to the ground as a heroic gesture. The spear remained in place until the warrior died or the battle ended. [See also **dog rope, war bonnet**.] *George Catlin captured the romance and pageantry of plains Indians by picturing them seated on ponies and in full uniform, with headdresses and trailers.*

Trail of Tears   the departure of 12,000 **Cherokee** from their ancestral homeland in Georgia to government **reservations** in Oklahoma, followed by a similar removal of **Choctaw, Chickasaw,** and **Creek** tribes. Beginning in October 1838, and ending March 26, 1839, the mass exodus caused Indians to suffer extremes of cold, bad weather, cholera, pneumonia, and hunger. More than 3,000 died and were buried in shallow graves alongside the trail, including the wife of Chief **John Ross**. The Cherokee who refused to leave the Smoky Mountains settled on what is now the Qualla Reservation in western North Carolina. [See also **Cherokee, Chickasaw, Indian Removal Act, Indian Territory, Long Walk, John Ross, Tsali**.] *In 1988, President Ronald Reagan proclaimed the Trail of Tears a national monument.*

travois [trav • wah' *or* trav' ihs *or* tra • voi']   an A-shaped carryall made of two poles harnessed to the shoulders of a dog or pony by strips of rawhide or **babiche**. Between the shafts was a bed of skin, wicker, or canvas to hold children; sick, injured, or old people; or parcels. In cold weather, a fur-lined sack replaced the open bed. As the animal moved forward, the travois was pulled along behind.

The dog travois proved inefficient because the animal was too small to pull heavy cumbersome loads. Also, a caravan of dog travois often came to a halt when a dogfight broke out or a group of dogs dashed after a rabbit, trailing their burdens behind them. After the introduction of the **horse** to the plains, **tepees** could be made much larger because horses were able to pull long, awkward tent poles and were easier to train. Thus, families, carrying their homes and goods with them, could accompany hunters on long journeys. *The Cheyenne used the travois to carry bundles weighing up to 80 pounds across the prairie.*

travois

treepies [tree' peez]   pieces of animal intestine that were stuffed with chopped meat and eaten as a delicacy, like sausage. Treepies, like **pemmican**, allowed native cooks to preserve extra meat and fat during times of plenty for the winter months or for use by travelers. [See also **tripe**.] *The Gilikum family preferred treepies and pone for a winter meal.*

tribe   a group of families or **clans** who share a common history and culture, including religion, language, values, territory, laws, and traditions. Tribes are more loosely organized than the political units of European culture. Tribal **sachems**, **chiefs**, **sagamores**, and **mikos**, who some-times resemble masters of ceremonies, advisers, or spokespersons, rarely have complete control of tribal members. The major North American tribes fall into geographical and linguistic groupings. Note that some tribes have migrated from one geographical location to another and thus appear in more than one division. *At one time, the United States was home to more than 1,000 Indian tribes.*

Eastern Woodlands and Great Lakes
(speakers of Algonquin, Iroquoian, and Siouan)

Abenaki	**Algonquin**	**Cayuga**	Chickahominy
Delaware	Erie	**Fox**	**Huron**
Illinois	**Iroquois**	**Kickapoo**	Lumbee
Mahican	Maliseet	Massachusetts	**Menominee**
Miami	**Micmac**	Mississauga	**Mohawk**
Monacan	Montauk	Nanticoke	**Narragansett**
Neutrals	**Ojibwa**	**Onandaga**	**Oneida**
Ottawa	Pamlico	Pamunkey	Passamaquoddy
Pennacook	**Penobscot**	Peoria	**Pequot**
Piankashaw	**Potawatomi**	Powhatan	**Sauk**
Seneca	**Shawnee**	Susquehanna	**Tuscarora**
Tutelo	**Wampanoag**	**Winnebago**	**Yamassee**

Southeast or South Atlantic
(speakers of Caddoan, Iroquoian, Hokan-Sioux, Muskogean, Tunican, and Yucan)

Acolapissa	Ais	Alabama	Apalachee
Atakapa	Bidai	Biloxi	Caddo
Calusa	**Catawba**	Chakchiuma	Chatot
Chawasha	Cheraw	**Cherokee**	Chiaha
Chickasaw	Chitamacha	**Choctaw**	**Creek**
Cusabo	Eno	Guale	Hasinai
Hitchiti	Houma	Karankawa	Koasati
Mobile	Monacan	**Muskhogean**	**Natchez**
Nepochi	Ofo	Pedee	Pensacola
Quapaw	Saponi	**Seminole**	Sugeree
Taensa	Tekesta	**Timucua**	Tunica
Tuscarora	Tuskegee	Tutelo	Waccamaw
Waco	Wateree	Wichita	Woccon
Yazoo	Yuchi		

Southwest
(speakers of Athapascan, Keresan, Tanoan, Uto-Aztecan, and Zunian)

Acoma	**Anasazi**	**Apache**	Aravaipa
Athapascan	Chiricahua	Cibecue	Cocopa
Concho	Coyotero	Halchidhoma	**Hohokam**
Hopi	Hualapai	Jicarilla	Jumano
Keres	Laguna	Lipan	Manso
Mescalero	Mogollan	**Navaho**	Opata
Papago	**Pima**	Piro	**Pueblo**
San Carlos	San Ildefonso	Tanoan	Taos
Tarahumara	Tewa	Tonto	Towa
Uinta	Uto-Aztec	Walapai	White Mountain
Yaqui	Yavapai	Zia	**Zuñi**

Great Plains-Prairie
(speakers of Algonquin, Athapascan, Caddoan, Siouan, and Uto-Aztecan)

Arapaho	Arikara	**Assiniboin**	Atsina
Blackfoot	Blood	**Cheyenne**	**Comanche**
Cree	**Crow**	**Gros Ventre**	**Hidatsa**
Iowa	Kansa	**Kiowa**	**Mandan**
Menominee	Miami	Misouri	Oglala
Omaha	**Osage**	**Pawnee**	Piegan
Plains	Ponca	Santee Dakota	Sarsi
Sioux	Sisseton	Teton Dakota	Wahpeton
Wind River	Yankton Dakota		

---

ih = sit; oh = soak; oo = soup; ow = sound; uh = such; y = side

Basin-Plateau
(speakers of Salish, Shahaptin, and Uto-Aztecan)

Bannock	Chemehuevi	**Flathead**	Havasupai
Kaibab	Kawaiisu	Klikitat	Lillooet
Mono	**Nez Percé**	Owens Valley	**Paiute**
Shoshone	Thompson	Umatilla	**Ute**
Walapai	Walla Walla	**Washo**	Wenatchi
Yakima	Yavapai		

California
(speakers of Hokan-Sioux, Penutian, Uto-Aztecan, and Yuki)

Achomawi	Atsugewi	Cahuilla	Castanoa
Chimariko	Chumash	Cochimi	Costano
Cupeno	Diegueño	Esselen	Fernandino
Gabrieleno	Gosiute	Hupa	Juaneno
Kamia	Karok	Kern River	Kiliwa
Kitanemuk	Konkow	Koso	Las Vegas
Luiseño	Maidu	**Mission Indians**	Miwok
Mohave	Mono	Nakima	Nakipa
Nomlaki	Panamint	Patwin	Pericu
Pomo	Salina	Serrano	Shasta
Tolowa	Tubatulabal	Waicuri	Wappo
Wintun	Wiyot	**Yahi**	Yana
Yokuts	Yuki	**Yuma**	Yurok

Northwest or Pacific Coast
(speakers of Athapascan, Hokan-Sioux, Penutian, and Salish)

Alsea	Chastacosta	Chehalis	**Chilkat**
Chimakum	Chetco	**Chinook**	Clatskanie
Clatsop	Coast **Salish**	Coeur d'Alene	Columbia
Coos	Duwamish	Haisla	Humptulips
Hupa	Karok	Katapuya	Klamath
Kutenai	Kwalhioqua	Makah	**Modoc**
Nisquali	**Nootka**	Okanoga	Puyallup
Quileute	Quinault	Sanetch	Shasta
Shuswap	Siletz	Siuslaw	Skagit
Skokomish	Snoqualmie	Spokane	Swinomish
Takelma	Tillamook	Tolowa	Totowa
Tututni	Twana	Umpqua	Wiyot
Yaquina	Yurok		

Canadian Pacific
(speakers of Athapascan, Eskimo-Aleut, Salish, and Wakasha)

Bella Bella	Bella Coola	Chemakum	Comox
Cowichan	**Déné**	Eyak	Gitksan
Haida	Haisla	Heiltsuk	**Kwakiutl**

a = s*a*ck; *ah* = s*o*b; *aw* = s*au*ce; *ay* = s*a*fe; *ee* = s*ee*k; *eh* = s*e*t

Lumni	Makah	Nanaimo	Niska
Nooksack	Puntlatch	Seechelt	Semiahmoo
Skagit	**Tlingit**	Tongass	**Tsimshian**

Canadian Plains
(speakers of Algonquin, Macro-Algonquin, and Na-Déné)

Abitibi	**Algonquin**	Beaver	Beothuk
Carrier	Chilcotin	Chipewyan	Colville
Cree	**Déné**	Dogrib	Han
Hare	Ingalik	Kaska	Kutchin
Kutenai	Lakes	Lillooet	Mistassini
Montagnais	Naskapi	Nicola	Nitlakyapamuk
Ojibwa	Okanagan	**Ottawa**	Saschutkenne
Saulteaux	Sekani	Shuswap	Slave
Swampy	Tagish	Tahltan	Tanaina
Tanana	Tete de Boule	Tsetsaut	Tutchone
Western Wood	Yellowknife		

Arctic
(speakers of Eskimo-Aleut and Chukchi-Kamchatkan)

Aleut	**Athapascan**	Baffin Island	Caribou
Copper	East Greenland	**Inuit**	Kaviagmlut
Labrador	Mackenzie	North Alaskan	Polar
St. Lawrence	Siberian	South Alaskan	Southampton
Tahagmiut	West Alaskan	West Greenland	

Central American
(speakers of Aztec-Tanoan, Hokan, and Macro-Penutian)

Acaxee	Amate	Amusgo	**Aztec**
Bagaz	Cahta	Cazcan	Chatino
Chinipa	Chol	Chontal	Chorti
Coahuiltec	Coca	Cuyutec	Guahichil
Hevome	Huastec	Huave	Ixcatec
Janambre	Jicaque	Jumano	Kanjobal
Kekchi	Lacondon	Lagunero	Lenca
Manso	Matlame	Matlazinca	**Maya**
Mixtec	Motocintlec	**Nahuatl**	**Olmec**
Opata	Orotina	Otomi	Popoloca
Sayultec	Tahue	Tamaulipec	Tapachultec
Tarahumara	Tarascan	Teco	Tepetixtec
Tezcatec	Tlatzihuiztec	Tlaxcala	**Toltec**
Totonac	Trique	Tuxtec	Tzeltal
Xocotec	Yucatan	Zacatec	Zapotec
Zoque			

---

*ih = s**i**t; oh = s**oa**k; oo = s**ou**p; ow = s**ou**nd; uh = s**u**ch; y = s**i**de*

Caribbean
(speakers of Andean-Equitorial,
Ge-Pano-Carib, and Macro-Chibchan)

Arawak	Boruca	**Carib**	**Ciboney**
Ciguano	Coiba	Corobici	**Cuna**
Guaymi	Guetar	Igneri	Jicaque
Lucayo	Matagalpa	Mosquito	Paya
Rama	Silam	Sumo	**Taino**
Talamanca	Ulva	Voto	Yosco

South American
(speakers of Andean-Equitorial,
Ge-Pano-Carib, and Macro-Chibchan)

Abipón	Alacaluf	Arara	Araucania
Arawak	Ashluslay	Atacama	Aymara
Barbacoa	Bororo	Camacán	Campa
Cañar	Cayapa	Charrua	Chimu
Chono	Colorado	Conibo	Coroado
Diaguita	Goajiro	Guaraní	Guató
Guayaná	Huarpi	**Inca**	Jívaro
Lipe	Macú	Mataco	Mbayá
Mojo	Mundurucú	Mura	Nambicuara
Omagua	Ona	Payaguá	Puelche
Querandí	Sherente	Sirionó	Taulipang
Tehuelche	Timbira	Tucuna	Tupina
Uru	Witoto	Yagua	Yahgan
Zamuco			

trickster a curious, mischief-making man-animal in Indian lore. Called **Old-Man** or Old Man Coyote, but who might appear as a raven, rabbit, bluejay, fox, hare, or mink, the trickster was studied in great detail by many anthropologists, particularly Franz Boas and Paul Radin. He demonstrated negative character traits, such as stubbornness, cruelty, dishonesty, and gluttony and sometimes cleverly foiled the plans of the Creator or pulled pranks on human beings. He also amused by outwitting and frustrating himself or causing himself pain or embarrassment, such as ripping off his own tail or getting his head or foot caught in a container.

- To the **Abenaki**, the trickster is Azeban the raccoon.

- In **Arapaho** lore, the trickster is a spider called Iktomi.

a = sack; ah = sob; aw = sauce; ay = safe; ee = seek; eh = set

- To the **Catawba**, he is an opossum called One Tail Clear of Hair.

- To the **Kiowa**, he was the hero-trickster Saynday.

- To the **Micmac** or Wabanaki of Nova Scotia, the trickster is Glooskap the frog, a wily rascal who taught humans how to weave, tan, fish, hunt, and do beadwork. Among the Maliseet the story of Glooskap centers on Mikumwesu, the older brother. The **Penobscot** of Maine vary the spelling to Gluscabi.

- In Lakota **Sioux** stories, the trickster is the hare.

- In **Nootka** or Tanaina lore, the trickster is either Guguyni the raven or Chulyen the crow.

- In **Ojibwa** legends, the trickster, Nanabozho or Wenabozho the hare, assisted Indians by outwitting natural forces.

- To the Passamaquoddy, the turtle Mikchich was Glooskap's deceitful uncle.

[See also **amaguq, coyote, inua, Micmac, Old-Man**.] *Like Br'er Rabbit of West African lore, the trickster demonstrated how a small animal could use native intelligence and instinct to overcome great foes and combat dangers.*

tripe a section of bear, moose, elk, deer, or buffalo intestine that could be used as a casing for spiced meat stuffing or cleaned and tied at one end to serve as a cooking vessel. [See also **stone boiling, treepies**.] *Indians allowed nothing to go to waste, a fact demonstrated by tripe or treepies, a kind of sausage.*

Tsali [sah' lee] a **Cherokee** martyr who killed two soldiers, then hid in the Great Smoky Mountains. In 1838, following the removal of Indians on the **Trail of Tears**, General Winfield Scott offered freedom for the remaining Cherokees if Tsali gave himself up. Tsali chose to face a firing squad so that his people could be free. [See also **Cherokee, Trail of Tears**.] *The story of Tsali gives him mythic characteristics, particularly the ability to predict his future.*

Tsimshian [sihm' shee • uhn]   a **tribe** of salmon fishers, gatherers, traders, and sea hunters native to British Columbia. Like those of the **Haida**, **Tlingit**, and **Kwakiutl**, Tsimshian villages once boasted **plankhouses**, carved **totem** poles and horn utensils, and **dugouts** and masks made from cedar. *During the eighteenth century, Russian traders and explorers pushed into Tsimshian territory to tap its source of rich furs and other trade goods.*

tsindi [sihn' dee]   a dice game played with two-sided markers made of shell, seeds, bone, fruit pits, bark, horn, pottery, wood, or ivory. *Tsindi players keep score by accumulating short sticks.*

tule [too' lee]   rushes or **cattails**, which are found on stream banks or wetlands. The **Pomo** Indians of California and Oregon pulled tule reeds and roots, dried them, then wove them into baskets and mats. Among the Indians of the Southwest, tule powder is used as a ritual offering and appetite stimulant. [See also **cattail, healing**.] *The damming of California rivers greatly reduced natural wetlands, which had flourished with tule and other wild plants.*

woman carrying a load with a tumpline

tumpline [tuhmp' lyn]   a strap made of **babiche**, slippery elm or cedar bark, **Indian hemp**, or basswood and used for securing loads to a carrier's forehead. The word, taken from the **Algonquin** term for pack strap, could also refer to a shoulder or chest harness or **bandolier**. A **cradleboard** was frequently attached to a tumpline. [See also **babiche, burden frame, cradleboard, mocuck, water bag**.] *Waneka slipped the tumpline around her forehead, then leaned forward to balance the loaded basket on her back.*

tuna   See **prickly pear**.

tundra [tuhn' druh]   poorly drained, treeless land or bogs in the frozen areas of the Arctic. The tundra, covered by a shallow layer of black soil that remains permanently frozen underground, is marshy and topped with herbs, grasses, lichens, and shrubs in summer. It is the

a = sack; ah = sob; aw = sauce; ay = safe; ee = seek; eh = set

home of large populations of migratory birds, geese, and ducks as well as lemmings, **caribou**, bears, hares, and musk oxen. [See also **Déné**.] *Inuit villagers gathered moss, lichen, vines, roots, and handfuls of berries and wildflowers from the thawing tundra.*

Tuscarora [tuhs • kuh • roh' ruh] a peaceful North Carolina **tribe** known as the shirt wearers. The Tuscaroras were the sixth member nation of the **Iroquois League**. Tuscaroras lived among European tobacco planters until Swiss adventurers led by Baron Christoph von Graffenried forced them from ancestral lands in 1711. The resulting hostilities, named the Tuscarora War, inflamed race relations along the Neuse River and Pamlico Sound. Outnumbered and outgunned, King Hancock signed a treaty with Colonel John Barnwell in 1712. The following year, a colonial troop sold 400 Tuscaroras into slavery. The remainder settled in New York State. [See also **Iroquois League**.] *To strengthen and stabilize Indian relations, survivors of the Tuscarora Wars joined the Iroquois League.*

tuttu [tuht' too]   the Alaskan Eskimo word for **caribou**. [See also **caribou**.] *Naigo helped to grade tuttu hides.*

ugruk [oo' gruk] or **oo-gruk** the **Eskimo** word for bearded seal, a major source of valuable skin, **blubber**, bone, and ivory. *The Inumarik hunted ugruk by making holes in the ice, then waiting until the animals came up for air.*

ulu [oo' loo] or **oolu** a sharp, fan-shaped utility knife or cleaver featuring a bone handle and curved blade. It is mainly used by **Eskimo** women to bone and skin animals; chip ice; chop moss for wicks; whittle sticks; perform minor surgery, such as cutting the umbilical cord on newborn babies or removing splinters; or trim hair. [See also **buckhorn, Dorset, pana.**] *The stranger used an ulu to slice up bits of caribou tongue for his dinner.*

umiak [oo' mee • ak] a 30-foot long, seaworthy boat with a driftwood or bone frame covered with sealskin, propelled by eight paddles, and guided by a steersman. Umiaks, which were at one time called women's boats because women paddled them, hold up to 25 passengers and are often used to transport cargo or for hunting whales. Common to Alaska and Greenland, umiaks were sometimes fitted with skin sails. Their coverings weather icy waters well and can easily be repaired with needle and thread. *The remains of Oogruk's umiak were washed ashore downstream from where it capsized.*

umialik [oo • mee' uh • lihk'] a whaling captain; the owner of an **umiak** or whaling boat; a prestigious community member. *Oogruk, an umialik among lesser villagers, took pride in owning a boat.*

Ute [yoot] a native **tribe** of stocky hunter-gatherers, farmers, and raiders of the Rocky Mountains and parts of the Northwest who followed the ancient Fremont and **Anasazi** tribes into the western basin of the Colorado

River and hunted elk and deer in the tablelands adjacent to the Wasatch Mountains. The Ute, whose name means "people at the mountaintops," were famous for innovative irrigation methods and equestrian skills. For a time, they utilized their remote location to dominate the area northwest of Santa Fé, New Mexico.

During the nineteenth century, the Ute produced notable leaders, including Chief Wakara, Tintic, and **Black Hawk**. Chief **Ouray**, one of the most outstanding tribal ambassadors, journeyed to Washington to plead for the resettlement of the Ute nation. In 1869, John Wesley Powell recorded a visit with Chief Tsauwiat, whose wife, The Bishop, occupied a high place on the local council. In 1879, Utes were forcibly resettled at the Uintah **reservation** in Utah. [See also **Black Hawk, Ouray**.] *In 1906, Virginia McClurg negotiated with Ute Chief Ignacio for the protection of the Mesa Verde cliff dwellings, where his tribe grazed their animals.*

southern Ute men of the nineteenth century

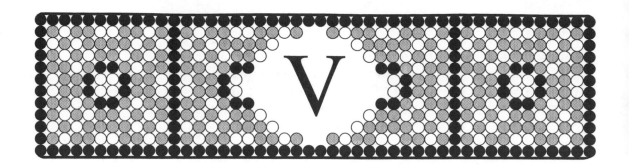

vision quest   a spiritual journey into self. Many teenage boys of the **plains Indians** entered manhood by communicating with the **Great Spirit** through ordeals of fasting and solitude. After purifying the flesh in the **sweat lodge**, the vision seeker stripped, rubbed down with dried **sage** or other herbs, and went to a secluded spot or entered a vision pit, where for several days he abstained from food, water, and human contact while whipping his flesh, breathing the smoke of incense or sweetgrass, and waiting for contact with the spirit world. Led by his father or a mentor, he returned to the village to announce the success of his quest. If the first experience proved unsatisfactory, the youth might return several times on his vision quest. He abandoned his childhood name and adopted an adult name derived from some part of his experience or dream. His **medicine bundle** featured plants, animal parts, or stones that symbolized his vision quest. [See also **medicine, medicine bundle, sweat lodge**.] *Cloud Walker's adult life began with a vision quest, which ended with a dream of his future success as a breeder of fine Appaloosa horses.*

voladores [voh' luh • dor' ayz]   among southwestern Indians, a group of four ritual fliers or acrobats dressed like brightly colored birds, who hang suspended from rigging atop a pole 100 feet in the air, then form a square representing the four winds and make a graceful descent. *The Totonac Indians are famous for their voladores, who wind cords up a pole, then descend in well-choreographed spirals.*

*a = s**a**ck; ah = s**o**b; aw = s**au**ce; ay = s**a**fe; ee = s**ee**k; eh = s**e**t*

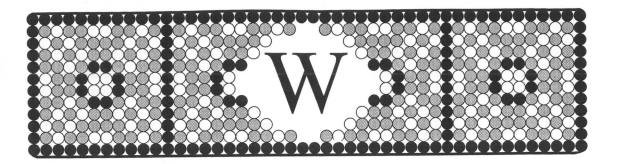

Wabanaki Confederacy [wah' bah • nah' kee] a free alliance of **Abenaki** tribes formed in 1750 and lasting a century. Emulating other Indian confederacies, particularly the **Iroquois League**, the Wabanaki Confederacy brought together Abenaki, Maliseet, **Micmac**, and Passamaquoddy for a **caucus** three times a year at Caughnawaga, Quebec. [See also **league, Samoset**.] *The Wabanaki Confederacy used wampum belts as symbols of honor and peaceful intent.*

wacanga [wuh • kahn' guh] a sweet-smelling grass used in cooking, medicine, and incense, which was burned in religious ceremonies as an enticement to beneficial spirits and as part of the **vision quest**. *For the plains Indian, wacanga was a basic need.*

Wahunsonacook See **Powhatan**.

Wakan Tanka [wah' k'n • tahn' kuh] the Lakota **Sioux** name for the **Great Spirit** or creator, equivalent to **Manitou**, **Quetzalcoatl**, and other Indian terms for a supreme being. Worshippers of Wakan Tanka, or the **Great Mystery**, concentrated on the unknown and supernatural powers of the spirit world. [See also **Great Spirit**.] *White Buffalo Calf Woman used the sacred pipe as a means of directing prayers through smoke upward to Wakan Tanka.*

Walum Olum [wah' luhm oh' luhm] a pictographic history of the **Delaware** recorded on bark scrolls. Discovered in 1820 by botanist Constantine S. Rafinesque, the remnants of the original text were not translated until 1833. [See also **Beringia, Delaware, pictograph**.] *Scholars doubt the authenticity of the Walum Olum, which describes the migration of the Delaware from Siberia over the land bridge called Beringia.*

---

ih = sit; oh = soak; oo = soup; ow = sound; uh = such; y = side

Wampanoag [wahm' pah • noh' ahg]   an **Algonquin tribe** of eastern forest Indians. Once native to Bristol County, Rhode Island, and Bristol County, Massachusetts, the Wampanoag, whose name means dawn people, dwindled after their first encounters with European settlers. Many died of scarlet fever and measles; others died during King Philip's War of 1675, during which **Massasoit**'s son Metacomet, or **King Philip**, fought for their survival. [See also **King Philip, Massasoit**.] *Today, around 500 Wampanoag reside around Martha's Vineyard and Nantucket, Massachusetts.*

detail from a Seneca wampum belt

wampum [wahm' puhm]   belts, strings, **bandoliers**, or sashes made from **sinew** strung with cylindrical shell beads. The beads, ⅛-½ inch long, were fashioned from whelk, periwinkle, conch, and the valve of freshwater clams. Their colors ranged from white to deep purple, which was the most valuable. Wampum, made by skilled female workers, served East Coast Indians as invitations, messages, condolences, treaty settlements, peace covenants, or ceremonial badges and decorations.

After the coming of European colonists, wampum became the equivalent of currency among colonists and was used in exchanges among Dutch and English settlers, who established local laws against counterfeiters. The most valuable wampum were judged for smoothness and color. When used as messages, dark wampum signified bad news; white wampum meant good news. As settlement in a civil suit, a victim's family might accept six strings of beads as restitution. The tribe often selected a Keeper of the Wampum, who recited verses commemorating events connected with a special wampum. [See also **beading, Delaware, dentalia, otekoa, quahog**.] *Wampum derives from the longer Algonquin term wampumpeag, which means white strings.*

Wananikwe [wah • nuh • nihk' way] (?-1878)   a **Sioux** prophet or seer who in 1876 initiated the Dream Dance, which followers believed would protect Indians from white settlers and restore the old order to the plains. Wananikwe's Dream Dance spread from the Greak Lakes as far south as Kansas and was practiced by **Ojibwa**, **Potawatomi**, **Fox**, and **Kickapoo** Indians. [See also **Ghost**

a = sack; ah = sob; aw = sauce; ay = safe; ee = seek; eh = set

Dance, Gray Hair, Wovoka.] *Through the influence of Wananikwe and his followers, the Sioux enjoyed a nostalgic resurgence of tribal pride and hope.*

wapatoo [wah' puh • too]   a low-growing plant common to marshes and stream banks; the arrowhead plant. Similar to **manioc** and **camas**, the wapatoo was valued among the **Cherokee** for its tasty roots. *Cindy Byrd gathered wapatoo roots and placed them to dry in a circle about her cooking fire.*

war bonnet   a ceremonial headdress decorated with feathers, fur, horsehair, horns, and often a single quill jutting from the scalp. The war bonnet, a symbol of tribal prestige, was worn for specific ceremonial occasions, such as historical enactments of tribal victories, and to protect a favored leader in battle. [See also **trailer**.] *Lame Deer's war bonnet reminded his visitors that the tribe had reached a crucial moment in their history.*

war club   a multipurpose weapon sometimes featuring a long, ironwood handle pierced at one end by a spike made from an animal tusk, iron blade, or piece of sharpened quartz, **obsidian**, shell, or bone and occasionally anchored with a wristband. When not in use, the war club could be suspended from the waist by a **thong**. [See also **tomahawk**.] *Rain-in-the-Face's war club bore extensive battle markings, each reminding him of his long military career.*

Ward, Nancy   or **One Who Travels** (1738?-1824)   a **half-breed Cherokee** heroine of the Creek War of 1755, who is thought to have been the daughter of a British officer and a member of a royal Cherokee family. She was born near Knoxville, Tennessee, and married to Brian Ward. Nancy elevated the flagging spirits of her nation, aiding its victory over its enemies, then served as go-between for white settlers and as negotiator at the council table. [See also **Cherokee**.] *Nancy Ward is credited with unselfish acts to both whites and Cherokees, including support of schools and animal husbandry and encouragement of humane treatment for military prisoners.*

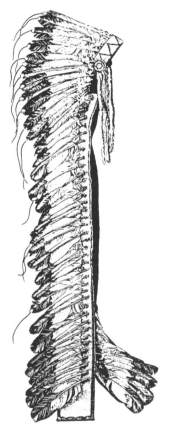

Bannock war bonnet

Washakie [wah • shah' kee] or **Pinaquana** [pee' nuh • kwah' nuh] (1798-February 20, 1900)   son of an Umatilla father and a **Shoshone** mother who became a Shoshone chief and Episcopal convert. He distinguished himself by serving as a diplomat during treaty negotiations in 1868, as a guide for the U.S. Cavalry, and as a protector of wagon trains. For his loyalty to the United States, Washakie was awarded a military funeral. [See also **Shoshone**.] *In 1878, in a protest directed at Wyoming Governor John Hoyt, Washakie accused the white man of killing game, capturing furs, and pasturing herds in Indian meadows.*

Washakie

Washo [wah' shoh] or **Washoe**   a scattered and dispossessed Hokan tribe of hunter-gathers native to Nevada. The Washo, one of the few tribes who did not keep horses, were limited in their ability to seek better living conditions. [See also **Datsolali**.] *Datsolali's baskets feature traditional Washo patterns.*

water bag   a waterproof pouch made from an animal stomach or a piece of hide laced together at the top to form a carrying bag. A large water bag could be suspended from the forehead on a **tumpline**. It was woman's work to carry the water bag to the stream each morning, empty the water from the night before, and fetch fresh water for household use. Young girls often used water bag-carrying duties as an excuse to meet their boyfriends away from the watchful eyes of adults. Young men who were too shy for courtship sometimes playfully shot darts into the water bags of attractive girls. [See also **tumpline**.] *Lennie slipped the strap of the water bag over her head and shoulder as she ducked through the flap of the tepee.*

wattle-and-mud   a primitive style of architecture based on a foundation of woven mats attached to a pole frame. The mats were glazed over with clay mud, which hardened in the sun. *Mesa Indians stayed cool in summer in their wattle-and-mud huts.*

weir [weer]   an artificial channel or dam in a stream or tidal creek that forces fish and eels into a net. A weir could be formed of stones arranged in a tight arrow formation; fashioned into a fencelike baffle of vertical canes, reeds, hardwood splits, or sticks; or designed as a cone-shaped

*a = s**a**ck; ah = s**o**b; aw = s**au**ce; ay = s**a**fe; ee = s**ee**k; eh = s**e**t*

enclosure or trap. Fishers beat the water to drive schools of fish toward the weir. South American Indians poisoned the water with shredded buckeye leaves and bark, devil's shoelace, cubé, or barbasco, a common toxic pea, similar to rotenone, that is harmless to human beings. Gathering fish from a weir was such easy work that children could be entrusted with the task. [See also **dip net, fish poison**.] *Wolverine's father and uncles laid out stones in a V-shaped pattern, then left him and his cousins to trap the fish that swam into the weir.*

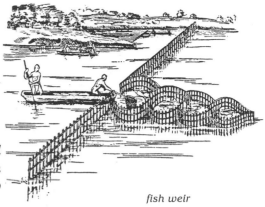

fish weir

Wheeler-Howard Act See **Indian Reorganization Act**.

White Bear See **Satanta**.

wickiup [wihk' ee • uhp] or **wikiup** an oval or circular bark house or hut of the **plains Indians**, formed of brush, grass, bark shingles, or woven reed mats over a framework of cedar timbers lashed with basswood strips. Inside, the wickiup featured overhead shelves for storage and low platforms for sleeping and lounging. [See also **Paiute**.] *The plains wickiup varied in style from temporary shelters to permanent dwellings, depending on how long the tribe planned to remain.*

wigwam a domed or cone-shaped lodge named for the **Abenaki** term for residence. The wigwam was woven from saplings or branches planted one foot in the ground, then arched, overlapped, and lashed together with basswood, walnut, slippery elm, or hickory bark to form a 15-foot oval or circular dome. The structure was covered with a patchwork of skins, rolls or shingles of birch, fir, cedar, spruce, walnut, or elm bark, or with mats woven from bulrushes or **cattails**.

Each wigwam had a smoke hole in the center, which could be covered by a flap during heavy rains. During severe winters, the bottom edge could be sealed with a layer of dirt and sod to keep out wind. The floors were covered by mats and platforms, which served as seats or beds. Under the platforms, Indian women stored bags of meal and baskets of **corn**, dried beans, fruit, and **squash**, gourds, and nuts. Overhead, they suspended strings of dried deer **jerky** or root crops, such as onions and herbs.

The father and mother guarded each side of the doorway, which was protected by a hide or blanket. Because of the rigidity of its construction materials, the wigwam, unlike the **tepee**, was a permanent dwelling and could not be easily moved. *Among Piñon Indians, erecting a wigwam was considered man's work.*

D. Timmons

bark wigwam

wigwassawigamig [wihg • wahs' suh • wihg' uh • mihg] an extended **wigwam** made from a single horizontal pole with vertical supports radiating outward. *The wigwassawigamig was one of many varied plains Indians' dwellings.*

wikiup See **wickiup**.

willow or **osier** a tree native to creek banks and watery shores across North America as far as the Arctic Circle. Native Americans relied on willow twigs and branches for pliable weaving material for backrests, **snowshoes**, fishing nets, and other lightweight goods. When boiled into a tea, the bark of the willow served as strong medicine against fever and pain. [See also **healing**.] *The discovery of aspirin was a natural outgrowth of Native American use of willow bark as a painkiller.*

Wilson, Jack See **Wovoka**.

winkte [wihnk' tee] a **Sioux** male who chose to live, dress, and behave like a woman, often becoming skillful at **quilling** and decorative arts. [See also **berdache**.] *Although Sioux warriors scorned the winkte and made him live on the outskirts of the village, they respected his wisdom and magical power.*

Winnebago [wihn' nuh • bay' goh] a major **tribe** of planters, fur traders, and bison hunters located in Wisconsin and allied with the **Sauk**, **Fox**, and **Kickapoo**. The Winnebago, who observed compassionate and humanistic treatment of women and children, referred to themselves as People of Real Speech. They believed in hospitality, modesty, perseverance, and generosity toward the elderly. In 1827, their most famous leader, medicine man, and prophet, White Cloud, supported **Black Hawk**, leader of a war against U.S. forces. Nearly exterminated by European diseases, in 1865 they followed Chief Little Hill and migrated from the Wisconsin River south to Nebraska; some returned to their original homeland and settled in Minnesota. Anthropologist Paul Radin preserved the lore and culture of the Winnebago, particularly the **trickster** cycle, which comprises stories of the wily Winnebago con man. [See also **Black Hawk**.] *Folklorist Mountain Wolf Woman grew sad on the empty plains and prayed to the Winnebago earth goddess.*

Winnemucca, Sarah [wihn' nuh • muhk' kuh] or **Tocmetone** [tahk • muh • toh' nay] (1844?-October 17, 1891) a **Paiute** teacher, interpreter, and guide. Born near Humboldt Lake, Nevada, Sarah Winnemucca was the daughter and granddaughter of **chiefs**. With only three weeks of formal education, she became a lecturer. In 1883, with her *Life among the Piutes: Their Wrongs and Claims* (Bishop, Calif.: Chalfant, 1992), she became the first Native American to publish in English. She also started the first school for and by Indians, which was built near Lovelock, Nevada. [See also **Paiute**.] *Sarah Winnemucca's book accuses the Bureau of Indian Affairs of corrupt dealings with Native Americans.*

witkowin [wiht' koh • wihn] a madwoman or woman of bizarre behavior and unconventional morals. [See also **heyoka**.] *Sioux wives tied the witkowin to a pine tree to stop her rambling around the camp.*

wooden face See **false face**.

Woquini See **Roman Nose**.

Wounded Knee the site of a pivotal **Sioux** massacre on December 29, 1890, at Pine Ridge Reservation, South Dakota. Five hundred men of the 7th U.S. Cavalry used cannon, lances, and rifles to kill 200 men, women, and children for supporting the **Ghost Dance**. Just two weeks after the murder of **Sitting Bull**, the shamefully one-sided battle ended with Indian corpses left to freeze on the battlefield. The Wounded Knee massacre was cited as the turning point in the defeat of **plains Indians**. [See also

Battle of Little Big Horn, Charles Alexander Eastman, Ghost Dance, Sitting Bull, Wovoka.] *According to the testimony of Turning Hawk concerning Wounded Knee, the Indians lost everything, even their hunting rifles.*

Wovoka [woh • voh' kuh] or **Jack Wilson** (1856?-September 20, 1932) a **Paiute** prophet and humble holy man from Walker Lake, Nevada, who studied Christian ways and was proclaimed the Red Messiah. Following a trance while he lay ill with scarlet fever, he predicted the coming of a messiah and a return to former greatness through the ritual **Ghost Dance**. He urged his followers to remain at peace while awaiting the overthrow of the white culture. Among his commandments were injunctions against fighting and quarreling and encouragements of good behavior so that followers could reunite in heaven. After the massacre at **Wounded Knee**, Wovoka's message lost favor with the **Sioux** nation. In 1926, Wovoka was visited by movie star Tim McCoy and told McCoy about his holy visions. Wovoka died in Schurz, Nevada. [See also **Ghost Dance, Gray Hair, Paiute, Sioux, Wananikwe, Wounded Knee.**] *Of his vision of a resurgence of the plain Indians' golden age, Wovoka commanded Indians to dance so that game would return to the land and dead Indians would return to life.*

Wyandot or **Wyandotte** See **Huron**.

Wovoka in 1891

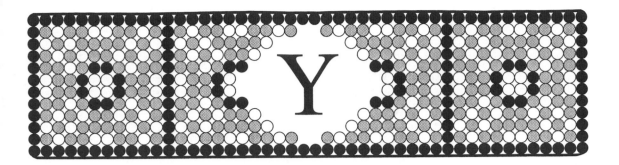

Yahi [yah' hee]   a Hokan tribe of hunter-gatherers native to the Sacramento Valley that was virtually wiped out by white settlers and gold seekers. [See also **Ishi**.] *Ishi, the last of the Yahi, outlived his tribe and its language, gods, and culture.*

Yakima [yah' kee • mah]   a Pacific Coast **tribe** of salmon fishers, gatherers, and hunters native to the Columbia River Basin. The Yakima met the **Lewis and Clark expedition** in 1806. Their experience with white settlers reached an impasse in September 1855 after miners violated treaties guaranteeing land rights. Led by Chief Kamiakin and his nephew Qualchin, the Yakima initiated a series of unsuccessful raids, but in general, the Yakima preferred peaceful fishing and hunting expeditions to warfare. *In 1915, the Yakima Chief Meninock declared that God created Indians to live on the land.*

Yamassee [yahm' uh • see]   a coastal agricultural tribe native to South Carolina that lived at peace with European settlers until April 15, 1715, when it followed the lead of the **Tuscarora** and rebelled against exploitation, forced labor, and deception by land grabbers and plantation owners. The result of the Yamassee War, which pushed colonists back to Charleston, was virtual genocide. *The few Yamassee who survived conflict with Europeans took refuge with Creeks and Choctaws in Florida.*

yankee   the **Algonquin** pronunciation of the word *English. Indians of the Northeast developed the terms* yengeesh *or* yinglees *into* yankee.

Yellow Feather   See **Massasoit**.

York (?-ca. 1806)   the black house slave of the Clark family, who accompanied Lewis and Clark on their westward expedition (1804-1805) as a scout and interpreter. York was the first black person that the Arikara and **Mandan** had ever seen. As pictured in artist Charles M. Russell's drawing of this historic meeting, the Indians held a celebration so that they could examine York's bare chest to determine why his skin was black. A year after the expedition's return, York, whom Clark had freed and set up in the shipping business in Tennessee, died of cholera. [See also **Lewis and Clark expedition**.] *The Mandan tried to rub black from York's skin and were amazed that he was not covered with paint.*

Young, Lucy (1845-?)   chronicler of the Wintun. In 1939, Young narrated her story of the California Gold Rush. According to her recounting of tribal events, the discovery of gold in Humbolt and Mendocino counties, California, caused the displacement and/or death of more than 50,000 Indians in a three-year period. *In her description of her grandfather's death, Lucy Young gives a clear picture of Wintun burial customs, which include digging a hole, putting brush above and below the corpse and selected personal items, and setting the mass on fire.*

yuca [yoo' kuh]   the tuber of the **manioc** or cassava plant. The **Taino** grated and strained yuca, then formed the pulp into cakes, which they baked on terra-cotta dishes. They boiled the poisonous juice several times, then fermented it and served it as a beverage. [See also **manioc, tapioca**.] *One of the food staples that Christopher Columbus found in San Salvador was the yuca.*

yucca

yucca [yuhk' kuh]   a sturdy, fibrous, versatile plant found in sandy arid regions of the southwestern United States. The yucca, which is a member of the agave family and is related to bear grass, produces a single vertical stalk covered with fragrant white flowers. Indians ate the cucumber-shaped, melonlike yucca pods and used the roots in a soap to control dandruff. A tea brewed from the paste of yucca roots was used to treat diabetes, rheumatism, and stomach ailments. The **Anasazi** wove yucca fibers into a coarse cloth, nets, fish traps, rabbit snares, sandals, and bags. Other uses included cord, **cradleboard** ropes, scrub

*a = s**a**ck; ah = s**o**b; aw = s**au**ce; ay = s**a**fe; ee = s**ee**k; eh = s**e**t*

brushes, brooms, paintbrushes, dolls, or games; they made sewing needles from the leaves' sharp tips. **Hopi** priests braided yucca strands into ritual whips, with which they flogged children who were being presented to the **kachinas**, and washed the hair of the bride and groom at wedding ceremonies and the deceased at funerals with soap made from yucca. Yavapais priests performed a similar ceremonial washing with yucca suds on a mother and newborn baby. [See also **Anasazi, bear grass, cactli, healing**.] *Because they were stored in a hot, dry climate, prehistoric garments and containers woven from yucca fibers remain intact.*

yuk   See **Yupik**.

Yuma [yoo' muh]   a small southwestern agricultural **tribe** that grew **pumpkins**, **corn**, **squash**, melons, and beans along the fertile banks of the Colorado River but relied on **acorns** as a staple food. The Yuma dressed simply in aprons or **breechclouts** and fiber sandals and decorated their faces and chests with **tattoos**. They are famous for decorating baskets and blankets with bird feathers and for conducting elaborate ceremonies honoring the dead. To appease wandering spirits, the Yuma made life-size models of their deceased family members on the anniversary of their deaths. They burned the models with gifts that they thought would be useful in the spirit world. *The tribal leader of the Yuma was known as the Brave Man.*

Yuma chief Pasqual

Yupik [yoo' pihk] (singular: **yuk** or **Yupiq**)   the language of the **Eskimo** in southern Alaska. Also the term by which central Alaskan Eskimos refer to themselves. [See also **Eskimo, Inuit, Inupiaq, Inupik**.) *An updated Yupik dictionary was published in 1970.*

yuwipi [yoo • wih' pee]   a **Sioux shaman** or **medicine man** who has the power of prophecy, which he uses to locate missing people and articles, discover the cause of disease, pinpoint schools of fish or herds of animals, or predict the outcome of tribal elections. [See also **medicine man, shaman**.] *Lame Deer sat in the medicine tent with his elders, waiting to hear what the yuwipi man would say about his lung weakness.*

---

ih = sit; oh = soak; oo = soup; ow = sound; uh = such; y = side

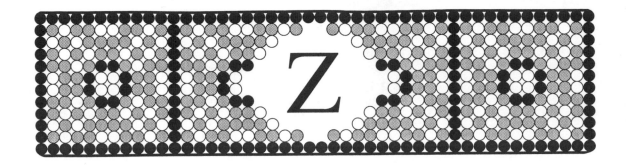

zarape [zah • rah' pay] or **sarape** [sah • rah' pay] a circular, sleeveless, unisex mantle of woven wool with a hole in the middle for the head. The zarape, native to southwestern U.S. Indians as well as those of the Yucatan Peninsula, can be adapted for use as a blanket, raincoat, sling, baby pouch, or carryall. *The zarape, a graceful draped garment, is still worn by Mexican Indians.*

zemi [zeh' mee] an idol, oracle, or household god of the **Carib** or **Taino** Indians. [See also **Carib, Taino**.] *Worshippers offered gifts of scented tobacco to the zemi in the village temple.*

Zuñi [zoon' yee *or* zoo' nee] a tribe of farmers and sheepherders of western New Mexico. Confronted with their first black visitor in 1539, the Zuñi of the Hawikuh Pueblo killed former slave Estevanico, who, as scout for Francisco de Coronado's exploratory party, was searching for the legendary lost cities of gold. Coronado visited Hawkiuh in 1540 on his way to the Grand Canyon and the Colorado River. Living in seven villages in New Mexico, the Zuñi formed one **pueblo** in 1695 as a means of protecting themselves from outsiders.

The modern Zuñi are famous for their turquoise-studded silverwork, which they learned from Spanish settlers. The **squash blossom** design is typical of Zuñi workmanship. Today, in November and December in Zuñi, New Mexico, they continue to hold religious rites, which are open to the public. [See also **Hopi, Pueblo**.] *The Zuñi pray to their sun god with a sunrise chant and a petition for long life, old age, water, seed, riches, power, and spirit.*

Zuñi design on a shield

*a = s**a**ck; ah = s**o**b; aw = s**au**ce; ay = s**a**fe; ee = s**ee**k; eh = s**e**t*

Sources

Academic American Encyclopedia. Danbury, Conn.: Grolier, 1983.

Adams, Alexander B. *Sitting Bull.* New York: Putnam, 1973.

Adler, David A. *A Picture Book of Christopher Columbus.* New York: Holiday House, 1991.

Aikman, Lonnelle. *Nature's Healing Arts.* Washington, D.C.: National Geographic Society, 1977.

Anthony, Suzanne. *Haiti.* New York: Chelsea House, 1989.

———. *West Indies.* New York: Chelsea House, 1989.

Arrowsmith's. Winter, 1976-1977.

Ashabranner, Brent. *Dark Harvest.* New York: Dodd, Mead, 1985.

———. *Morning Star, Black Sun.* New York: Dodd, Mead, 1982.

Averill, Esther. *King Phillip.* Eau Claire, Wis.: E. M. Hale, 1950.

Baldwin, Fred D. "With the Very Best Intentions," *Apprise* (February 1992), 52-54.

Baldwin, Gordon C. *America's Buried Past.* New York: Putnam, 1962.

———. *Indians of the Southwest.* New York: Capricorn, 1973.

Bancroft-Hunt, Norman, and Werner Forman. *The Indians of the Great Plains.* London: Orbin, 1981.

———. *North American Indians.* Philadelphia: Courage Books, 1992.

Banks, Lynne Reid. *The Indian in the Cupboard.* New York: Avon Books, 1980.

———. *The Return of the Indian.* Garden City, N.Y.: Doubleday, 1986.

Batherman, Muriel. *Before Columbus.* Boston: Houghton-Mifflin, 1981.

Baugh, Albert C. *A History of the English Language.* New York: Appleton Century Crofts, 1957.

Beals, Frank L. *Chief Black Hawk.* Chicago: Wheeler, 1943.

Beck, Barbara L. *The Aztecs.* New York: Franklin Watts, 1966.

Bedini, Silvio A., ed. *The Christopher Columbus Encyclopedia.* New York: Simon & Schuster, 1992.

Begay, Shonto. *Ma'ii and Cousin Horned Toad: A Traditional Navajo Story.* New York: Scholastic, 1992.

Bemister, Margaret. *Thirty Indian Legends of Canada.* Vancouver, B.C.: Douglas & McIntyre, 1973.

Bernath, Stefen. *Trees of the Northeast.* New York: Dover Publications, 1973.

Black Elk. *The Sacred Pipe.* Baltimore: Penguin Books, 1972.

Bleeker, Sonia. *The Aztec.* New York: Morrow, 1963.

———. *Mission Indians of California.* New York: Morrow Jr. Books, 1956.

———. *The Navajo.* New York: Morrow, 1958.

Borland, Hal. *When the Legends Die.* New York: Bantam Books, 1963.

Bothwell, Jean. *The Lost Colony.* Philadelphia: John C. Winston, 1953.

Brandon, William. *The Last Americans.* New York: McGraw-Hill, 1974.

Breeden, Robert L., ed. *Mysteries of the Ancient World.* Washington, D.C.: National Geographic Society, 1979.

———. *Trails West.* Washington, D.C.: National Geographic Society, 1979.

Brewster, Benjamin. *The First Book of Indians.* New York: Franklin Watts, 1950.

Brooks, Barbara. *The Seminole.* Vero Beach, Fla.: Rourke, 1989.

———. *The Sioux.* Vero Beach, Fla.: Rourke, 1989.

Brower, Kenneth. *Yosemite: An American Treasure.* Washington, D.C.: National Geographic Society, 1990.

Brown, Dee. *Bury My Heart at Wounded Knee.* New York: Henry Holt, 1970.

Bruchac, Joseph. *The Boy Who Lived with the Bears.* New York: Highsmith, 1991.

———. *New Voices from the Longhouse.* New York: Highsmith, 1989.

Buchman, Dian Dincin. *Herbal Medicine.* New York: Wings, 1979.

Burt, Olive W. *Chief Joseph.* New York: Bobbs-Merrill, 1967.

Caduto, Michael J., and Joseph Bruchac. *Keepers of the Earth.* Golden, Colo.: Fulcrum, 1988.

Camusso, Lorenzo. *The Voyages of Columbus.* New York: Dorset, 1991.

Sources

Canby, Thomas Y. "The Search for the First Americans." *National Geographic* (September 1979): 330-63.

Cantor, George. *Historic Landmarks of Black America.* Detroit: Gale Research, 1991.

Carpenter, Allan. *Enchantment of Central America: Panama.* Chicago: Children's Press, 1971.

Catlin, George. *North American Indians.* New York: Viking-Penguin, 1989.

Cavendish, Richard, ed. *Man, Myth and Magic.* New York: Marshall Cavendish, 1970.

Chaffee, Allen. *The Story of Hiawatha.* New York: Random House, 1951.

Chambers, Bradford. *Aztecs of Mexico.* New York: Bobbs-Merrill, 1965.

Clark, Ann Nolan. *The Desert People.* New York: Viking, 1962.

———. *In My Mother's House.* New York: Viking, 1969.

Cleven, Cathrine S. *Black Hawk.* New York: Bobbs-Merrill, 1966.

Codd, Carol. *Chooki and the Ptarmigan.* New York: Walker, 1976.

Cody, Colonel William F. *The Adventures of Buffalo Bill.* New York: Bonanza, 1954.

Collier, John. *Indians of the Americas.* New York: New American Library, 1947.

Cooke, David C. *Tecumseh.* New York: Julian Messner, 1959.

Cooper, James Fenimore. *The Deerslayer.* New York: Penguin, 1987.

———. *The Last of the Mohicans.* New York: Bantam Books, 1981.

———. *The Prairie.* New York: Holt, Rinehart and Winston, 1950.

Copeland, Peter F. *Indian Tribes of North America.* New York: Dover Publications, 1990.

Core, Dr. Earl. *Common Forest Trees of West Virginia.* Conservation Commission of West Virginia, 1959.

Craven, Margaret. *I Heard the Owl Call My Name.* New York: Dell, 1973.

Crowe, Amanda. *Cherokee Legends and the Trail of Tears.* Cherokee, N.C.: Cherokee Publications, 1979.

Crump, Donald J., ed. *Canada's Wilderness Lands.* Washington, D.C.: National Geographic Society, 1982.

Cuevas, Lou. *Apache Legends: Songs of the Wind Dancer.* Happy Camp, Calif.: Naturegraph, 1991.

Curtin, L. S. M. *By the Prophet of the Earth: Ethnobotany of the Pima.* Tucson: University of Arizona Press, 1984.

Dalgliesh, Alice. *The Columbus Story.* New York: Charles Scribner's Sons, 1955.

Dana, Mrs. William Starr. *How to Know the Wild Flowers.* New York: Dover Publications, 1962.

D'Apice, Rita, and Mary D'Apice. *The Algonquian.* Vero Beach, Fla.: Rourke, 1990.

D'Attilio, Anthony. *Seashore Life.* New York: Dover Publications, 1973.

de Brébeuf, Father Jean. *The Huron Carol.* New York: Dutton Children's Books, 1990.

de las Casas, Bartolome. *The Devastation of the Indies: A Brief Account.* Baltimore: Johns Hopkins University Press, 1992.

de Leiris, Lucia. *Shells of the World.* New York: Dover Publications, 1983.

Deuel, Thorne. *American Indian Ways of Life.* Springfield: Illinois State Museum, 1958.

Deur, Lynne. *Indian Chiefs.* Minneapolis, Minn.: Lerner, 1972.

Dial, Adolph L., and David K. Eliades. *The Only Land I Know: A History of the Lumbee Indians.* San Francisco: Indian Historian Press, 1975.

Dickens, Roy S., Jr. *Cherokee Prehistory.* Knoxville: University of Tennessee Press, 1976.

Dictionary of Daily Life of Indians of the Americas. Newport Beach, Calif.: American Indian Publishers, 1981.

Dines, Glen, and Raymond Price. *Dog Soldiers.* New York: Macmillan, 1961.

Dobelis, Inge N., ed. *Magic and Medicine of Plants.* Pleasantville, N.Y.: Readers Digest Press, 1986.

Dobrin, Norma. *Delawares.* Chicago: Melmont, 1963.

Dorian, Edith, and W. N. Wilson. *Hokahey!* New York: Whittlesey House, 1957.

Dunn, J. P., Jr. *Massacres of the Mountains: A History of the Indian Wars of the Far West.* New York: Capricorn Books, 1969.

Dutton, Bertha, and Carolina Olin. *Myths and Legends of the Indians of the Southwest.* Santa Barbara, Calif.: Bellerophon, 1993.

Eastman, Charles A. *Indian Boyhood.* Williamstown, Mass.: Corner House, 1975.

Edmunds, R. David, ed. *American Indian Leaders.* Lincoln: University of Nebraska Press, 1980.

Edwards, Cecile Pepin. *King Phillip.* Boston: Houghton Mifflin, 1962.

Ehle, John. *Trail of Tears: The Rise and Fall of the Cherokee Nation.* New York: Anchor, 1992.

Elting, Mary, and Franklin Folsom. *The Story of Archeology in the Americas.* Irvington-on-Hudson, N.Y.: Harvey House, 1960.

Encyclopedia Americana. Danbury, Conn.: Grolier, 1987.

Encyclopaedia Britannica. London: Encyclopaedia Britannica, 1981.

Engel, Dolores. *Voyage of the Kon-Tiki.* Milwaukee: Raintree/Steck Vaughn, 1979.

Erdoes, Richard. *The Sun Dance People.* New York: Alfred A. Knopf, 1972.

Famous Indians: A Collection of Short Biographies. Washington, D.C.: Bureau of Indian Affairs, Department of the Interior, 1973.

Farnsworth, Frances Joyce. *Winged Moccasins.* New York: Julian Messner, 1954.

Farquhar, Margaret C. *The Indians of Mexico.* New York: Holt, Rinehart & Winston, 1967.

Feldman, Susan, ed. *The Story-Telling Stone.* New York: Dell, 1965.

Fenton, Carroll Lane, and Alice Epstein. *Cliff Dwellers of Walnut Canyon.* New York: John Day, 1960.

Ferrell, Robert H., and Richard Natkiel. *Atlas of American History.* New York: Facts on File, 1990.

Ferris, Jeri. *Native American Doctor: The Story of Susan LaFlesche Picotte.* Minneapolis, Minn.: Lerner, 1991.

Finger, John R. *The Eastern Band of Cherokees, 1819-1900.* Knoxville: University of Tennessee Press, 1984.

Fitzhugh, William W., and Susan A. Kaplan. *Inua: Spirit World of the Bering Sea Eskimo.* Washington, D.C.: Smithsonian Institution Traveling Exhibition Service, 1983.

Flaherty, Robert. *The Story of Comstock the Eskimo.* New York: Simon & Schuster, 1968.

Fleischer, June. *Pontiac.* Mahwah, N.J.: Troll, 1979.

Forbis, William H. *The Cowboys.* New York: Time Life, 1973.

Fraser, Frances. *The Bear Who Stole the Chinook.* Vancouver, B.C.: Douglas & McIntyre, 1968.

Fullerton, Lynne, et al. *The Nuvuk News.* Brockport, N.Y.: Edwin Hall, March, 1987 (Newsletter).

Garst, Shannon. *Buffalo Bill.* New York: Julian Messner, 1948.

George, Jean Craighead. *Julie of the Wolves.* New York: Harper & Row, 1972.

Gibson, Michael. *The American Indian.* Norwich, England: Wayland, 1974.

Gill, Sam D., and Irene F. Sullivan. *Dictionary of Native American Mythology.* Santa Barbara, Calif.: ABC-Clio, 1992.

Goodnough, David. *Christopher Columbus.* Mahwah, N.J.: Troll, 1979.

———. *John Cabot and Son.* Mahwah, N.J.: Troll, 1979.

Gorham, Michael. *The Real Book About Indians.* Garden City, N.Y.: Garland, 1953.

Grant, Bruce. *Concise Encyclopedia of the American Indian.* New York: Wings, 1989.

Grant, Matthew G. *Buffalo Bill.* Gallery of Great Americans series. Mankato, Minn.: Creative Education, 1974.

———. *Chief Joseph.* Gallery of Great Americans series. Mankato, Minn.: Creative Education, 1974.

———. *Columbus.* Gallery of Great Americans series. Mankato, Minn.: Creative Education, 1974.

———. *Crazy Horse.* Gallery of Great Americans series. Mankato, Minn.: Creative Education, 1974.

———. *Geronimo.* Gallery of Great Americans series. Mankato, Minn.: Creative Education, 1974.

———. *Jim Bridger.* Gallery of Great Americans series. Mankato, Minn.: Creative Education, 1974.

Sources

————. *Kit Carson.* Gallery of Great Americans series. Mankato, Minn.: Creative Education, 1974.

————. *Osceola.* Gallery of Great Americans series. Mankato, Minn.: Creative Education, 1974.

————. *Pontiac.* Gallery of Great Americans series. Mankato, Minn.: Creative Education, 1974.

————. *Squanto: The Indian Who Saved the Pilgrims.* Gallery of Great Americans series. Mankato, Minn.: Creative Education, 1974.

Green, John. *Life in Ancient Mexico.* New York: Dover Publications, 1991.

Grosvenor, Gilbert M. *We Americans.* The Story of Man Library. Washington, D.C.: National Geographic Society, 1975.

Hahn, Elizabeth. *The Inuit.* Vero Beach, Fla.: Rourke, 1990.

Hamel, Paul B., and Mary U. Chiltoskey. *Cherokee Plants.* Published by author, 1975.

Harrell, Mary Ann, ed. *Builders of the Ancient World.* Washington, D.C.: National Geographic Society, 1986.

Harris, Moira F. *Between Two Cultures: Kiowa Art from Fort Marion.* New York: Highsmith, 1989.

Heatter, Basil. *A King in Haiti.* New York: Farrar, Straus & Giroux, 1972.

Hedrick, Basil C. *Historical Dictionary of Panama.* Metuchen, N.J.: Scarecrow Press, 1970.

Heizer, Robert F. *The Indians of California.* Berkeley: University of California Press, 1962.

Heizer, Robert F., and Albert B. Elsasser. *The Natural World of the California Indians.* Berkeley: University of California Press, 1980.

Henry, Edna. *Native American Cookbook.* New York: Julian Messner, 1983.

Heyerdahl, Thor. *Kon-Tiki.* New York: Permabooks, 1963.

————. *Kon-Tiki: A True Adventure of Survival at Sea.* New York: Random House, 1984.

————. *The Ra Expeditions.* Garden City, N.Y.: Doubleday, 1971.

Hill, Ruth Beebe. *Hanta Yo: An American Saga.* New York: Warner Books, 1979.

Hirschfelder, Arlene. *Happy May I Walk.* New York: Charles Scribner's Sons, 1986.

Hodge, Frederick W. *Handbook of American Indians North of Mexico.* Totowa, N.J.: Rowman and Littlefield, 1975.

Hofsinde, Robert. *The Indian Medicine Man.* New York: Morrow Jr. Books, 1966.

————. *Indian Picture Writing.* New York: Morrow Jr. Books, 1959.

Holling, Holling C. *The Book of Indians.* New York: Platt and Munk, 1935.

Hughes, Jill. *Eskimos.* New York: Gloucester, 1984.

Incas, Aztecs, and Mayas. Santa Barbara, Calif.: Bellerophon, 1992.

The Indian Historian. Vol. 2 (Summer) 1969.

Indians, Eskimos, and Aleuts of Alaska. Washington, D.C.: Bureau of Indian Affairs, Department of the Interior, 1966.

Jacobson, Daniel. *The Gatherers.* New York: Franklin Watts, 1975.

————. *Great Indian Tribes.* Maplewood, N.J.: Hammond, 1970.

————. *Indians of North America.* New York: Franklin Watts, 1983.

Jassem, Kate. *Chief Joseph.* Mahwah, N.J.: Troll, 1979.

————. *Pocahontas.* Mahwah, N.J.: Troll, 1979.

————. *Sacajawea.* Mahwah, N.J.: Troll, 1979.

————. *Squanto: The Pilgrim Adventure.* Mahwah, N.J.: Troll, 1979.

Jenness, Aylette. *Dwellers of the Tundra.* Toronto: Thomas Y. Crowell-Collier, 1970.

Johnson, Ann Donegan. *The Value of Truth and Trust: The Story of Cochise.* La Jolla, Calif.: Value Communications, 1977.

Johnson, Spencer. *The Value of Curiosity: The Story of Christopher Columbus.* La Jolla, Calif.: Value Communications, 1977.

Jonaitis, Aldona, ed. *Chiefly Feasts: The Enduring Kwakiutl Potlatch.* Seattle: University of Washington Press, 1991.

Jones, Jayne Clark. *The American Indian in America,* Vol. 1. Minneapolis, Minn.: Lerner, 1973.

————. *The American Indian in America,* Vol. 2. Minneapolis, Minn.: Lerner, 1991.

Joseph, Frank. *Sacred Sites: A Guidebook to Sacred Centers and Mysterious Places in the United States.* St. Paul, Minn.: Llewellyn, 1992.

Kalman, Bobbie, and William Belsey. *An Arctic Community.* New York: Crabtree, 1988.

Katz, William Loren. *Black Indians: A Hidden Heritage.* New York: Atheneum, 1986.

———. *The Black West.* Seattle, Wash.: Open Hand Publishing, 1987.

Kennedy, Paul E. *North American Indian Design.* New York: Dover Publications, 1971.

Kimball, Yeffe, and Jean Anderson. *The Art of American Indian Cooking.* New York: Simon & Schuster, 1965.

Kohn, Bernice. *The Story of Sequoyah.* New York: Prentice-Hall Press, 1969.

Kroeber, Alfred. *The Arapaho.* Lincoln: University of Nebraska Press, 1983.

Kroeber, Theodora. *Ishi: Last of His Tribe.* New York: Bantam Books, 1964.

LaDoux, Rita C. *Iowa.* Minneapolis, Minn.: Lerner, 1992.

La Farge, Oliver. *The American Indian.* New York: Golden, 1965.

Lambert, R. S. *The World's Most Daring Explorers: 38 Men Who Opened Up the World.* New York: Sterling, 1956.

Lame Deer, John, and Richard Erdoes. *Lame Deer, Seeker of Visions.* New York: Washington Square, 1972.

Larrington, Carolyne. *The Feminist Companion to Mythology.* New York: Pandora, 1992.

Lavender, David. *Let Me Be Free.* New York: Doubleday, 1993.

Lavine, Sigmund A. *The Games the Indians Played.* New York: Dodd, Mead, 1974.

Leavitt, Dr. Jerome E. *America and Its Indians.* New York: Grosset & Dunlap, 1962.

Lee, Melicent Humason. *Indians of the Oaks.* New York: Ginn, 1937.

Levinson, Nancy Smiler. *Christopher Columbus: Voyager to the Unknown.* New York: Lodestar, 1990.

Lister, Robert H., and Florence C. Lister. *Those Who Came Before.* Tucson: University of Arizona Press, 1983.

Lodge, Sally. *The Cheyenne.* Vero Beach, Fla.: Rourke, 1990.

Longfellow, Henry Wadsworth. *The Song of Hiawatha.* New York: Dial Press, 1983.

Lummis, Charles F. *Pueblo Indian Folk-Stories.* Lincoln: University of Nebraska Press, 1992.

Lund, Duane R. *Early Native American Recipes and Remedies.* Cambridge, Minn.: Adventure Publications, 1989.

Lynch, Regina H. *Cookbook.* Chinle, Ariz.: Navajo Curriculum Center, Rough Rock Demonstration School, 1986.

Mandel, Jack Kent. *Significant American Indians.* Chicago: Children's Press, 1975.

Mankiller, Wilma P. *Mankiller: A Chief and Her People.* New York: St. Martin's Press, 1993.

Marriott, Alice. *Sequoyah.* Eau Claire, Wis.: E. M. Hale, 1956.

Marriott, Alice, and Carol K. Rachlin. *Plains Indian Mythology.* New York: Meridian, 1985.

Martini, Teri. *The True Book of Indians.* Chicago: Children's Press, 1970.

Mason, Antony. *The Caribbean.* Englewood Cliffs, N.J.: Silver Burdett, 1989.

Mason, Otis T. *Traps of the American Indians.* Seattle, Wash.: Extract from the Smithsonian Annual Report, 1901.

Massai Point Trail. National Park Service, Chiricahua National Monument, Arizona, n.d.

Maxwell, James A. *America's Fascinating Indian Heritage.* Pleasantville, N.Y.: Reader's Digest Press, 1978.

McCall, Barbara A. *The Cherokee.* Vero Beach, Fla.: Rourke, 1989.

McCracken, Harold. *George Catlin and the Old Frontier.* New York: Dial Press, 1959.

McCrum, Robert, et al. *The Story of English.* New York: Viking, 1986.

McIntyre, Loren. *The Incredible Incas and Their Timeless Land.* Washington, D.C.: National Geographic Society, 1975.

McKissack, Patricia. *The Apache.* Chicago: Children's Press, 1984.

Meltzer, Milton. *Columbus and the World Around Him.* New York: Franklin Watts, 1990.

Merrell, James H. *Indians of North America: The Catawbas.* New York: Chelsea House, 1989.

Mesa Verde Museum. *Spruce Tree House.* Mesa Verde, Colo.: Mesa Verde Museum Association, n.d.

Miers, Earl Schenck, ed. *Indians of the Great Basin and Plateau.* New York: Putnam, 1970.

Sources

Mirsky, Jeannette. *Balboa.* Eau Claire, Wis.: E. M. Hale, 1964.

Momaday, N. Scott. *The Ancient Child.* New York: Doubleday, 1989.

————. *House Made of Dawn.* New York: Harper & Row, 1968.

————. *The Way to Rainy Mountain.* Albuquerque: University of New Mexico Press, 1969.

Moquin, Wayne, and Charles Van Doren. *Great Documents in American Indian History.* New York: Praeger, 1973.

Morison, Samuel Eliot. *Christopher Columbus.* New York: Dorset, 1991.

Morrison, Dorothy Nafus. *Chief Sarah.* New York: Atheneum, 1980.

Mowat, Farley. *Never Cry Wolf.* New York: Bantam Books, 1963.

————. *The Snow Walker.* Boston: Little, Brown, 1973.

Nabokov, Peter. *Native American Testimony: A Chronicle of Indian-White Relations from Prophecy to the Present, 1492-1992.* New York: Viking, 1992.

New Book of Knowledge. Danbury, Conn.: Grolier, 1989.

Neihardt, John G. *Black Elk Speaks.* Lincoln: University of Nebraska Press, 1961.

Newman, Gerald. *The Changing Eskimos.* New York: Franklin Watts, 1979.

Niethammer, Carolyn. *American Indian Food and Lore.* New York: Collier, 1974.

O'Dell, Scott. *Island of the Blue Dolphins.* New York: Dell, 1960.

————. *Sarah Bishop.* New York: Scholastic, 1980.

————. *Sing Down the Moon.* New York: Dell, 1970.

————. *Streams to the River, River to the Sea.* New York: Fawcett, 1986.

Oppenheim, Joanne. *Black Hawk.* Mahwah, N.J.: Troll, 1979.

————. *Osceola.* Mahwah, N.J.: Troll, 1979.

————. *Sequoyah.* Mahwah, N.J.: Troll, 1979.

Ortiz, Simon. *The People Shall Continue.* San Francisco: Children's Book Press, 1988.

Owen, Roger C., et al. *The North American Indians: A Sourcebook.* New York: Macmillan, 1967.

Pastron, Allen. *Great Indian Chiefs.* Santa Barbara, Calif.: Bellerophon, 1993.

Paulsen, Gary. *Dogsong.* New York: Bradbury Press, 1985.

Peckham, Howard. *Pontiac.* New York: Bobbs-Merrill, 1963.

Peters, Russell M. *Clambake: A Wampanoag Tradition.* Minneapolis, Minn.: Lerner, 1992.

Pine, Tillie S., and Joseph Levine. *The Maya Knew.* New York: McGraw-Hill, 1971.

Pool, Raymond J. *Flowers and Flowering Plants.* New York: McGraw-Hill, 1941.

Powell, John Wesley. *Down the Colorado: Diary of the First Trip Through the Grand Canyon, 1869.* New York: Promontory Press, 1969.

Powers, William K. *Indians of the Northern Plains.* New York: Capricorn, 1973.

Pryde, Duncan. *Nunaga: Ten Years of Eskimo Life.* New York: Walker, 1971.

Pugh, Ellen. *Brave His Soul.* New York: Dodd, Mead, 1970.

Rachlis, Eugene. *Indians of the Plains.* New York: American Heritage, 1960.

Radin, Paul. *The Trickster: A Study in American Indian Mythology.* New York: Schocken, 1972.

Regguinti, Gordon. *The Sacred Harvest: Ojibway Wild Rice Gathering.* Minneapolis, Minn.: Lerner, 1992.

Richter, Conrad. *The Light in the Forest.* New York: Bantam Books, 1953.

Rickman, David. *Northwest Coast Indians.* New York: Dover Publications, 1984.

Rights, Douglas L. *The American Indian in North Carolina.* Winston-Salem, N.C.: John F. Blair, 1957.

Roberts, Arthur O. *Tomorrow Is Growing Old.* Newberg, Ore.: Barclay Press, 1978.

Robison, Nancy. *Buffalo Bill.* New York: Franklin Watts, 1991.

Ross, Allen. *Mitakuye Oyasin: "We Are All Related."* New York: Highsmith, 1992.

Russell, Francis. *The French and Indian Wars.* New York: American Heritage, 1962.

Salomon, Julian Harris, et al. *The Book of Indian Crafts and Indian Lore.* New York: Harper & Row, 1928.

Schouweiler, Tom. *The Lost Colony of Roanoke.* San Diego, Calif.: Greenhaven, 1991.

Seibert, Jerry. *Sacajawea.* Boston: Houghton Mifflin, 1960.

Seymour, Flora Warren. *Bird Girl: Sacagawea.* New York: Bobbs-Merrill, 1945.

————. *The Story of the Red Man.* London: Longmans, Green, 1929.

Sharpe, J. Ed. *The Cherokees Past and Present.* Cherokee, N.C.: Cherokee Publications, 1970.

Shipley, William. *The Maidu Indian Myths and Stories of Hanc'iby Jim.* New York: Highsmith, 1991.

Shorto, Russell. *Tecumseh.* Englewood Cliffs, N.J.: Silver Burdett, 1989.

Showers, Paul. *Indian Festivals.* New York: Thomas Y. Crowell, 1969.

Sides, Dorothy Smith. *Decorative Art of the Southwestern Indians.* New York: Dover Publications, 1961.

Sis, Peter. *Follow the Dream.* New York: Alfred A. Knopf, 1991.

Smith, Howard E., Jr. *All About Arrowheads and Spear Points.* New York: Holt, Rinehart & Winston, 1989.

Smith, J. H. Greg. *Eskimos: The Inuit of the Arctic.* Vero Beach, Fla.: Rourke, 1987.

Snow, Dorothea J. *Indian Chiefs.* Racine, Wis.: Whitman, 1959.

————. *Sequoyah.* New York: Bobbs-Merrill, 1960.

Snyder, Gerald S. *In the Footsteps of Lewis and Clark.* Washington, D.C.: National Geographic Society, 1970.

South, Stanley A. *Indians in North Carolina.* Raleigh, N.C.: State Department of Archives and History, 1959.

Speare, Elizabeth George. *The Sign of the Beaver.* New York: Yearling Books, 1983.

Stan, Susan. *The Ojibwe.* Vero Beach, Fla.: Rourke, 1989.

Stevenson, Augusta. *Tecumseh.* New York: Bobbs-Merrill, 1955.

Stuart, Gene S. *America's Ancient Cities.* Washington, D.C.: National Geographic Society, 1988.

————. *The Mighty Aztecs.* Washington, D.C.: National Geographic Society, 1981.

Stuart, George, and Gene S. Stuart. *The Mysterious Maya.* Washington, D.C.: National Geographic Society, 1977.

Sturtevant, William C., gen. ed. *Handbook of North American Indians.* Washington, D.C.: Smithsonian Institution, 1984.

Swentzell, Rina. *Children of Clay: A Family of Pueblo Potters.* Minneapolis, Minn.: Lerner, 1992.

Tamarin, Alfred. *We Have Not Vanished.* Chicago: Follett, 1974.

Tanner, Clara Lee. *Prehistoric Southwestern Craft Arts.* Tucson: University of Arizona Press, 1976.

Tanner, Clara Lee, and Richard Kirk. *Our Indian Heritage.* Chicago: Follett, 1961.

Taylor, Tom. *Native American Foods and Cookery.* Raleigh: North Carolina State Museum of Natural Sciences, 1986.

Thibert, Arthur. *English-Eskimo Dictionary.* Rev. ed. Ottawa, Ont.: Canadian Research Centre for Anthropology, 1970.

Thomson, Lucy. *To the American Indian: Reminiscences of a Yurok Woman.* New York: Highsmith, 1991.

Tomkins, William. *Universal American Indian Sign Language.* Published privately, 1968.

Townsend, Richard. *The Aztecs.* New York: W. W. Norton, 1992.

Truman, Margaret. *Women of Courage.* New York: Bantam Books, 1976.

Tunis, Edwin. *Indians.* New York: Thomas Y. Crowell, 1959.

Ulmer, Mary, and Samuel E. Beck, ed. *Cherokee Cooklore.* Norman, Okla.: Museum of the Cherokee Indian, 1951.

Underhill, Ruth M. *Red Man's America.* Chicago: University of Chicago Press, 1971.

————. *Red Man's Religion.* Chicago: University of Chicago Press, 1965.

Vallejo, Mariano Guadalupe. *Great Indians of California.* Santa Barbara, Calif.: Bellerophon, 1991.

Van Every, Dale. *Disinherited: The Lost Birthright of the American Indian.* New York: Avon Books, 1966.

Viola, Herman J. *After Columbus: The Smithsonian Chronicle of the North American Indians.* Washington, D.C.: Smithsonian Institution, 1990.

Voight, Virginia Frances. *Uncas.* New York: Funk & Wagnalls, 1963.

Vogel, Virgil J. *This Country Was Ours.* New York: Harper & Row, 1972.

Sources

Waldman, Carl. *Atlas of the North American Indian*. New York: Facts on File, 1985.

——. *Who Was Who in North American History*. New York: Facts on File, 1990.

Wax, Murray L. *Indian Americans*. Englewood Cliffs, N.J.: Prentice-Hall, 1971.

Weiner, Michael A. *Earth Medicine—Earth Food*. New York: Fawcett Columbine, 1980.

Wenger, Gilbert R. *The Story of Mesa Verde National Park*. Mesa Verde, Colo.: Mesa Verde Museum Association, 1991.

When Worlds Collide: How Columbus's Voyages Transformed Both East and West. (Fall/Winter Special Issue) *Newsweek* 1991.

Wigginton, Eliot, ed. *Foxfire 3*. Garden City, N.Y.: Doubleday, 1973.

Wilbur, C. Keith. *Indian Handicrafts*. Chester, Conn.: Globe Pequot Press, 1990.

Wilkes, John. *Hernan Cortes: Conquistador in Mexico*. Cambridge, Mass.: Lerner, 1977.

Winders, Gertrude Hecker. *Jim Bridger*. New York: Bobbs-Merrill, 1962.

Wolfson, Evelyn. *From Abenaki to Zuni*. New York: Walker, 1988.

Woods, A. J. *Errata: A Book of Historical Errors*. New York: Green Tiger Press, 1992.

World Book Encyclopedia. Chicago: World Book, 1991.

Wormington, H. M. *Prehistoric Indians of the Southwest*. Denver, Colo.: Denver Museum of Natural History, 1966.

Worthylake, Mary M. *Children of the Seed Gatherers*. Chicago: Melmont, 1964.

Wright, Barton, and Evelyn Roat. *This Is a Hopi Kachina*. Flagstaff, Ariz.: Museum of Northern Arizona, 1970.

Wright, Mabel Osgood. *Flowers and Ferns in Their Haunts*. New York: Macmillan, 1928.

Yue, Charlotte, and David Yue. *The Igloo*. Boston: Houghton Mifflin, 1988.

Subject Index

Note: Information under each subject is listed by alphabetic entry.

General Index

Note: Information under each subject is listed by alphabetic entry. For additional information on tribes, consult the individual tribe entry in the text.

Tall Bull dog soldier
Tallchief, Maria Osage
Tallchief, Marjorie Osage
Tall Men Assiniboin
Tamany Delaware
Tashquent cactli
tattoo Creek, Pomo, Yuma
Taza Cochise
Ten Bears Comanche
Tewa Popé, Pueblo
Thule narwhal
Thunder Black Hawk
thunderbird medicine
Tillamook Ghost Dance, Salish
Tilokaikt Cayuse
Timucua arrow, bow, mound
Tinker, Clarence B. Osage
Tiwa Pueblo
Tlingit chilkat, labret, tattoo, Tsimshian
Toahty, Lillian Arapaho
tobacco bear grease, calumet, catlinite, healing, Huron, lanyard, machete, medicine dance, medicine pipe, Midwinter Festival, peace pipe, pipe bag, zemi
Toltec milpa, Nahuatl
Tomahas Cayuse
Tonto Apache
toque beading, Pawnee, Sequoyah
totem Indian, Kwakiutl, thunderbird, Tlingit, Tsimshian
Totonac voladores
Továr, Pedro Hopi
Tree of Peace Deganawida
Tribbles, Henry Bright Eyes
trickster inua, Iroquois, longhouse, Winnebago
Tschoop Mahican
Tsimshian potlatch, totem
Turkey Foot Little Turtle
Tuscarora chinquapin, deer decoy, Yamassee
Two Moons Battle of Little Big Horn

Umatilla Washakie
Ute Comanche, lodge, long knives
Uthawah Iroquois League
Uto-Aztecan atlatl, Nahuatl

Verrazzano, Giovanni da Narragansett
Victorio Apache, Mangas Coloradas
Viracocha Inca
vision quest Crazy Horse, Native American Church, wacanga

Wabanaki trickster
Waioskasit Menominee
Wakara, Chief Ute
Walks-with-the-Moon Crow
Wampanoag Hobomak, maize
Wamsutta Massasoit, King Philip
Wanapum All-Mother, medicine man
Ward, John black Indian
Washington, George Cornplanter, Little Turtle
Washita River Battle of Little Big Horn, Black Kettle
Washo Ghost Dance
Wassaja Apache
The Way to Rainy Mountain Kiowa, medicine song
Wayne, Anthony Little Turtle
Weatherford, William half-breed
whale agvik, flense, maktak, umiak, umialik
When the Legends Die muckamuck
Where the Red Fern Grows Indian Territory
White Cloud Black Hawk, Winnebago
White Fang amaguq
White Hand Sand Creek Massacre
White Horse Geronimo
Whitewolf, Jim Kiowa
wigwam Algonquin, bast
Williams, Roger Narragansett
Wilson, Alfred Native American Church
Wilson, Peter Cayuga
Wilson, Woodrow Ben Kindle

Carib

Goajiro

Cuna

Guaymi

Chibcha

Arawak

Arawak

Cañar

Omagua

Timbira

Chimu

Mundurucú

Sherente

Inca

Nambicuara

Cayapa

Inca

Mojo

Aymara

Sirionó

Atacama

Coroado

Diaguita

Guaraní

Araucania

Abipón

Charrua

Puelche

Tehuelche

Alacaluf

Ona

Yahgan